THE EVOLUTION OF PROCUREMENT AND SUPPLY MANAGEMENT TRANSFORMATIONS

REMOVING OBSTACLES TO SUCCESS

MELISSA DREW

Part of the J. Ross Publishing Intelligent Procurement Series

J.ROSS PUBLISHING

ISBN: 978-1-60427-194-2

Printed and bound in the U.S.A. Printed on acid-free paper.

10 9 8 7 6 5 4 3 2 1

Library of Congress Cataloging-in-Publication Data can be found in the WAV section of the publisher's website at www.jrosspub.com/wav.

Direct all inquiries to J. Ross Publishing, Inc., 151 N. Nob Hill Rd., Suite 476, Plantation, FL 33324. For EU safety/GPSR concerns, email: gpsr@mare-nostrum.co.uk or contact: Mare Nostrum Group B.V., Mauritskade 21D, 1091 GC Amsterdam, The Netherlands.

Phone: (954) 727-9333
Fax: (561) 892-0700
Web: www.jrosspub.com

To my teenage daughters, Emma and Ava,
who support me in ways they may never understand

CONTENTS

FOREWORD

Procurement and supply management organizations are experiencing rapid change. Many of these changes are conducted through the ever-present *transformation project*. However, these projects failed 20 years ago, and now—20 years later—they are still failing. Most companies still chase the *shiny object* that seems easy on the surface but are not pausing long enough to ask the right questions. Companies are not taking time to plan for a flexible foundation, and everything stacked on top falls. This is supported by a 2023 McKinsey and Company report that 70 percent of digital transformations failed to reach their target, with root causes including inadequate leadership engagement, insufficient change management, poor planning, and not building the right capabilities.

Does doing the same things over and over again and expecting different results sound like the textbook definition of *insanity*? It should, and to resolve this, you need to dive into Melissa's book. From automation to sustainable sourcing to adaptable leadership, *The Evolution of Procurement and Supply Management Transformations* offers actionable strategies to help you navigate these transformations and drive long-term success. Melissa shows that regularly evaluating supplier performance, risk management, process efficiency, and stakeholder satisfaction provides transparency and fosters stronger collaboration across the organization. She promotes a different way of thinking and what questions to ask for success. It is a must-read for forward-thinking professionals looking to stay ahead and be fully informed in a constantly changing field.

Good luck on your transformation journey!

Mike Cadieux
Founder of Procurement Foundry and
Former Chief Procurement Officer

ABOUT THE AUTHOR

Melissa Drew is an international keynote speaker with over 30 years of data and digital transformation expertise. Her professional career has contributed to her breadth and depth of knowledge working in the private sector, with start-ups, and as a consultant with Kearney, Deloitte, and IBM. She focuses on how emerging technologies impact procurement and supply chain organizations. Ms. Drew was ranked #34 of the Top 100 Women in Supply Chain 2023, was named a Top 25 Global Consultant in 2021, and is a Top 50 Global Thought Leader and Influencer on Supply Chain 2024. She hosts the "Impact of AI and Data" podcast, interviewing procurement leaders worldwide about their perspectives on today, tomorrow, and beyond.

Melissa is a TEDX speaker who has been featured in AI Time Journal, Tech Exec Magazine, and various data and technology podcasts. Recently, she became the founder of the nonprofit organization, The AI Literate Citizen, with a mission to advance AI literacy for global citizens of all ages. Melissa is a guest lecturer at the Rutgers Business School Supply Chain Program on the topic of Emerging Technologies. When not writing or speaking, Ms. Drew mentors others, travels internationally, and tries to keep up with her twin teenage daughters. One of her most outstanding achievements is remaining cancer-free since October 2022.

At J. Ross Publishing we are committed to providing today's professional with practical, hands-on tools that enhance the learning experience and give readers an opportunity to apply what they have learned. That is why we offer free ancillary materials available for download on this book and all participating Web Added Value™ publications. These online resources may include interactive versions of material that appears in the book or supplemental templates, worksheets, models, plans, case studies, proposals, spreadsheets and assessment tools, among other things. Whenever you see the WAV™ symbol in any of our publications, it means bonus materials accompany the book and are available from the Web Added Value Download Resource Center at www.jrosspub.com.

Downloads for *The Evolution of Procurement and Supply Management Transformations* include various articles and whitepapers, a policy checklist, and the United Nations 2030 Agenda for Sustainable Development.

CHAPTER 1

INTRODUCTION

This book covers content across many topics and processes within the procurement and supply chain organization and will not dive deep into one area or another. It is intended to:

- Promote a different way of thinking
- Identify what questions to ask
- Understand what is blocking success
- Question traditional methods and make way for the new

The procurement and supply chain organization aims to broaden its influence within the larger organization, create revenue-generating opportunities, and prioritize value. While there is an ongoing discourse about how future technologies can aid in achieving these objectives, it is crucial to recognize that the future is already upon us. The organization must learn to transform immediately and effectively. This book is designed to help identify the areas that are not functioning optimally and eliminate the obstacles that hinder the success of a procurement and supply management organization. After reading this book, the hope is that you will no longer view large-scale transformations as multi-year initiatives but as a continuous process.

When the proper foundation is in place, the organization should only perform minor adjustments when encountering future disruptions, both with positive and negative impacts. When the organization no longer focuses its energy and resources on rebuilding that foundation every few years, the procurement and supply chain team can step out of the crazy circles where it has been stuck. However, a thorough spring cleaning is needed before this can happen. This means removing the irrelevant "stuff" that has not been touched in over 30 years.

Transformation, in its simplest definition, is the ability to change from one state to another to end up in a better place than where you were before. A consensus view from many industry leaders is that a real transformation is a journey; not something that is done once but is a continuous effort. I agree with this up to a point. The statement can be and has been interpreted to mean that continuous transformations are occurring one after the other. A successful transformation should create a sustainable foundation to be leveraged against future disruptions. If you need to perform a second or third transformation project, the first one was not completed correctly. It may have been too narrowly focused or, in most scenarios, not a true transformation.

In the future, the organization will continue to encounter known and unknown disruptions. Some of these disruptions may be perceived as having a positive or negative impact. For this book, the definition of a disruption is *a permanent interruption to an industry or market's current direction*. Therefore, the effect of a disruption will require a permanent change to an organization's strategic direction, goals, and processes. These disruptions are expected to happen more frequently in the future, which is why organizations must be alert and adjust more often.

The organization should not be required to perform multiple, comprehensive transformations whenever a disruption occurs. The ability to adapt more often may be the critical variable that allows for future successes such as strengthening competitive advantage, improving brand loyalty, gaining market share, developing new revenue streams, and creating value. Considering automation during a transformation will reduce the need for rework later, and right-sizing the organization will support a solid but flexible foundation that allows for smaller adjustments when needed.

WHAT IS A DIGITAL TRANSFORMATION?

The term *digital transformation* is used with meaningful purpose. It is the ability to use technology to support transformation goals and yield more robust results. Transforming through digital technologies or moving information into a digital footprint (digitalization) is also changing how we consume information. How that information is used significantly changes how we interact with internal and external stakeholders. For example, this can lead to reevaluating the current business model to better innovate or create more product variety.

One may say, "That is what the enterprise resource planning (ERP) applications were meant to provide, right?" ERP did shift information into a digital format, but it also created limitations that were not initially expected. It could not generate the desired significance across the entire organization compared to what can be achieved now. ERP is still necessary in a modern organization; however, with the accessibility and adoption of a wider variety of technologies across the enterprise, we can achieve much more significant results faster and with higher confidence.

Since 2005, there have been three main motivators for digital transformations within the procurement and supply management organization: technological changes, shifts in consumer demand, and the COVID pandemic. These external forces caused a reactive response from executive leadership and were used as leverage to build an internal case for transformation. However, the funds for these transformations were short lived because the leverage used in the business case was based on a short-term need rather than a strategic need.

This is a contributing factor to why organizations feel the need to start transformation projects repeatedly and why the term *transformation* has become generalized over the last decade. More recently, this term has been used to reference any project that benefits one or more departments in the short term but rarely features long-term, organization-wide sustainable results. Since 2005, in my experience, very few companies have successfully transformed their organization with a comprehensive overhaul of processes while leveraging technologies for automation that result in a data-driven, cultural, and improved stakeholder experience. When following up with those firms years later, they had completed their comprehensive transformation just once. They made additional adjustments as they reacted to changes in corporate strategies or changes to match consumer demand. Still, those adjustments were minor and could be accomplished in six months or less. These organizations were able to jump forward in capturing market share, sustaining brand loyalty, and adjusting more quickly when needed.

> If you are doing a second, third, or fourth transformation project, the first one was not done properly.

Around 2007–2008, there was an awareness and desire within the procurement and supply chain organization to shift from on-premise technology architecture (also known as behind the firewall) to cloud technology architecture. Skepticism of cloud technologies and the cost of migrating from an on-premise architecture to a cloud-based solution delayed most companies from immediately adopting these new technologies. Additional concerns included a lack of comfort in pushing organizational data outside the organization and the uncertainty of the security of that data in the cloud. A few companies, labeling themselves as *the bleeding edge*, were comfortable exploring emerging technologies that had not been proven yet. It was these companies who helped pave the way for everyone else.

The first substantial wave of projects started to emerge around 2010. At this time, some organizations at the top percent of the technology adoption bell curve saw themselves as early adopters. Their decisions were motivated by a return on investment, calculated by comparing the cost of development and maintaining technology infrastructures against the financial advantages of cloud-based applications.

At the same time, as software application providers were also shifting to the cloud, the definition of an application developer was slowly replaced with the phrase *configuration*. Configuration could be supported by a business user who could make small changes to the application themselves without the need for information technology (IT) resources or resources from the supplier. Full-time developers with application-specific knowledge were no longer required by the organization's IT department to implement or maintain cloud-based applications. Another financial advantage was that application providers could push updates directly into the application multiple times yearly. This benefit allowed organizations to match consumer demand in nearly real time instead of waiting one to two years for the IT organization to make similar enhancements.

The second substantial wave was between 2015 and 2017. During this time, there was more accessibility of information combined with increased consumer awareness. This combination created a more educated consumer who wanted to understand the organization's supply chain and procurement practices and what impact this had on them. One example of more accessible information was in 2016 when the U.S. Food and Drug Administration (FDA) updated the nutrition facts label. This was the first significant change to the label since it was introduced in 1994. Consumers now had more visibility into food and beverage ingredients and could start making better decisions about which products they wanted to consume. This had an immediate and sometimes profound impact on sales and profits. As consumer buying behavior changed more frequently, the procurement and supply chain organizations needed to adapt more quickly. Consumer behavior may have been a catalyst for change, but other factors during this time contributed to this second wave of digital transformation:

- **Organizational change in priority:** Although the business case of moving from on-premise to the cloud had been discussed for the prior five years, most organizations were not prepared to devote resources, time, and funding until now.
- **Shift in procurement's value:** Executive leaders were becoming more aware of how the procurement organization could directly impact other parts of the organization and how procurement-driven savings could be reallocated in different company areas. One example was reallocating savings to the marketing department to support a C-suite initiative to rebrand globally. The additional funds were used to create new branding and messaging television commercials.
- **Technology improvements:** Cloud-based applications now included automation across the supplier life cycle, including more data connectivity between sourcing and contracts and visibility into spending. Software applications were improved with an

end-to-end view of process automation through a unified and integrated suite of applications. This connected the awarded suppliers with a contract for the requisitions and invoicing modules. The integrated suite was vital for some companies when moving to cloud-based applications.

- **Technology confidence:** Cloud-based technologies had been mainstream for around seven years. As more organizations shifted to the cloud, the confidence to use cloud-based applications increased. Executive leaders had more confidence that the technology would and could deliver.
- **Technology competition:** The market now had more application providers from which to choose. The increase in competition naturally reduced application licensing costs and spurred the development of features and capabilities to differentiate between one application company and another.

The transformation wave in 2010 focused on procurement automation; then in 2015, the focus was on procurement optimization. The integrated suite's benefits included improved visibility in spending and controls, increased savings opportunities, and process efficiencies. The average time frame for global transformation initiatives was 18 to 24 months, and fees ranged between $3 and $5 million U.S. dollars.

The third wave began around 2021 to 2022, focusing on procurement intelligence with more value-based results. Examples of these results were higher confidence in data-driven decisions, automating tail-end tactical processes, and self-service capabilities. This third wave combined the negative impacts of COVID-related supply chain delays with technology advancements. Companies were pushed out of their comfort zones. They were now required to evaluate technologies to support daily needs for virtual meetings and global team workshops and define what a home-office employee looks like. Supply chain challenges and delays forced companies to find technologies to answer foundational questions such as "Who and where are the alternative suppliers who can meet our needs?" or "How can I know if this supplier can ship my products to my customers on time?"

More questions required more data and more resources to find answers. Often, the answers were discovered too late to make a difference or were derived with low confidence. The more data collected, the more challenging it became to identify patterns within the data quickly. At the same time, there were more discussions about how artificial intelligence (AI) technologies could help solve this problem. AI technologies could augment human thinking to supplement our limitations by evaluating historically complex data and real-time information.

The term *AI* is used in this book as a general term to house various types of technologies, such as machine learning, natural language processing, deep learning, computer vision, robotic process automation (RPA), and neural networks. These technologies can be used to access large amounts of customer and supplier data to address those questions in or near real time. For example, according to Jaggaer's website, their supply chain application uses "artificial intelligence and machine learning technologies to provide predictive analytics and recommend actions based on real-time data." Its use of neutral networks recognizes existing patterns in supplier behavior combined with real-time supply chain delays to provide insights into reducing risks of production downtimes, delayed deliveries, and increased costs.

As cloud-based applications stabilized, the overall time frame for these projects dropped to between 12 and 15 months with fees ranging between $1 and $2.5 million. However, the organization remained sensitive to the cost of a transformation. This meant critical workstreams like change management or project management were commonly removed from the transformation budget before it started. In other scenarios, the organization selected the lowest-cost supplier when choosing cloud-based applications. Selecting low-cost suppliers often leads to little or no thought to the skills of the project resources or the lack of experience those resources may have with similar projects.

When this happens, low-cost projects focus on the shortest timeline and lean into the technical side of a transformation initiative. The project is reduced to a lift-n-shift, meaning the existing processes and data are automated without considering process efficiencies, simplification, or optimization. A lift-n-shift does not emphasize data quality or stakeholder experience. Even though this is no longer a transformation initiative, it is still sold that way internally. These types of projects check a few boxes for the executive sponsor. Shortly after the application is live, leadership wonders why they do not see the significant value promised.

The blame is almost always placed on the application without considering other root causes. There is a large gap between the original business case and the results. This gap is caused by a domino effect of the decisions made before the project started, such as reducing the budget, removing critical workstreams, and limiting resources, all leading to a project that should not have been labeled a *transformation*. What was sold to the stakeholder was not the project that eventually occurred.

Another common stakeholder complaint is the lack of a follow-on phase that promises to integrate items from the current project backlog. These backlog items are a combination of processes considered out-of-scope before the project began, combined with business challenges identified throughout the project (i.e., during the configuration phase, integration testing phase, or user-acceptance phase). The cases that follow are specific examples of processes that should have been corrected but instead postponed until a future phase (that never happened):

- When shifting from paper to digital purchase orders, it was discovered that the printed version of the digital purchase order did not include the same terms and conditions already written in the paper purchase orders. These terms and conditions should be added and translated into the local language of the supplier's location. The project team decided to add the terms and conditions in English, but the translations were placed in the backlog to be executed in the next phase.
- When comparing the paper purchase order to the new digital version, the electronic version did not include several fields that had been included in the paper version. These fields were not considered mandatory, but they offered more information about the purchased items for customs agents. Over time, the logistics team noticed when they added more information on the purchase order, the purchases were detained for less time at customs. A few extra fields reduced the overall transportation cycle times, and it reduced the storage costs and other hidden fees at customs. Since

these were not mandatory fields, the project team placed them in the backlog list to add the requirements to the next phase.

- During the validation of the tax reconciliation process on an invoice, it was noticed the invoice was routed to a tax person to correct and approve. The organization should not modify a supplier's invoice. This is out of compliance with internal controls and policies. The correct process was to send the invoice back to the supplier, requesting they revise and resubmit. Instead of automatically updating the process to route the invoice back to the supplier, the project team told the tax department to route the invoice back to the supplier manually and then added this item into the backlog to fix during the next phase.

When these or similar items are encountered, the first question always asked is why these never came up during the requirements phase. The second question is why the business stakeholders did not say anything after the configuration phase. The response is always the same: the stakeholder signed off on the requirements and configuration phase but never mentioned it. Ultimately, the deciding factor compares how much more time and money these changes will add to the project and how significant these changes are to the business. The compromise is to add these into a backlog for a follow-on phase that never occurs. The company is left with an electronic process that does not include the critical elements needed from the original paper or manual processes.

EXAMPLES OF REAL-WORLD SCENARIOS

Real-World Scenario #1

I began working with a client who had implemented a cloud procurement application less than two years before our first meeting. They were unsure if the issues they were experiencing were because of the application they selected, the lack of process improvement during the application implementation, or because they had not included change management as part of the original implementation. After establishing a *listening tour* of key stakeholder groups, superusers, and executives, my last conversation was with the CEO, who had specific concerns about a requisition for $7.47. This requisition had been escalated to him because no one had approved it. The application had been configured so that when a requisition was not approved within a specific number of days, the requisition would be escalated to the approver's manager. It would continue moving upward in the chain until someone eventually approved it.

The CEO did not believe a requisition of that size should be escalated to him, and I agreed with him. This was also a quick fix because their cloud procurement application had an out-of-the-box option for executives. Once the CEO and other executives were placed in the *Executive Group*, any requisitions would be blocked. The total time to fix this within the application to ensure the CEO did not receive requisitions through an unnecessary escalation process was precisely six minutes.

Most companies would stop there. The immediate issue was resolved with some minor effort. In this specific example, there was still the underlying problem of why the requisition was not approved during the first, second, or third escalation. A band-aid had been applied to fix the symptom, which made everyone feel better. Yet, the requisition went unapproved for more than 45 days and caused additional costs due to project delays. The head of procurement operations commented on the listening tour, "The purpose of implementing an application was to reduce the requisition request to order cycle times, not increase them."

> The root cause of failure is not the application but, most often, the organization's decisions before, during, and after implementation.

Real-World Scenario #2

Resources in the accounts payable department manually coded invoices and wanted to reassess their processes. The company was using a cloud-based eInvoicing solution. When documenting the current process, all electronic invoices were automatically routed to offshore accounts payable resources as the first stop in the approval process. Those resources would manually enter the accounting code before the electronic invoice was routed to the stakeholder(s) for additional approval.

In looking at the original implementation documentation, this organization had defined the implementation of the eInvoicing application as a transformation project. Yet, all they ended up doing was automating the same process they had before, coding the invoice. The only difference was that the accounts payable resources no longer received a physical copy of an invoice but rather an electronic version. Some minor benefits may have been received, but deploying an application to automate the current resource did not leave them in a better place than before. Multiple and manual touchpoints remained without including a business and digital component. This led to increased errors and the lengthening of end-to-end process cycle times. The only difference was that before the project, the company used paper-based invoices; after the project, the company used electronic invoices.

Real-World Scenario #3

A global Fortune 75 organization expanded its supplier management program by manually adding 30 offshore resources to enter supplier data into the ERP system. Adding more resources offshore provided a low-cost option. The offshore resources performed repetitive, tactical tasks, but the organization continued to experience limitations in process standardization. Resources offshore had a higher turnover rate that contributed to an inconsistency in quality. Additionally, manual data entry required more resources to review, validate, and correct data entry errors.

When process changes were necessary because of policy updates, the 30 offshore resources did not immediately adopt those changes. More resources and time were required to communicate, train, and update standard operations procedures for those offshore resources to follow. What started as 30 resources quickly expanded to 45 resources. Adding 15 extra resources to the process did not make the process faster.

Lesson Learned

When a transformation initiative is not a deliberate and proactive decision by the organization, it loses its purpose and value. For a few companies, it has become a checkbox that allows leadership to say they reacted quickly to external forces. For other companies, it is an afterthought that loses funding before it can start or is deprioritized halfway through the project. For most companies, the transformation initiative is seeing only half of the larger picture. Either the company defines transformation as redesigning business processes with no automation or as a technology-only project where critical business and process decisions are not considered.

For example, when critical decisions are made to one part of the process without understanding the impact of that decision, it can hide potential issues that may not become visible to the organization right away. Not taking the time to understand the effects of other steps in the existing process or how that decision will impact the users six months from now delays potential issues until later. In all these scenarios, the transformation project fails immediately or has signs of failing less than 12 months after completion.

WHY TRANSFORMATION INITIATIVES FAIL

Transformation projects fail for many reasons, but several common obstacles appear across all transformation projects regardless of the industry. The remainder of this book will outline and dive deeper into some obstacles that block success, help you understand the underlying root cause of why transformation initiatives fail, and identify a few alternatives. The following list includes the top 20 variables contributing to failed transformation initiatives that will be explored later:

1. Starting a transformation as a reaction to an external event rather than proactively building a foundation to support future changes
2. Establishing temporary workarounds as long-term solutions
3. Belief that using technology alone will solve the problem
4. Lack of purpose or understanding of why we need a transformation
5. Working with policies established 100+ years ago
6. Not supplementing your team with pockets of expertise
7. De-emphasizing, then prioritizing, then de-emphasizing risk

8. Not questioning the current state; the status quo bias
9. Underestimating the value of culture
10. Inadequate processes that create more work (after automating)
11. Accountability is spread across too many individuals to be effective
12. The definition of success is not evolving to match the frequency of disruption
13. Lack of a bold digital vision
14. Limited opportunities for stakeholder feedback
15. Lack of enterprise collaboration in overlapping initiatives
16. Lack of a front-seat leader
17. Allowing unconscious bias in the workplace
18. Misaligning value with strategic goals
19. Not rethinking how we think
20. Not setting up employees to be successful

Section I

A Window into the Past

CHAPTER 2

EVOLUTION OF THE PROCUREMENT ORGANIZATION

When searching the internet for the earliest recording of procurement, there are references to the Egyptians during the building of the Pyramids. In 2500 B.C., scribes played a clerical role in documenting on papyrus the quantities of materials and the number of workers needed. The scribes tracked each order from when it was requested to when it arrived on site. This example resembles order management, logistics, and supply chain management today. Yet, similar references are made throughout history, including the Roman Empire. SCMglobe.com discusses a modern-day procurement and supply chain management process deep within the Roman empire around 300 A.D. using the example of buying olive oil from North Africa and bringing that product back to Rome.

Trading has been frequented throughout history, as have the fundamental concepts of procurement, logistics, and supply chain. Further examples include the Silk Road trade routes, which connected Asia with the Mediterranean, including North Africa and Europe. These routes were in use until 1452 when the Ottoman Empire boycotted trade with China and closed the routes. In 1492, Columbus' "discovery" of the New World saw an expansion of procuring and trading commodities between the British Empire and items found in the New World.

In 2015, Ardent Partners published an illustration of the evolution of the procurement organization from 1870 to 2015. What made this study more notable than previous chief procurement officer (CPO) studies was the visual diagram outlining distinct phases in the evolution of the procurement organization. It was also the first formal announcement outlining a shift from the Strategic Phase in 2014 into the Agile Phase (see Figure 2.1).

As a procurement professional who began working in procurement, supply chain, and data management in 1995, I would like to share an alternative perspective. Specifically, starting the Clerical Phase in 1830 instead of 1870 and splitting the Strategic Phase into two distinct groups (see Figure 2.2):

- Transactional Phase (1990s–2006)
- Strategic Phase (2007–2014)

As we explore procurement history, be mindful of what your procurement organization looks like today. Stepping backward can often provide a perspective for seeing the path in front of us more clearly. It offers opportunities to understand how we previously met obstacles, the decisions we made at that time, and the impact of those decisions. We call these *lessons learned.*

These lessons learned, when evaluated properly, provide the tools needed when we encounter similar challenges in the future so that our

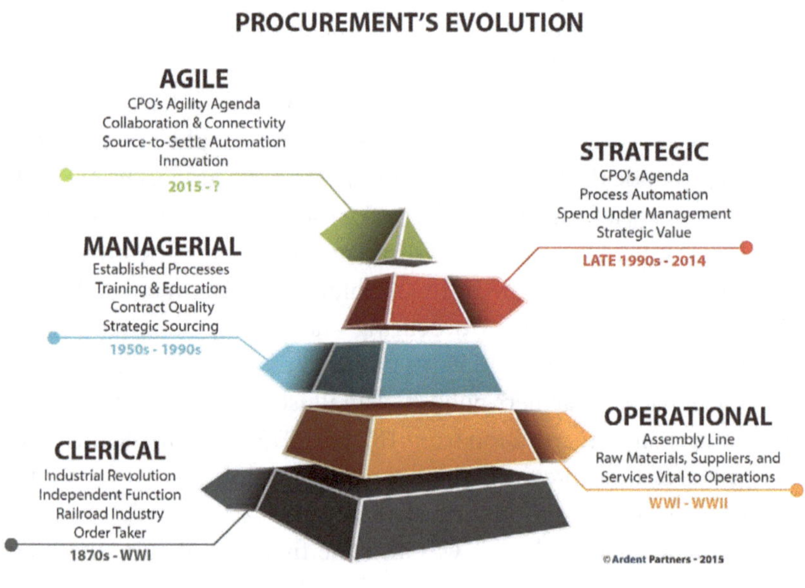

Figure 2.1 Procurement evolution (Ardent Partners 2015)

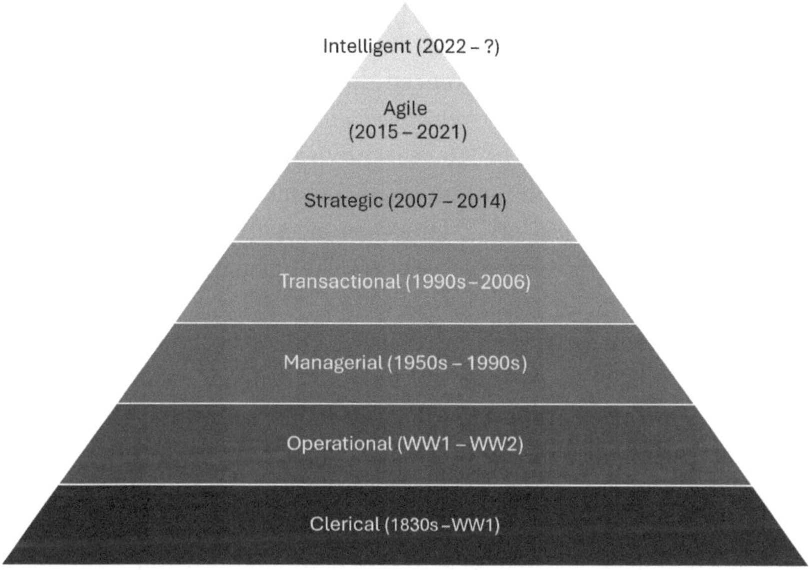

Figure 2.2 Reimagined Procurement evolution

decisions will lead to better results. Without a proper retrospective and reflection, the transformation initiative doesn't yield the intended outcomes. The organization then attempts another initiative to fix the problems from the first one that failed, and it becomes a never-ending cycle. Not being able to move the organization forward is an obstacle of our own making. Sometimes, it is harder to break free when obstacles are created by us than when those obstacles are created by someone else.

The remainder of this section will focus on the evolution of the modern-day definition of procurement and supply chain, starting with the 1830s during the American Industrial Revolution. This was a direct result of the War of 1812 when Britain stopped shipping goods to the United States. This marked the beginning of industrialization within the United States, first in the textile industry and then in other manufacturing areas.

> Stepping back to reflect can provide a clearer path to moving forward.

CLERICAL PHASE (1830–WORLD WAR I)

In 1832, Charles Babbage referenced the formal role of purchasing in his book *On the Economy of Machinery and Manufactures*. He said the book was written because of "10 years of visiting workshops and factories in England and on the continent to acquaint myself with the various resources of mechanical art." Many references from this book can be directly translated into activities still relevant to modern-day procurement and supply chain organizations.

Babbage's book focuses on the division of labor in the organization. In Section 252, he states, "In one of the most difficult arts, that of mining, great improvements have resulted from the judicious distribution of the future; and under the arrangements which have gradually been introduced, the whole system of the mine and its government is now placed under the control of the following officers." Of the 10 officers listed, number nine, is "a materials man selects, purchases, receives, and delivers all articles required."

In Section 253, the introduction of competition combined with the subdivision of labor (the ten officers listed) "renders it necessary for each producer to be continually on the watch, to discover improved methods by which the cost of the article he manufactures may be reduced . . . and also affords them a better chance of suggesting to the manufacturer changes in the fashion of his goods, which may be suitable either to the tastes or finances of his customers."

In the chapter titled "On the Cost of Each Separate Process in Manufacture," Babbage outlines the importance of understanding the end-to-end process and, more specifically, the costs associated with each process step to improve processes and reduce costs over time. In modern-day procurement, this would be a means of process improvement. The goal is to simplify each step in the process or the end-to-end process to reduce process cycle time and directly reduce overall cost.

Finally, Section 254 focuses more on the impact of process improvement. It provides a specific example: ". . . if a method could be contrived of diminishing by one-fourth the time required for fixing on the heads of pins, the expense of making them would be reduced by about thirteen percent." It is impressive that a book published in 1832 references a dedicated procurement individual focusing on the total cost of ownership and improving processes to reduce costs and meet customer demands.

Later, in 1887, Marshal M. Kirkman authored the book *The Handling of Railway Supplies: Their Purchase and Disposition* while he was the Chicago & North Western Railway controller. According to the preface, "the purchase, care, and use of railway supplies influences directly the cost . . . and affect, therefore, the reputations of officers and the profits of owners."

Kirkman's book takes a very tactical view of purchasing, covering all aspects from purchasing supplies, requisitions, supervision, receipt and inspection of material, storage, fuel, and the disbursement of materials and inventories. However, he only briefly introduces the idea of corrupt practices and the negative impact of a distributed purchasing model. He cites, "a person hired for his skill as a blacksmith is not likely to possess the qualities necessary to enable him to cope successfully with the veteran merchant in purchasing goods that a blacksmith requires." Kirkman's perspective was that the skills of purchasing goods for a blacksmith were quite different from the skills needed as a blacksmith and, therefore, should not be the same person. This involves a different department with skilled resources who can successfully cope with more experienced suppliers. The term *distributed purchasing model* did not exist in the 1870s. Still, Kirkman's book does provide a perspective on having separate resources for those who purchase supplies for the business and those who consume those supplies.

By 1887, Babbage's "materials man" from 1832 had a formal title with expanding roles and responsibilities. In Chapter 3, Kirkman references "the office of the purchasing agent (whose) duties not only familiarize him with all new devices, but his observation enables him to point out those most likely to lessen expenses or add to the efficiency of a property." This statement not only outlines the purchasing agent as an individual who considers improvements continuously but also includes learning about and understanding innovation (i.e., all new devices).

Kirkman also states, ". . . to be able to buy its supplies at the lowest possible figure is enormous value to a company, and a capable purchasing agent, it is probable, can save his employer a greater sum through the exercise of experience and intelligence than any other officer" where "one of the most effective avenues for accomplishing this will be to publicly and generally invite bids from manufacturers, and others for supplies for a considerable period ahead." In the late 1800s, the concept of competitive bidding and "looking forward" to consider prior purchasing while estimating future demand was used to outline the early beginnings of a procurement and supply management department. In Kirkman's eyes, a purchasing agent was no longer an entry-level individual but an experienced one who gained knowledge or intelligence over time and should become more valued than other officers. Having this level of experience meant the development of a purchasing department with a group of individuals who acquired knowledge over time and were no longer seen as short-term contractors.

OPERATIONAL PHASE (WORLD WAR I–WORLD WAR II)

There were no significant changes to procurement operations after Kirkman's book in 1887, except in small pockets of industries like textiles, railroads, and mining manufacturing. In the early part of the 20th century, two groups contributed to advancing a purchasing organization: the United States War Department and the National Association of Purchasing Agents (N.A.P.A.).

During World War 1, between 1914 and 1918, purchasing and logistics were formalized and evolved into a central activity. The manufacture of consumer goods shifted to support the military. The Council of National Defense, established by Section 2 of the Army Appropriation Act of August 29, 1916 (39 Stat. 649), paved the way to coordinate industries and resources for national security and welfare. It quickly established a National Defense Advisory Commission divided into seven committees, each focusing on a different area(s) impacting the war:

1. Raw materials, metals, and minerals
2. Munitions, manufacturing, and industrial relations
3. Engineering and education

4. Labor
5. Medicine and sanitation
6. Supplies
7. Transportation and communications

These committees categorized items based on similarities in their purchasing behavior. For example, procuring and shipping labor differed from procuring and shipping raw materials or finished goods such as munitions. Private organizations eventually mimicked these categories, further expanding and breaking them into smaller subcategory groupings, which set the foundation for category-based purchasing.

Key Milestones Between 1917 and 1946

Between 1917 and 1946, a series of events occurred that by themselves did not do much to advance the forward momentum of a procurement organization. However, when viewed over time, each event contributed in one way or another to the eventual development of a formal and centralized department coordinating all efforts to procure, pay, and distribute materials for the war effort:

- On December 28, 1917, Storage and Traffic Services was established (General Order 167) to supervise the transport of troops and supplies and the storage of supplies.
- On January 11, 1918, the War Department's finance activities centralized the Purchase Service in the Office of the Chief of Staff to supervise the acquisition of supplies and munitions and coordinate army procurement.
- On February 9, 1918, the Purchase Service in the Office of the Chief of Staff was redesignated as the Purchase and Supply Division
- On April 16, 1918, multiple offices were consolidated to form a centralized Purchase, Storage, and Traffic Division (General Order 36).

There was also a noticeable overlap in purchasing activities across military divisions during this time. For example, on November 15, 1918, the supply functions of the Medical Department of the U.S. Army were transferred to the Office of the Director of Purchase and Storage.

The Purchase, Storage, and Traffic division merged with the Office of Finance at the end of World War I.

Between World War I and World War II:

- On July 14, 1920, the War Department was reorganized, with most operational purchasing responsibilities shifting to the Office of the Quartermaster General.
- On August 16, 1921, Supply and Transport planning functions were reassigned to the newly established Supply Division (G-4).

During World War II:

- On March 9, 1942, the Operational functions of the Supply Division (G-4) were renamed the newly established Services of Supply Division.
- On June 11, 1946, the Services of Supply Division was redesignated as the Service, Supply, and Procurement Division.

Examples of the centralized efforts to consolidate purchasing and provide transparency to the public can also be seen in the *Official Bulletin*, a daily newspaper from 1917–1919, under the order of the President by the Committee on Public Information, first published on May 10, 1917, just one month after the United States entered World War I. This publication brought visibility into procurement, bidding, and contract activities. It also illustrated a purchasing department with resources fully dedicated to these activities. Throughout the war, this was widely read by the public and potentially influenced the private sector to strengthen its purchasing function as an essential department outside the military.

For example, just three months after its first publication in the *Official Bulletin*, the Bureau of Supplies and Account of the Department of the Navy issued a list of proposed items needed for purchase and how bidders (or suppliers) could access the complete list of the schedule of materials. Two examples are shown in Figures 2.3 and 2.4.

In the *Official Bulletin* from February 1919, the word "Purchase" is introduced as part of the office title: Office of Director of Purchase and Storage (see Figure 2.5). Also in Figure 2.5, the notice highlights a dollar threshold for a purchase order of $25,000, a threshold that has been carried forward through the decades from 1919 to the present.

NOTICE GIVEN OF PROPOSED PURCHASE OF LONG LIST OF MATERIALS FOR NAVY

The Bureau of Supplies and Accounts of the Navy Department has issued notice of proposed purchases of the following materials.

Bidders desiring to submit proposals should request the Bureau of Supplies and Accounts, Navy Department, Washington, D. C., to send schedules covering the material which they propose to offer, giving schedule numbers.

MISCELLANEOUS.

Articles.	Quantity.	Delivery at navy yard.	Sch.	Articles.	Quantity.	Delivery at navy yard.	Sch.
Crane, locomotive, 15-ton	1	Charleston, W. Va.	1395	Machines, universal grinding	4	South Charleston, W. Va.	1399
Drill, radial, motor-driven	1	Mare Island, Cal.	1396				
Lathe, engine, back-geared	1	Key West, Fla.	1404	Material, building, for 30 houses		Las Animas, Colo.	1398
Lathe, engine, motor-driven	1	Fort Mifflin, Pa.	1400	Pump, centrifugal, motor-driven	1	Norfolk, Va.	1397
Lathe, 24-inch, turret, motor-driven	1	do.	1400	Press, hydraulic, forging, 200-ton	1	Key West, Fla.	1404
Machine, boring, drilling, 66-inch, horizontal.	1	Key West, Fla.	1404				

Figure 2.3 An example of an official bulletin notice of proposed purchases

NOTICE OF PROPOSED PURCHASES FOR THE NAVY

WASHINGTON, D. C., February 6, 1918.

Bidders desiring to submit proposals for the following material should give the schedule numbers desired and forward same without delay. Applications will be filled as soon as the schedules are received from the Public Printer. Schedules can also be obtained upon application to the navy purchasing office in or near to each navy yard.

MISCELLANEOUS.

Articles.	Quantity.	Delivery at navy yard.	Sch.
Cable, interior communication, leaded and armored	12,000 feet	Brooklyn, N. Y.	1685
Hose, fire, linen, unlined	5,000 feet	Puget Sound, Wash.	1683
Hose, fire, cotton, rubber lined	10,000 feet	do.	1683
Lead, sheet, in rolls	82,000 pounds	Boston, Mass.	1680
Sets, ventilating, portable	50	Puget Sound, Wash.	1684
Wire, single-conductor, leaded and armored	90,000 feet	Brooklyn, N. Y.	1685
Wire, lighting and power	50,000 feet	Puget Sound, Wash.	1682
Wire, lighting and power, two-conductor, leaded and armored.	5,000 feet	do.	1685

Figure 2.4 A second example of an official bulletin notice of proposed purchases

This provided a real acknowledgment that the government saw the value in a department dedicated to purchasing activities with a management role that had oversight. This reference also mentions purchase orders under $25,000, illustrating that not all purchases were equal. Depending on the dollar amount, purchase orders under a specific threshold followed a different path or policy. Additionally, an example of receiving and opening sealed bids was mentioned in the *Official Bulletin* on March 18, 1919 (see Figure 2.6). This concept is still used in modern-day procurement with local, state, and federal agencies.

Around the same time, in 1915, the N.A.P.A. was founded as a not-for-profit educational association serving professionals and organizations with a keen interest in supply management, education, training, qualifications, publications, information, and research. Before 1915, local purchasing

PURCHASE AND STORAGE

The following is a list of purchase orders and contracts passed by the Board of Review, Office of Director of Purchase and Storage:

February 26, 1918.

Purchase orders under $25,000, made on open market purchase or left to lowest bidder and submitted to the board for consideration after execution and delivery:

6722. United States Steel Products Co., San Francisco, Cal., boiler tubes No. 9 BWG, $6,-669.10.

2701. N. A. Gunst Branch, San Francisco, Cal., 1,100 cigars, Londres Alb; 1/10 box, at $2.34; 660 cigars, Perfectors; 1/10 box at $3.795—$5,078.70.

2726. California Packing Corporation, San Francisco, Cal., 64,800 cans cherries, No. 2½, extra black, at $0.21⅝, $14,040.

261. Frye & Co., Seattle, Wash., 17,500 pounds fresh pork, hams, 30 cents; 15,000 pounds fresh pork, loins, 32.5 cents; 17,500 pounds fresh pork, shoulders, 235 cents—$14,237.50.

Figure 2.5 Office of Director of Purchase and Storage

associations had formed in at least ten major cities in the United States, including one of the most active groups in Buffalo, New York (founded in 1904). The plan was to organize nationally to grow the profession and further improve the value of the purchase organization within a company. It was not until 1915, after developing a national organization, that things moved forward more quickly. The N.A.P.A. had three strong affiliates when it held its first convention in New York in 1916, with 100 of its 250 members in attendance. That year, the N.A.P.A. launched a magazine called *The Purchasing Agent*.

The N.A.P.A. was vocal about the War Department's lack of consolidated procurement processes. Specifically, in the editorial section of Volume 5, Issue 2 (February 1918), of *Purchasing Agent* magazine, titled "War Department Centralization," the N.A.P.A. was not shy about offering its opinion on how the War Department could improve: "The methods the War Department employs in purchasing supplies, demanding the maintenance of five separate purchasing divisions, have been criticized during the past few weeks . . . Secretary of War Baker has shown his desire to bring about more efficient buying in the War Department by creating a Director of Purchases. It remains to be seen how much real

SEALED PROPOSALS INVITED

War Department.

U. S. SOLDIERS' HOME.

Sealed proposals will be received until 10 o'clock a. m., April 24, 1919, for furnishing a 500-kilowatt turbo generator. For specifications, blanks, and further information apply to Secretary-Treasurer, United States Soldiers' Home, Washington, D. C.

Treasury Department.

BUREAU OF ENGRAVING AND PRINTING.

Sealed proposals will be received by the Bureau of Engraving and Printing for furnishing and delivering the following articles:

Until 2 p. m., March 31, 1919: One 1-gallon porcelain evaporating dish for silver bath; six 1-quart measuring jugs with removable funnel tops; 4 tanks of oxygen gas, approximately 200 cubic feet to tank (tanks when empty to be returned to contractor at his expense).

Until April 1, 1919: Five thousand feet of one and one-eighth inch No. 1 maple flooring, 2½-inch face.

Department of the Interior.

ST. ELIZABETHS HOSPITAL.

Sealed proposals will be received by St. Elizabeths Hospital for furnishing and delivering the following materials:

Until 4 p. m., April 1, 1919: Four hundred pounds of farina (or equal); 2,500 pounds of evaporated apples; 200 pounds of baking powder; 300 pounds of pearl barley; 600 pounds of lima beans; 600 pounds of kidney beans; 6,000 pounds of navy beans; 100 pounds of chocolate; 1,500 pounds of hominy, coarse; 1,500 pounds of hominy grits; 200 dozen cans of corn; 150 dozen cans of peas; 100 dozen No. 10 cans of tomatoes; 1,500 pounds of macaroni (in bulk); 3,600 pounds of rolled oats; 500 pounds of evaporated peaches; 3,000 pounds of prunes (state size_; 800 pounds of seedless raisins; 15 dozen 1-gallon cans of rhubarb; 3,500 pounds of rice; 8,000 pounds of fine table salt; 600 pounds of cornstarch; 300 gallons of sirup, golden.

Figure 2.6 Sealed proposals invited

coordination will result . . . but the fact they have been taken is evidence the administration realizes the necessity for at least reasonable centralization of war purchases."

The editorial continues to call for "one executive possessing real buying authority, but it realizes that this development cannot be brought about in a day." However, the editorial ended positively: "The War Department should be credited with the good it has accomplished up to the present time under adverse conditions."

Other issues of the *Purchasing Agent* magazine discuss procurement ethics (January 1919), the development of a formal purchasing course (January 1921), and the advantages of standardization (January 1925).

Key milestones throughout the 1920s and 1930s continued to illustrate the value and importance of the purchasing agent through the influence of the N.A.P.A.:

- In 1920, the N.A.P.A.'s ethics committee developed a *Purchasing Agents Creed*, a predecessor to the Principles and Standards of Purchasing Practice.
- In 1923, the N.A.P.A. created the National Business Survey, polling members on their industry sector knowledge and consolidating the results into a national report. This survey eventually changed its name to the Report on Business.
- In January 1925, an issue of *Purchasing Agent* mentioned a purchasing course at the University of Chicago facilitated by John C. Dinsmore, a purchasing agent at the University. The course description reads, "Functions of the purchasing department in the modern industrial organization. The course deals not only in the theory and ethics of modern purchase methods but also discusses standards, analyses, sources of supply, and price tendencies."
- In 1928, the N.A.P.A. developed the *Standards for Buying and Selling*. Along with the *Principles and Standards of Purchasing Practice* of 1923, these two guides to ethical conduct remained relevant for decades.

MANAGERIAL PHASE (1950s–1990s)

The priorities during World War II, which set the initial focus on purchasing, were no longer applicable post-war. During the war, there was a direct link between the need to procure items to support the war effort. Unfortunately, the role of procurement was prioritized for this specific need because when the war was over, so was the perception that procurement professionals were needed as part of the normal day-to-day operations of an organization. Bruce D. Henderson commented about purchasing during this time, noting that purchasing was neglected in most organizations because it was unimportant to mainstream problems. He said that some executives found it hard to visualize a company becoming more successful than its competitors because of its superior procurement.

Purchasing was not seen as a valuable contributor to the organization as executives considered other priorities, such as marketing, sales, and profit. This viewpoint did not last too long. Those returning from World War II took advantage of the GI Bill, which provided a larger pool of educated consumers. The concept of buy now, pay later with the first revolving credit card in 1958 issued by Bank of America enabled consumers to purchase and pay over time. This increase in consumer spending required organizations to reconsider stocking inventory to ensure the product was on hand when the consumer wanted to buy.

There were still many competing priorities, and the purchasing organization was also competing for attention. For example, the finance department prioritized cost reduction while increasing profit margin. At the same time, the need to communicate product differentiation to consumers strengthened the voice of the marketing department. In parallel, in the mid-1960s, television improved its reach into most consumer's homes. Marketing and advertising quickly gained executive sponsorship over the finance department because of its direct link to consumers, sales, and revenue.

In 1968, the N.A.P.A. changed its name to the National Association of Purchasing Management (NAPM) to better reflect the evolution of the purchasing group as a fundamental management function supporting corporate goals. The association continued to be a prominent voice for the role of purchasing in modern-day manufacturing organizations. Yet, it was not gaining much traction, as seen in Dean Ammer's 1974 article in the *Harvard Business Review.*

Ammer's article included comments about the negative perception of purchasing that could be overcome through accomplishing active purchasing, which is measured in terms of meeting overall company objectives and contributing to bottom-line profitability. He noted that the purchasing executive should be part of nonpurchasing decisions, for the entire organization loses when purchasing is not part of the organization's consensus on major decisions. Finally, Ammer suggested that the function should have sufficient stature to report to top management or a division manager. However, according to his survey, this only happened in 37 percent of the responding firms.

Other external forces during this time included the impact of the Vietnam War (1955–1975) and, more notably, the Organization of the Petroleum Exporting Countries oil embargo (1973–1974). The manufacturing organization was beginning to recognize the direct and indirect impacts of global economic and political forces, of which the United States did not have significant control over the outcomes—specifically, the direct and indirect impacts on sales and revenue. Within a very short time, there was acknowledgment of the need for improving efficiencies, particularly in purchasing, transportation, inventory storage, control, and management.

Also, the ability to coordinate and exchange information through electronic mail (i.e., email) beginning in the 1970s allowed organizations to purchase products outside their local geographic regions with opportunities to consider multiple suppliers. In the 1990s, purchasing had finally become a separate department within the larger enterprise that operated in multiple countries or was buying from suppliers in multiple countries. The purchasing department, however, continued to report to the finance department because of the overlapping theme of cost reduction.

TRANSACTIONAL PHASE (1990s–2006)

The Transactional Phase marked a significant jump forward for the procurement organization with dedicated resources, a well-defined procurement department, and a single individual to oversee procurement-only functions. In most manufacturing and nonmanufacturing organizations, the procurement department remained under the finance department and reported to the CFO (chief financial officer). It maintained its primary purpose: to issue an order or piece of paper to secure supplies, services, or materials. This order was an agreement to purchase from a supplier in exchange for a cost the buyer and the supplier agreed on. Once the organization confirmed the receipt of the supplier's invoice, based on the mutually agreed upon cost documented on the purchase order, the order was paid based on the payment terms.

The transactional or tactical sourcing methodology used during this time remains mostly a reactive approach to address an immediate need. This phase was most notable for the following:

- Purchase orders were the primary method of buying
- Enterprise resourcing planning (ERP) was the primary application to generate purchase orders
- Policies supporting a purchase order for all goods and services
- Cost was the primary variable when comparing suppliers
- More frequent use of requests for proposals
- The *spend cube* defined data collection
- The term *strategic sourcing* was used
- Attention to indirect spending was improving
- Supplier and organization relationships were most often confrontational
- The highest-ranking procurement resource was at the VP level
- The procurement VP commonly reported to the CFO
- Introduction of the purchasing card
- Procurement and IT (information technology) resources were challenging ownership of procurement processes
- Advancements during this phase set the path for early-stage process automation

There were numerous improvements and leaps forward during this time, many of which resulted in efficiency gains within the purchasing process. Others became the foundation for understanding the impact of evaluating total spending. Still, other improvements may have been ineffective, but they have led the way for future improvements, and three warrant more discussion:

- The blanket purchase order
- Spend cube
- Migrating from ERP to procure-to-pay (P2P)

The Blanket Purchase Order

During this time, the concept of no-PO/no-pay was used to signal to the supplier and to the internal business stakeholders that without a current purchase order number on an invoice, the supplier would not receive payment. Depending on the organization's payment terms, once the invoice tied to a purchase has been received and approved, it may take another 45 days before the supplier receives its payment. This was before electronic invoicing, and it was common to see stacks of paper invoices being routed through the organization to collect a physical signature. Even if the payment terms were 45 days, approving the invoice and entering the information into the ERP system took longer.

Consider this real-world scenario: in one of my projects, my role was to walk the steps of the invoice from beginning to end to understand where process improvements could be made. I discovered that people sorted invoices and walked them to a department for the first signature. A stack of invoices was delivered to a central department bin. At some point over the next 24 hours, a department resource would pick up the stacks of invoices and deliver them to an individual's desk, placing them on a tray called *IN*. From there, the invoices stayed in that tray on the individual's desk until they were processed. Mostly, the invoices were not a priority or were forgotten. At other times, the invoices continued to be stacked on top of the prior stack. This meant the older invoices were now at the bottom of the tray. Still, other times, the desk person would receive a phone call to find an invoice and move it to the top of the pile as it was urgent.

When the invoices were signed, they were placed into a different bin on the individual's desk labeled *OUT*. A couple of times a day, someone would walk through the office, pick up anything found in the *OUT* tray, and take them back to a central department location. The paper invoices were then placed in a department tray labeled *internal department* where they waited for another individual to pick them up and drop them off in another department for approval. When all the approvals were completed, the invoice was placed in a different department tray labeled *A/P*, where they would travel to the accounts payable department to be further processed and entered into the ERP system.

In one company, it was explained to me how common it was to pick up damaged invoices because the department bins were often next to the coffee machine (see Figure 2.7). It was supposed to be convenient for the department staff to have all the department bins and coffee machines in the same area, but it ended up causing more harm than good. If the invoice details could not be read, the invoice had to be returned to the accounts payable department to be reprinted and rerouted for approval. The approver was supposed to document this and return the damaged invoice to the accounts payable department for a reprint. Often this did not happen. When I asked the interdepartmental messenger what happens when they pick up a damaged invoice by mistake, the response was, “My job is to deliver this stack of invoices to the next department. Even if I thought it was a damaged invoice, I will take it to the next department for approval. The approver is responsible for marking the invoice as damaged and placing it into the *AP* bin for pick up by that messenger.” What a mess!

Figure 2.7 Coffee in the mailroom

While interviewing resources in another company, one anonymously told me that invoices were frequently lost or misplaced. For example, occasionally, the interdepartmental messengers would stop to use the restroom and leave the invoices there by mistake. Sometimes, the stack of invoices was still in the bathroom when he/she returned, but other times, someone else would pick them up, and it was never known where those invoices ended up. At the same company, because some departments were so far apart, the interdepartmental messenger would arrive to discover no invoices to pick up. If this happened repeatedly in a department, the messenger would decide not to walk to that department daily. As you can imagine, this led to further delays in paying the supplier regardless of any payment term arrangements already negotiated.

As a result, the supplier's workaround for receiving faster payments was to generate and send more invoices. For example, instead of sending an invoice once per month, the contract may outline that invoices would be issued twice or every two weeks. For the business stakeholders, this meant they created purchase orders more frequently and most often for the same price as the last purchase order. The approvers were approving more invoices, which meant more paper and a slower response time in the approval process. The purchase order was created, approved, and physically mailed, faxed, or emailed to the supplier. The business stakeholders needed a solution to minimize their data entry efforts for multiple purchase orders for the same amount going to the same supplier every two weeks. In the ERP system, this workaround was to create a *blanket purchase order*.

A blanket purchase order is an open-ended purchase order that does not close until the contract is finished or all the work is completed. It is advantageous when a supplier requires multiple invoices over a long period. Once the blanket purchase order is created, the supplier can issue invoices against the same purchase order number until no funds remain or the date on the blanket purchase order has passed. There were many disadvantages to using a blanket purchase order, including, but certainly not limited to:

- Year-end reconciliation of budgets became more challenging
- A disconnect between the work completed and no invoice from the supplier

- Lack of understanding of actual money spent compared to the departmental budget

It was and is still common that if the monies allocated for the departmental budget were not used, the finance department would absorb them and redistribute them to another over-budget project. Many business stakeholders didn't want to lose their funding. They would rather keep the funds tied to their department and move unused funds to a project in their department, not elsewhere. It became a real problem with blanket purchase orders remaining open 6–12 months after the work was completed.

Finally, blanket purchase orders caused the procurement organization problems in understanding exactly what was purchased. They required someone to review every invoice issued that may or may not have some information on the work performed. The supplier created invoices and rarely included the same level of detail documented on the purchase order. If understanding this was necessary, someone reviewing the invoices would need to pull the purchase order referenced on the invoice. This was time-consuming, with an inconsistent process depending on the individual tasked with the job. It was never 100% reliable that all the money was discovered.

The Spend Cube

The spend cube was a concept created to aid the procurement department in understanding total spend. It was the foundation for how companies began understanding how to find patterns in the data across three primary areas: spend, supplier, and business unit. Its objective was to know who purchased what from whom or, more specifically, to answer the following questions:

1. What did we purchase? (i.e., category of spend)
2. Who did we purchase from? (i.e., the supplier)
3. Who made the purchase? (i.e., the business unit or department)

The goal was to provide the procurement department with a database (often an MS Access database or SQL) of information they could sort through and understand their addressable spend. The term *addressable spend* looks at all the revenue collected, reconciles it with financial statements, and subtracts areas of spend that could not be sourced or negotiated, or where the procurement department could not have an impact. These may include removing salaries, taxes, penalties, bank fees, and utility payments. Additionally, the spend cube helped overcome other preexisting challenges with data, such as:

- General ledger (GL) codes were often too broad or generic, with two to five words as a description
- Invoices coded incorrectly by accident or on purpose
- Spend data or purchasing details were stored across multiple systems
- The accounts payable department could not provide the transactional detail needed to understand what exactly was purchased
- Commodity or materials codes in the ERP were not supportive of indirect spend
- GL codes did not match the sourcing categories used by procurement professionals

Many consulting firms working for Fortune 500 companies included the development of the spend cube as part of their basic services. It became the foundation of a procurement assessment phase, where the results identified opportunities for savings or improvement. This phase would last several months because the consulting teams cleaned up the data manually as they collected it, often categorizing the data for the first time into sourcing category groups (see Figure 2.8).

Once the data was collected, one dedicated resource, such as myself, would typically format, harmonize, clean, and classify the data using the global standard code—the United Nations Standard Products and Services Code (UNSPSC). Working around 70–90 hours a week for nine weeks, I would manually scrub the data. Procurement organizations could see for the first time if they were buying the same item across multiple suppliers, or how much money was spent in one sourcing category or subgroup (i.e., office supplies), or if business units were buying from the same suppliers.

On the surface, those nine weeks of hard work created visibility into who purchased what, from whom, and how many times. This was a

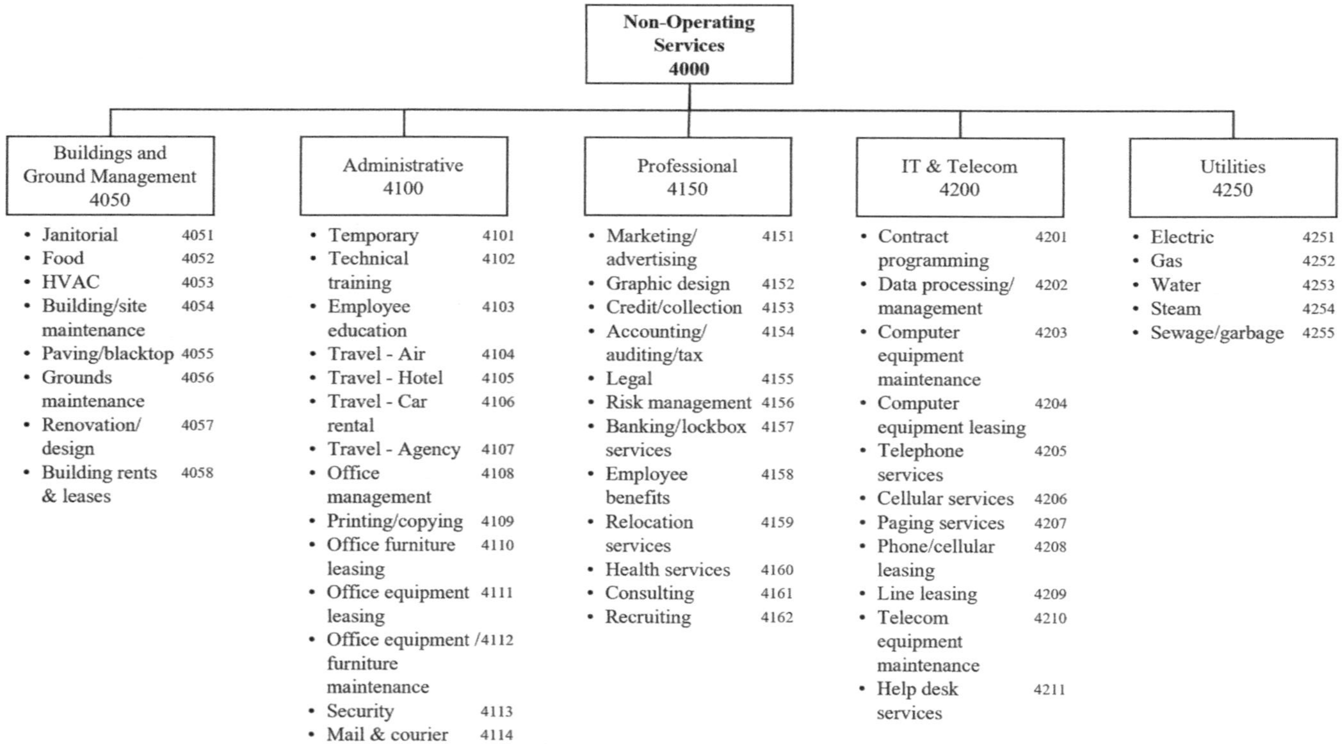

Figure 2.8 Procurement category taxonomy

good thing in a snapshot, but this manual process also brought a few disadvantages. Once the task was completed, the results were reviewed with the organization. The final deliverable for the assessment phase was a database with the raw data and cleansed data. PowerPoint slides offered insights and an implementation wave strategy documenting which sourcing categories the procurement team should tackle first.

This database had a time limitation. After 6 months, the cleansed data was no longer relevant, and the procurement organization was frustrated that it could not continue with the great work completed during the assessment phase. There was no way to repeat the assessment without devoting a lot of time and resources or through hiring a consulting firm to return and do it all again.

In addition, the assessment phase was flawed. The data classification was completed manually 100% of the time. This meant I would review every line of data from the organization and consider each line of purchase while also considering the supplemental data for that purchase. For example, to classify a line of data to the correct UNSPSC, all of the data had to be taken into context: the supplier name, the item description, the GL account, the ERP material code, etc.

Other considerations also had to be explored, such as whether this was a product or service or if the item was related to a capital project. If it was a separate purchase, it would be classified differently. Because this process was manual, I could not consider myself or the results of my work 100% accurate. Working 70–90 hours a week meant little sleep and that my decisions may not have always been consistent. Over time, as a consultant doing many of these each year, I had the UNSPSC, the Supplier Industry Code (SIC), and the National American Industry Classification System (NAICS) codes memorized for suppliers used most often. The U.S. government created SIC codes in 1937. They are four-digit codes for classifying a company's primary industry based on the company's highest revenue category. When Staples was first founded, its code was Stationary. SIC codes can be updated because they reflect the highest revenue category. If you are unsure about a supplier, specifically a start-up supplier, the SIC codes provide a good reference.

The U.S. Census Bureau assigns one NAICS code to each establishment based on its primary activity (generally the activity that generates the most revenue for the establishment) to collect, tabulate, analyze, and disseminate statistical data describing the economy of the United States. The codes are broadly defined and do not provide much value in understanding more information about a supplier. The U.S. Census Bureau created the NAICS codes for economic reporting and supplier purchasing classification.

The primary challenge with this approach was all of the knowledge I had collected and memorized was in my head. I was a highly valued resource, but when the project was over, all of the knowledge I brought with me and all the knowledge I learned left with me.

Migrating from ERP to the Cloud

Some newer technologies offered applications that connected directly to the end user. This means end users can access the buying solution directly and not have to depend on centralized resources in another department. For example, by 1990, the research firm Gartner coined the term *enterprise resource planning*. This new industry term was used to signal that many organizations, not just manufacturing, were now using technology to increase the efficiencies of their entire operations. In 1993, Microsoft released Excel v5.0 for Windows, including VBA (Visual Basic for Applications)—as noted in *The History of Microsoft Excel—Microsoft | Excel Help*. In Excel, the capability of macros made it easier for the general user to create formulas. This opened almost unlimited possibilities in automating repetitive tasks, specifically in crunching numbers and improving the time it took to assess data and present it to business stakeholders. Excel had become the standard application for developing proposal requests within the procurement department.

In 1999, Ariba went public with its Ariba Buyer application, which provided a new web-based interface for end users to create and approve purchase orders more efficiently than the ERP system. In 2000, Gartner introduced the idea of ERP II, referencing internet-enabled systems that could pull data from other sources, including front-office applications like customer relationship management (CRM). All the technological changes during this time were installed on-premise or behind the organization's firewall. This meant the application must be installed and maintained by the organization, not the application provider.

Budgets for these projects were held by the IT department because that part of the organization was the most impacted by these types of endeavors. These projects were staffed with more IT than procurement resources because IT resources were needed to install and integrate Ariba Buying with the ERP system during the project. Additionally, the IT department needed to hire resources with specific skill sets for the application just purchased. As a result, the IT department also had to increase its long-term budget for resources responsible for installing software patches, troubleshooting application issues, and providing developer resources to make changes to the application.

These on-premise solutions were sold at a very high cost, commonly purchased only by Fortune 100 companies who were considered financially stable and could afford such an investment. Advantages did include some savings in licensing fees, where a user who previously required an ERP license to create a purchase order was now bundled into the new buying application. The user license shifted to the volume of spending pushed through the Ariba Buying application. Since the organization installed and maintained this application, there was also a sense of greater security as individuals outside the internal network could not access these on-premise applications.

Disadvantages included more significant capital investment in procuring additional servers and other hardware components before installing the application. If the company was growing, the ability to scale quickly could be stalled due to the requirement of purchasing additional hardware and resources to develop the new systems. Finally, on-premise solutions, particularly in the financial or healthcare industries, must comply with regulatory agencies, and these firms are responsible for maintaining that compliance across all systems they own.

The procurement organization didn't see a lot of value. These early applications focused on the purchase order, receiving, and invoice processing, but with a better user interface and additional capabilities that the ERP systems didn't have. The procurement department became more involved when it recognized the results of the spending cubes were directly connected to how the data was entered into the purchase order by the end user. A distributed process to enable any end user to create a purchase order did achieve shorter cycle times from purchase order to supplier payment. It also created a new challenge in the consistency of data entry. The procurement department began to exert more influence on the buying process and take ownership to outline policies on how data was entered into these systems.

By 2006, significant changes began to emerge regarding how other departments viewed the procurement organization. The procurement technology landscape was to be forever changed because cloud technologies were becoming more accessible due to lower cost structures for cloud computing and, therefore, cloud procurement. This enabled procurement to create a different narrative about its value and potential. It was the milestone that ushered procurement into the next phase of its evolution.

STRATEGIC PHASE (2007–2014)

The Strategic Phase of the procurement organization saw changes in how the organization viewed the relationship with the supplier and a more proactive approach through category management and planning. As a result, a dedicated department called "Strategic Sourcing" was established under the procurement organization, and evaluating the total cost of ownership, instead of just the purchase price, was becoming the standard method for approaching proposals. Additional changes also occurred during this phase:

- There was a shift from on-premise to cloud-based procurement and supply chain applications.
- Cloud procurement applications were used in sourcing, contracts, buying, and invoicing.
- Catalogs and purchase cards expanded how the internal user bought goods and services.
- Cost plus other variables were considered in a total cost of ownership approach when comparing suppliers (i.e., shipping, customs, storage, tariffs, and switching costs).
- Negotiating longer term contracts with line-level (item) savings became the norm.

- Dedicated resources performed tactical activities, such as data entry, calculating total cost analysis across multiple suppliers, and analyzing cost versus savings.

Cloud technology was the primary contributing factor that allowed the evolution into a strategic procurement organization because it provided new capabilities to the application providers that directly impacted the procurement organization. These factors included the following:

1. The organization no longer owned or maintained the hardware, which pushed the responsibilities of maintaining regulatory compliance onto the application provider.
2. Expanded application development into non-transactional products and processes (sourcing, contracts, and supplier performance) and improved workflow.
3. Multi-tenancy, a single instance of a software application utilized by multiple customers, became available. Software patches were automatically pushed to the customer and did not rely on their IT resources to schedule, test, and update. This improved the customer experience since the internal user no longer had to wait for IT resources to prioritize, schedule, test, and eventually push an update.
4. Global users could now access an application without latency or delays, which improved performance. Often, users who were further away from the server where the application was installed would see significant delays in processing. For example, if the server was in California, users in India would notice a lag when clicking a button to see the results. The further from the server, the more lag time was observed.
5. Improved productivity was realized since global users could work on the application simultaneously. Previously, as users logged into an on-premise application, the application became slower. It used to be so common that users would purposely modify their daily routine to stop working on specific applications at the same time that users in other time zones started working.
6. Changes in the application life cycle provided more frequent product changes that were now available across all customers

simultaneously. For example, if Customer A customized their on-premise application, Customers B and C might also find it valuable. There was no method for sharing customizations that might benefit other customers.

7. Removing the requirement for servers and additional IT resources reduced the overall cost of the application to the customer. Customers no longer needed to hire procurement application developers to maintain data, apply software patches, and require developers (unique to that procurement application) to support customization and ongoing changes.
8. Cloud computing paved the way for competition by reducing the cost of entering the market. For example, Coupa was founded in 2006 using cloud technology.

Other key milestones contributed to the Strategic Phase of procurement. They were selected because they contributed to the foundation of what we know today. The following companies either built the foundation of cloud architecture, were among the early adopters of cloud technology, became a voice highlighting the potential value, or helped to educate users on cloud technologies and architecture:

- 2006: Amazon introduced its Simple Storage Service, followed by Elastic Compute Cloud. These products pioneered the ability to deliver *infrastructure-as-a-service* at a cheaper and on-demand pricing basis. This paved the way for global users to experience no delays due to distributed data centers and realized cost reductions in the capital investment of servers and hardware. IT resources were no longer needed, but special capabilities were required to maintain applications.
- 2007: Coupa launched a *software-as-a-service* product called Coupa On-Demand for small and midsize businesses. The original barriers to entering the procurement application market were gone, allowing more competition.
- 2007: IBM partnered with Google to promote cloud computing in universities, donating hardware and providing a curriculum to teach cloud computing to students.
- 2008: Google released the beta version of Google App Engine. The App Engine was a *platform-as-a-service*, one of the first of

its kind. It provided a fully maintained infrastructure and a deployment platform for users to create web applications using a common language. This was another technological advancement supporting improved user interfaces. It led to a shift from needing specialized developers to make back-end application changes and moving toward front-end capabilities to make configuration changes.

- 2008: Gartner saw an opportunity for cloud computing "to shape the relationship among consumers of IT services, those who use IT services and those who sell them."
- February 2010: Microsoft released Microsoft Azure to compete with Amazon Cloud Computing, which was previously announced in October 2008.
- March 2011: IBM announced the IBM Smart Cloud framework (to compete with Amazon Web Services), linked to its Smarter Planet campaign launched in November 2008. IBM claimed that technology could make an industry smarter.

During this time, companies were not immediately jumping at the opportunity to shift from on-premise solutions to cloud solutions, noting security as one of the fundamental reasons. I recall many times when I was introducing cloud-based applications to Fortune 200 companies. Dealing with the security issue meant spending 2–3 months talking with the IT departments about cloud user security, data security, and the change from development to configuration. IT departments would push back hard and become obstacles to moving forward out of fear for job security. Often, I would be asked to list other companies in their industries who were taking steps toward the cloud and coordinate calls with their IT departments. Projects were stalled for 3–6 months until this was sorted.

It should not be surprising that if a company wanted to promote the safety of a cloud-based architecture, it should also provide resources that could address some of the industry's concerns to support a quicker path to adoption. That is precisely what IBM did in April 2011. They founded the Cloud Standards Customer Council as an end-user advocacy group to accelerate the adoption of cloud services. The Council created guidelines for companies to use in charting their path to cloud adoption, outlined options to remove barriers due to security concerns, and contributed to the development of organizational standards. This foundational framework helped move cloud adoption more quickly. As more Fortune 50 companies adopted cloud-based technology, other companies would follow suit. If a Fortune 50 company could overcome the negative perceptions of data and end user security issues, so could they.

AGILE PHASE (2015-2021)

In 2015, Ardent Partners published their annual CPO Rising Study—The Agility Agenda. The study received feedback from 318 CPOs across 25 industries, plus interviews with 26 CPOs, of which 21 also responded to the survey. What was notable about 2015 was the formal announcement that the procurement organization was shifting out of the Strategic Phase and into the Agile Phase. Ardent Partners summarized, "The procurement teams that adeptly connect their tools, resources, and expertise to support the evolving needs of the business will succeed above all others. Agility will define the next wave of procurement success."

In 2015, Agile was used primarily in software development as an iterative process to develop smaller application capabilities to reach a faster production state. With cross-functional collaboration throughout the software life cycle, this continual improvement of processes enabled companies to release new application capabilities more frequently, with the expectation that each release brings improvement. Therefore, the agile process never ends until the application is considered end-of-life and terminated.

The 2015 CPO Rising study used this concept to summarize the overall theme from CPO feedback. It noted that an agile procurement organization translates into the "ability to quickly leverage alternative suppliers for a given commodity, part, or service in the event of a supply disruption or new business requirement." Current procurement practices of revisiting their supply base once every three to five years were no longer in alignment with expectations of corporate goals. Brands now needed to adjust more often to meet the behavioral changes of consumers who were becoming more educated. For example, information online helped educate users on the potential health concerns of certain food ingredients, such as artificial sugars and synthetic colors. Using alternative, healthier ingredients is often more expensive for manufacturers, but companies must adapt to maintain sales once consumers possess that knowledge. Some examples of brands changing ingredients in 2015 include:

1. Nestlé announced it would remove artificial colors and flavors without affecting product quality or increasing prices. Pressure from consumer behavior was the primary factor. This decision affected over 250 products across 10 brands, including the popular Butterfinger, Nestlé Crunch, and Baby Ruth candy bars. Instead, Nestlé planned to use ingredients from natural sources. For example, Butterfinger bars would now contain annatto, which comes from seeds found in the fruit of the Achiote tree, as the replacement for red dye #50 and yellow dye #5. Additionally, Nestlé Crunch bars began using natural vanilla instead of the artificial variety.
2. Kraft removed all artificial flavors, preservatives, and synthetic colors, including yellow dyes #5 and #6, and used paprika, annatto, and turmeric instead.
3. Pepsi announced it would stop using aspartame, commonly sold under the brands Equal and NutraSweet, as the sweetener in Diet Pepsi and other Pepsi products and replace it with sucralose, an artificial sweetener commonly known as Splenda. Pepsi executives referenced the driving factor as the consumer perception that aspartame is unsafe.

"Waste and Opportunity 2015," a report from *As You Sow* and the Natural Resources Defense Council, analyzed the packaging practices of 47 fast food chains, beverage companies, and consumer goods and grocery firms. The report was forthright about calling out major global brands and highlighting leaders and laggards. This report was just one of many that inspired consumers to reevaluate what was essential and change how they spent their money and who they spent it on. This renewed sense of consumer empowerment impacted how brands made and packaged goods.

For example, suppose consumers prioritized avoiding filling landfills and reducing plastics in the ocean. In that case, they may either share their concerns with the specific brand out of loyalty or spend their money elsewhere. The choice to spend their money elsewhere does not go unnoticed. Recognizing a decline in sales is often the loudest metric for any company. The new agile procurement organization was coined to increase the organization's ability to adjust to consumers' changing needs.

The overall top strategies for all procurement organizations noted in the 2015 study were:

1. Improve collaboration with line-of-business leaders (42%)
2. Improve the use of technology (40%)
3. Implement stronger policies and processes (39%)

These strategies sparked a renewed interest in the procurement business and digital transformation initiatives with objectives to:

- Shift procurement and supply chain processes to cloud-based technologies
- Simplify and standardize processes
- Automate to reduce the end-to-end process cycle time
- Enable sharing of procurement information across global employees

Unfortunately, what did not change in 2015 was the pressure to find and drive more savings. This meant the procurement organization would be measured primarily by annual savings numbers or how much money the department could save the company. The focus on savings was a large obstacle and hindered CPOs from achieving the objectives outlined in the 2015 study (see Figure 2.9). Each year, the savings goals were increased or set higher than the year before.

Between 2015 and 2021, the procurement organization took a few steps forward by leveraging procurement cloud technologies to automate some processes, but automation alone could not fully realize its goals. In 2021, the following gaps still existed:

- Lack of confidence in procurement and supply chain data
- Lack of visibility in evaluating supplier risks
- Inaccuracies in data, limiting the ability to make actionable decisions

- Slow growth in foundational skills for procurement professionals to be effective
- Lingering tactical-level tasks and activities
- Limitations in understanding how to utilize digital technologies to their fullest potential

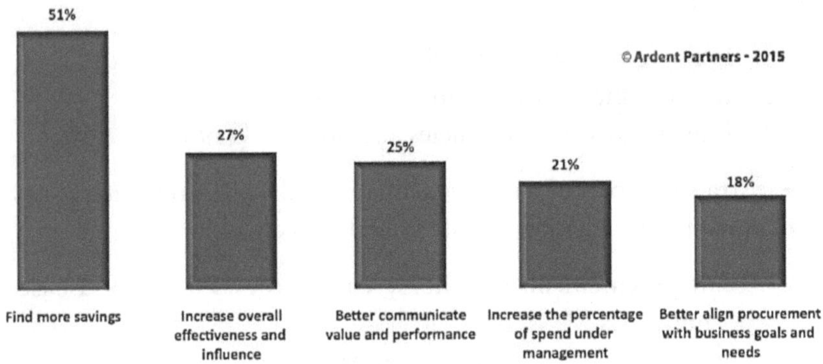

Figure 2.9 Prioritize savings above all

INTELLIGENT PHASE (2022–TBD)

The underlying shift in focus and data priority drives the Intelligent Phase. In other words, to use data to make better-informed decisions. Recognizing that data is not just about the right data at the right time but also about being able to pull that data when the decision is most impactful to the organization. Terms like *data competency*, *data literacy*, and *data culture* are standard in this phase. Other factors contributing to the Intelligent Phase are:

- The advancement of technology architectures and subsequent reduction in cost so more organizations utilize them
- Improvements in silicon chip processing power and speed to support artificial intelligence (AI) technologies that can analyze petabytes of data (or one million gigabytes)
- The acceptance of global remote collaboration because of the COVID pandemic to better cooperation and diversity of thought
- The use of application program interfaces connecting to more data sources to supplement large enterprise applications

The term AI used in this book is not about robots thinking for themselves or driverless taxis but the augmentation of the human thought process by assisting in day-to-day activities such as solving complex problems and performing repetitive tasks. The goal of this phase is to shift resources into more value-added roles. At the same time, technologies take over repeatable tasks, analyze large amounts of data quickly, reduce human bias, and improve the decision-making process in a shorter period. You might think, "Um . . . yeah, we heard this before. That same goal was supposed to be a benefit in the Agile Phase, so what is different?" The answer is that now we can access the technology and capabilities to back up that statement.

> Procurement and supply chain professionals are working with technologies that were not accessible five years ago and will more than likely work with technologies five years from now that do not yet exist today.

The goal is to set up a procurement organization for ongoing success that is scalable and sustainable to any future disruptions. More specifically, the procurement organization cannot continue to evolve without the combination of both business and digital transformation. One cannot truly sustain without the other.

Section II

Obstacles Blocking Success

CHAPTER 3

SETTING UP FOR FAILURE

Chapter 1 highlighted 20 common variables that contribute to failed transformation initiatives. One variable alone will not cause a failure; it is a combination of them that creates the obstacles blocking the desired outcome. These obstacles may be encountered at any time throughout the transformation journey. To achieve long-term, repeatable success from a digital transformation, the process must start in the early stages of the planning phase. To that end, this chapter will focus on four critical aspects of successful transformations:

- Guideline principles
- Underestimating current state value
- Setting up for failure before kickoff
- Workarounds offer temporary relief

GUIDING PRINCIPLES

In many projects, *2-in-a-box* refers to two individuals paired together, working side by side. One individual is the employee, and the other is a contractor or consultant with more experience. The *box* refers to the workstream or area of focus, like *sourcing* or *procuring-to-pay*. For example, two individuals in the procure-to-pay box are the workstream leads responsible for day-to-day activities, from understanding the business requirements and process, coordinating with stakeholders, and documentation to the final go-live phase. Depending on the size and scope of the project, these individuals perform the following activities themselves or will collaborate with team members in other workstreams, such as change management, configuration, and testing.

The 2-in-a-box concept was designed to empower individuals to make frequent, low-risk decisions without the need for constant escalation. This approach enables the team to keep the project moving forward and minimizes the opportunity for a complete work halt; it helps to maintain the budget and stay within the targeted timeline. The challenge to this approach is ensuring the workstream leads have the responsibility and authority to make these decisions while staying aligned with the vision and expectations.

Guiding principles are the guard rails for these project decisions. They emphasize the foundational values and provide guidance in decision making throughout the end-to-end project life cycle. They aim to ensure alignment and focus on project key objectives. Consider guiding principles as a proxy for executive management so they do not have to be engaged in every decision.

The first step in drafting the guiding principles is a workshop with the executive sponsors and other executives with a professional stake in the transformation project's results. This workshop aims to understand why the transformation project was initiated and what the outcomes need to be. For example, the transformation project could be initiated because the company was changing its strategic position in the market by acquiring other companies or the company was looking to expand its procurement and supply chain into the Asia Pacific region. If the company's goal was to leverage AI technologies to automate areas of processes, this carries a different set of expected outcomes. Once this workshop is completed, the project team members can draft, refine, and approve the guiding principles. These activities are strongly recommended to be the first workshops scheduled during a project's planning phase or immediately after a formal project kickoff.

Guiding principles are coupled with leadership expectations of the results they expect to achieve. They are designed to prevent the team from making decisions that fall off the rails or go too far beyond expectations. Like a cheat sheet, if a decision is required, the workstream can refer to the guiding principles for assistance and feel confident their decisions align with the project charter, project goal, and executive vision.

Guiding principles should be a series of 7–10 bullet points, no more than two sentences in length. The following list contains several examples of guiding principles for transformation initiatives:

- Prioritize the user experience
- Our culture cannot embrace a high degree of change at one time
- The 80/20 rule is in place, so we will not focus on the 20 percent of the process that cannot be achieved in this phase
- Aim for timely decisions, not perfect ones
- Simplify before leveraging technologies to automate
- Prioritize processes that impact the user's ability to perform their job
- If a decision negatively impacts a critical process supporting the core business of this organization, escalate

Consider a scenario where the team feels one guiding principle conflicts with another. When teams experience these scenarios, they often follow an escalation process. If a decision cannot be made at the next level, it may flow to a change control board or a steering committee to make the final decision. The outcome may result in no change, an approved scope change with more resources, or a change in the timeline.

Next, assume the project's goals are to simplify and automate the requisition-to-pay process. Leadership seeks results that improve data quality to support better-informed decisions and reduce end-to-end process cycle times for greater efficiency. They also want to reduce or eliminate tactical tasks so the user can focus on more strategic activities. This would tie back to the guiding principle: *prioritize the user experience.* Consider a decision that could make the process more manageable and optimized for the supplier or the internal business user. If the wrong decision is made, the results may not be fully known until after going live or when all organizational users apply the new technology and process. In alignment with our leadership expectations, which focus more on internal users, a process decision should lean toward improving the user experience, not the supplier experience.

Contemplate a decision to redesign process flow. During the solution part of the project (where the workstream team outlines the future state), a highly efficient process is developed. However, to move from the current state (the process today) to the future state (the highly efficient process) requires a high degree of change. Balancing leadership expectations with how much the organization's culture can absorb is critical during decision making. If the decision is in the wrong direction, it may not be known until the user-testing phase. This is when the users will experience the new future state process themselves. A poor decision may require the team to reconfigure the process and extend the timeline. This will cause resource and budget constraints. This decision could tie back to several guiding principles listed above, such as *the 80/20 rule*, *aim for timely decisions, not perfect ones*, and *our culture cannot embrace a high degree of change at one time.*

Imagine a decision that evaluates redesigning three manual processes executed initially in Excel. Of these three processes, one process requires more time and effort to develop a future state process than the other two. The workstream leads must decide whether to continue working through the third process or set it aside for a future phase. It would be great to no longer have an Excel-based process, but continuing to focus resources and time may also not be in the best interest right now or may exceed the team's ability to complete milestones in time. Decisions should tie back to the guiding principle of *prioritizing processes that impact the user's daily ability to perform their job.*

The above examples of tough decisions that must be made in transformation projects must be steered by the guiding principles. Otherwise, there is no alignment to a common end goal and no real chance of long-term success. Unfortunately, this activity is almost always forgotten or deprioritized over other planning activities. Without the critical first step of designing guiding principles, the transformation project may yield delays, miscommunication, and conflicts in feedback.

UNDERESTIMATING THE CURRENT STATE OF VALUE

Teams often underestimate the value of documenting the current state of a business or process in the run-up to a transformation. They believe that learning about the current state does not directly correlate to the development of the future state, that learning about the current state takes too much effort, and that it just elongates the overall timeline. Consider the change management workstream, which supports communication and helps control the impact of changes on the business user. It is responsible for evaluating the degree of change, creating a training approach, and executing training to match that degree of change. Its purpose is to maximize user adoption after the go-live phase. To do this effectively, understanding the degree of change is critical to achieving the organization's goals. If end users do not understand the true extent of the change(s), there is a risk of a lower rate of adoption that directly impacts the return on investment (ROI) of the transformation.

Documenting the current state process and then comparing it to the future state results in a list of all changes, no matter how big or small. The change management team will create a document called *Change Impacts* that outlines what is stopping and starting. *What is stopping* refers to a step, task, or activity in the current state that may no longer exist in the future state. *What is starting* refers to how a step, task, or activity will now exist in the future.

This team will create communications around change impacts to start the change process as early as possible. It will refine its training approach to the level of change for each stop/start. For example, a small amount of change may equate to a quick reference guide, whereas a large amount of change may equate to detailed training materials, a three-minute video, and a quick reference guide.

Change management teams will create metrics and key performance indicators for the processes with the highest degree of change. This will enable them to prioritize their time to the more critical future state process with a higher degree of change. Post go-live, they will review reports to monitor the adoption of essential processes. When they do not see adoption improving, they can quickly offer ad hoc virtual training to large groups and reach out to individuals for one-on-one training.

Another consideration for understanding the current state is how it impacts buying in the future—specifically, how the user will buy or purchase that same thing in the future state compared to how they purchase that same item in the current state. Take, for example, buying ads for websites or for placement in digital newspapers and magazines. In the current state process, digital ads are purchased and paid for online with a credit card. It is not a purchase that requires a purchase order, and the organization will not receive an invoice after the service is done. Advertisements are paid for at the time of the request or purchase. The payment is made before the digital ad is published. The service is confirmed when the digital ad is published and publicly available. For a retail organization that relies heavily on magazine insertion orders, missing a deadline can directly impact sales and revenue. A technology project may not take into consideration how the company buys products and services across each department. If all future purchases are bucketed into either purchase orders or contracts, procurement policies may be updated to reflect that credit cards are not allowed. This will have ramifications for departments that need to use credit cards to secure advertising.

A good transformation project considers all types of purchases in every department. This ensures no purchase types are missed in the future state process. It also strengthens short-term user adoption because every user will know how and where to buy the same products and services in the current state compared to the future state. Because the user knows how and where to purchase, their purchases will promote long-term sustainable behaviors.

Beyond understanding the current state, it is also essential to understand technological capabilities that could be used to improve future-state processes. Online catalogs are a good example of this. Assume in the current state, users must create a purchase order that requires them to perform a lot of data entry to purchase an item, such as giving an item description, selecting a commodity code, and inputting technical specifications. Manually entering a lot of data presents a challenge to the organization since these inputs will not match across all users. This mismatch of data impacts the organization's ability to make better-informed decisions driven by quality data.

An online catalog allows an organization to create a predefined menu of available purchases with predetermined pricing, items, item descriptions, and commodity codes. Predefined financial accounting combinations can also guide users in choosing the correct general ledger accounts and cost centers based on their department. Online catalogs are designed to facilitate an easier path to purchasing goods and services. The goal is to reduce the end-to-end purchase cycle time, minimize tactical purchasing activities, and allow business users to focus more on relationships with internal stakeholders or external suppliers.

If the team does not take the time to understand how the user is currently purchasing the item, an opportunity can be missed to determine the best use of the new capabilities offered. When is it best to use a catalog not associated with a formal contract? Small purchases like postage stamps or toner from a local supplier are good examples. A local toner supplier may not require a formal agreement, but the products will have *agreed-to* prices and terms, making them suitable for the catalog.

These are just a few examples of the value of understanding the current state. It can lead to improved user adoption and higher ROI. It can also improve the efficiency of how goods and services are purchased and strengthen communication with business users.

SETTING UP FOR FAILURE BEFORE KICKOFF

It is common for leadership to hear the following phrases 12 to 15 months after deploying or implementing a procurement or supply chain application:

1. "We implemented an enterprise cloud application globally, but we are not getting the value we were told we could get out of it."
2. "This application is not working; we are considering implementing a different application provider."
3. "We don't understand why our business transformation didn't work.
4. "The purpose of implementing technology was to facilitate a transformation."

Setting up for success means arming a person or team with the necessary skills and tools. However, setting up a person or team to fail is also possible. This could be defined as not providing the individual with the budget, resources, or timeline to meet expectations but still expecting them to succeed without one or all of the above. The same can be said about setting up the procurement organization to succeed or fail before a transformation project starts.

There are many underlying reasons why the aforementioned phrases can be heard, such as a lack of a change management plan, implementation while under budget constraints, part-time project management, or perhaps pausing a project due to changes in executive leadership or other internal politics. All these reasons have an underlying theme:

the organization makes decisions before a transformation initiative begins without understanding the consequences of those decisions. Typically, there are four types of "failed" approaches, each contributing to a botched transformation before it even begins:

1. The leapfrog approach
2. The switchback approach
3. The lack of commitment approach
4. The do-it-yourself approach

Approaches 1 and 2 can start the same way—an executive is new to the organization and looking to prove their value by attempting to make a tangible change to how things are done. A long list of user pain points and complaints is used as ammunition to, for example, build a case for replacing an application provider with the belief that a new application will resolve many of these issues. Time and resources are dedicated to application evaluation, requests for information, and requests for proposals—plus, you can add time for implementation and post go-live support. This can result in 15 to 24 months of wasted effort, especially if the work processes were not examined and streamlined before a new technology partner was chosen. Often, this work does not lead to long-lasting value or improve on the prior technology platform.

> There is more value in improving the existing process than changing the application that supports the process.

1. **The leapfrog approach:** This approach is one where the organization leaps to a different application provider every handful of years but never returns to any of the previous application providers. For example, a company purchases from provider *A*, then four to six years later leaps to provider *B*, and then several years later leaps to provider *C*. This approach is often seen when the organization hires a new procurement officer or executive leader. There are many reasons why an executive may believe this is the easiest option, including internal politics to

personal bias from prior jobs. Challenges with the leapfrog approach include:

- *End users*: The high degree of switching negatively impacts the end user. Even if the process is mostly standardized, some changes are required to meet the application's functionality requirements—even small changes can require the end user to learn a new process. When the organization is on its third application in a decade, user adoption is highly challenging or no longer exists. This approach has contributed to the departure of procurement and supply chain employees from the company. Feedback from users experiencing this approach shows many have finally given up on their organization.
- *ROI*: The cost of purchasing and implementing previous applications contributes to the company's inability to fulfill its ROI requirements on these types of projects. Slow user-adoption rates directly and negatively impact the organization's ROI. Ironically, this can often cause leadership to mistakenly conclude that a lack of ROI must mean a new application should be tried.
- *Executive leadership*: In this scenario, the new executive was hired and decided to move from application provider *A* to application provider *B*. It is also possible that after four to five years, the same executive will move to a new application provider, *C*, with similar claims of a lack of ROI or that the current application cannot meet the end user's needs. Even though the leader has a limited number of times they can claim the application is the issue, they lose credibility because they are perceived as not knowing what they are doing or looking out for themselves rather than the betterment of the end users.

2. **The switchback approach:** This approach is when companies purchase a procurement application from provider *A* and then leap to application provider *B* only to switchback later to application provider *A*. Challenges with the switchback approach include:

- *End users*: This approach is often worse than the leapfrog approach because leadership circled back to a previous provider, causing more confusion. Users will assume there must have been a good reason to leave application provider *A*, so why are we returning to them? User adoption in this approach is still strained, but not as much as the leapfrog approach.
- *ROI*: The ROI in this approach is still negative but not as much as in the leapfrog approach. When switching back to the previous version, processes and training documentation are already created from the earlier implementation, which tends to speed up the current implementation. While users may not enjoy switching back to a previous application, they do have some familiarity with it.
- *Executive leadership*: Leadership does lose some credibility, but not as much as in the leapfrog approach. That is because the end user is familiar with application provider *A*.

3. **The lack of commitment approach:** In this approach, companies purchase one or two modules from application provider *A*. Two years later, they purchase another module from the same application provider, *A*, and continue to add on over the years. Challenges with the lack of commitment approach include:

    - *End users*: This approach is often more challenging to end users than the other approaches because users are left with part of a process inside *and* outside of the application. Additionally, other steps in the process could remain in different systems. This means users are performing duplicate data entry tasks across multiple systems. While there are some benefits to a partially electronic process, users will find little value in this approach, and it elongates the end-to-end process life cycle with increased errors.
    - *ROI*: ROI is affected negatively due to the failure to automate effectively. In these situations, 40 percent or more of a process

is often outside of an application—another system, MS Excel, an MS Access Database, or even paper-based. For example, users receive a PDF invoice through a supplier portal but must manually type the accounting codes from the invoice into an enterprise resource planning system. Once additional modules are purchased, there is no consideration to reevaluate the existing end-to-end processes. This can lead to disconnected processes, even if they are digital. Users will create workarounds on top of workarounds. This will be observed as a quick fix to resolve the symptoms but does not consider the underlying root cause. A good example would be purchasing approval flows. Instead of reevaluating the approval flows to optimize or simplify the older and newer modules, more approvals are added to the purchasing requisition, increasing the end-to-end cycle times.

- *Executive leadership*: In this scenario, leadership does not experience an immediate negative impact from end users. Most often, leadership explains this approach as an opportunity to *try first before committing* to a more extensive application footprint or, due to a limited budget this year, deciding to purchase just a few modules. It is commonly communicated to the users that the expectation is to buy additional modules the following year. Future budgets can change, and priorities for funds earmarked to the procurement and supply management organization tend to be the first to be reallocated. When additional modules are not purchased, end users are stuck with a half-manual, half-digital process when they might prefer an end-to-end manual process. The negative perception from users will not start immediately but will continue to grow every year.

If you hire an expert, such as an electrician or a general contractor, to support a kitchen remodel, then why do you believe you can be successful with a transformation project on your own?

4. **The do-it-yourself approach:** This approach still exists in some organizations. No funding is given to the procurement or supply chain organization, but there is an expectation for them to transform their areas. The goal may be to support future acquisition strategies or reduce their internal budgets year over year. In this scenario, leadership is either not equipped or is so *in the weeds* fighting daily fires they cannot step back and think strategically. This ultimately leads to a do-it-yourself transformation initiative with no outside support from subject matter experts or consultants. Challenges with the do-it-yourself approach include:

    - *End users*: At first, this seems like a great approach to keeping costs down and empowering end users to succeed. However, these projects have no formal project management resources. After a few months, users will experience challenges balancing project-related activities with day-to-day activities, which are prioritized. Eventually, they will stop working on the transformation activities and return 100 percent to their job. One real-world example is a procurement organization attempting its fifth transformation initiative in 17 years. The word *transformation* was used as a label each time, but the project was far from transformational. Users became so frustrated that they no longer supported their procurement leader when another transformation project was announced to start again. The procurement organization saw many resources leaving the company each year. Other departments outside the procurement and supply management organization soon siloed themselves because of the lack of effectiveness. These users created their purchasing channels by buying off contracts and working around processes, contributing to poor metrics and negative perceptions.
    - *ROI*: ROI does not exist with this approach. This is because the project had no formal budget from executive leadership. Department resources stop working on the project in favor of different priorities. When the project stalls, it is never revisited nor officially finished, yielding no results every time.

- *Executive leadership*: With this approach, executive leadership is often between a rock and a hard place. They are given many things they must achieve without funding or other support. From the user's perspective, leadership is seen as doing very little while expecting a lot. In addition, leadership feels limited in what they can accomplish. Skill sets within the team do not support the strategic activities needed to drive transformational projects.

WORKAROUNDS ARE TEMPORARY RELIEF

In some of the previous examples, users will create work efforts and processes *around* the current process they are expected to follow. Every time a user does this, it may provide immediate relief and be perceived as effective, but this relief is temporary. When more users do the same, the temporary relief is shorter, and the negative impacts grow more quickly.

Consider a process like building a highway from Washington, D.C., to Baltimore, MD. The cars are the users moving through a process. An optimized highway runs straight from D.C. to Baltimore to make travel time one hour. Winter comes, and a storm causes several trees to fall on the road, blocking the direct path. A workaround is created, routing the cars around the blocked portion of the road. This increases the time to one hour and 30 minutes (see Figure 3.1).

Unfortunately, some of the fallen trees also damage the pavement on the highway (see Figure 3.2). What started as one workaround becomes several workarounds, and as total travel time continues to rise, vehicles eventually stop traveling this route (process). Users search for more optimal or direct paths (i.e., processes) because their current path is no longer viable from their perspective.

In this scenario, someone decided creating a workaround was quicker than fixing the problem. These workarounds are like band-aids. They cover the problem with the goal of keeping users on the primary path or process. As more workarounds are applied, more construction occurs, adding more delays and increasing the total time. Users grow tired of the constant process delays and the increased time it takes to navigate

Figure 3.1 Alternative path

Figure 3.2 A pothole creates the need for another workaround

the end-to-end cycle time. They eventually find alternative ways to get where they need to go by navigating outside the process initially confirmed for them. However, workarounds are not adequate for the following reasons:

- They are not designed as long-term solutions, which leads to continuous problems that require an increase in resources to maintain
- They contribute to inconsistent processes, and users have difficulty knowing which procedures to follow
- They are the opposite of efficient and simplified processes
- They lead to miscommunications and mistakes, thereby increasing risks
- They create negative impacts on user adoption
- They address the symptoms instead of the underlying root causes of problems
- They instill negative user perceptions of deprioritizing quality and standards
- They make it more difficult to enforce accountability
- They cause a lack of confidence in the organization's ability to deliver

CHAPTER 4

POLICIES

THE VALUE OF POLICIES

The term *policy* can have slightly different meanings across industry sectors, public versus private, or government versus corporate. The following list describes two examples that provide a common understanding of *procurement policies.*

- "The purpose of a procurement policy is to ensure that best value—the most advantageous balance of price, quality, and performance—is obtained when purchasing business-related products and services and to minimize fraud, waste, and abuse in purchasing." Legal Services Corporation
- "Your procurement policy outlines the overarching principles and standards used to set direction and influence decisions. It guides employee decision making under a given set of circumstances within the framework of objectives and goals established by senior management." Vendor Centric

A policy is a set of guidelines the organization outlines for its employees to comply with regulatory, federal, or state requirements, organizational standards, and culture. Procurement policies are used to maintain control, confirm fairness, and improve the effectiveness of purchasing decisions. They help the employee understand what the employee can expect from the company and what the company can expect from the employee. It also guides the establishment of a formal relationship between the supplier and the employee acting on behalf of the company.

Another way to think about it is that a policy provides the *why* and the *what*, whereas a procedure provides the *how* with step-by-step instructions. Companies believe procurement policies are essential but often do not fully realize their value, and as a result, little attention is dedicated to creating and maintaining policies. The following sections explain some common reasons procurement policies exist and where they have provided value to the organization.

Consistency and Fairness

Consistency and fairness are necessary in procurement policies to ensure a standardized purchasing approach across all global departments and users. These building-block attributes help create corporate guidelines that all suppliers are treated fairly and consistently regardless of who the employee is or where they physically reside. They help reduce the potential for favoritism and bias in procurement and supply management activities.

A corporate procurement policy should outline transparency, equality, nondiscrimination, and conflicts of interest. The procedures would outline what steps an employee can take to support this policy and may include training and the use of audits. The best-known example of a procurement procedure is the request for proposal, which provides explicit directions for employees when the company's money is needed for goods and services.

Cost Control

The procurement department was created to achieve this goal. Procurement policies help manage and control costs, and the supporting procedures evaluate suppliers and negotiate prices, ensuring that purchases are made at the best possible value. They aim to align with the financial objectives of the executive committee or board.

Examples of cost control policies may include annual budgeting and what to do when budget requests are outside annual planning. Approvals on purchases, delegation of authority, and dollar thresholds at each approval level tie back to ensuring costs are consistent across the organization. A travel expense and entertainment policy outlines what and how the company will reimburse employees for face-to-face meetings with suppliers and vendors (illegal or inappropriate expenditures should be flagged and dealt with based on these policies).

Compliance and Risk Management

Policies help organizations comply with legal and regulatory requirements and mitigate risks related to fraud, corruption, and other unethical practices. This may include local laws for some industries operating at a state or government level, such as banks and other financial institutions, and specific guidelines and annual reporting they must follow that may not exist in other industries.

The company must be capable of monitoring new laws and reporting requirements, such as the Corporate Transparency Act (CTA), which became effective in the United States in January 2024. The CTA requires small business owners to provide transparency through annual reports documenting ownership. Its purpose is to apply the same level of visibility that exists in large organizations to smaller organizations to limit tax fraud, money laundering, and other financial misconduct. There is also a long list of types of companies that are exempt from the annual reporting requirement. Each company is responsible for knowing this regulation exists and confirming whether it is exempt. If the company is not exempt, it must know how, when, and where to submit its reports. Failure to comply with this regulation carries a daily fine.

Efficiency

Clear guidelines streamline the procurement process, making it more efficient and less prone to delays or errors. Efficient policies aim to maximize productivity and minimize waste to improve resource utilization and speed up turnaround times. Depending on the industry, policies could outline the optimization of employee and contract resources, when and how to leverage seasonal resources, improvements to processes, efficiency audits, and the use of innovation within the organization.

Quality Assurance

Procurement policies should include criteria for evaluating the quality of purchased goods and services. This ensures that the organization receives products that meet its standards and requirements and extends to internal employees, contractors, seasonal supports, suppliers, and alliance partners. Examples include how goods and services will meet or exceed customer expectations, continuous improvement initiatives, and compliance with industry and global standards such as the International Organization for Standards (ISO) 9000 groups of standards. Companies with ISO 9000 certifications have an advantage when providing goods and services to other companies. It minimizes the need for closer evaluation because they have already met the global standards required for the ISO 9000 certification. According to Statista's website, in 2023, China had the most ISO certifications globally, with over 551,000 certifications. Italy, India, and Germany rank second, third, and fourth; their total certifications are approximately 94,000, 61,000, and 47,000, respectively.

Transparency

Procurement policies must enhance transparency and accountability throughout the organization. The goal is to ensure all stakeholders have access to the relevant information needed to do their job successfully while fostering trust and responsibility. This is especially important for public sector organizations or those subject to a higher standard than corporations in the private sector.

Examples of policies that support transparency may include communication requirements for different levels of information distributed to other groups of people. Accountability and confidentiality are policies that balance the principles of transparency while supporting the company's goals. Reporting requirements, training, and annual audits are also aspects of policies to facilitate awareness and compliance.

Strategic Alignment

Effective procurement policies align purchasing decisions to the organization's strategic goals, ensuring that procurement supports overall business objectives. Equally important, organizational policies must align with the operational (or tactical) activities needed to support those goals. Consider the following two scenarios.

Scenario 1. An example of an organizational policy is one that encourages employees to work in different departments within the company every two to three years. These policies foster cross-functional training and experience of its employees. They create employees with a broader understanding of the company instead of a deeper understanding of one department. It can reduce turnover, encourage loyalty, and improve the organization's ability to execute the operational activities needed to support the executive direction of the company. However, not all organizational policies that positively impact employees will have the same effect on procurement policies. Consider a procurement approval policy that outlines the workflow to approve requisitions. The workflows are designed around the role of the individuals and the dollar amount each role can authorize. A lower threshold amount requires fewer individuals in the approval workflow.

When a requester (or the person who raises the requisition) submits a requisition for more than a specific dollar threshold (e.g., $50,000 USD), the requisition automatically flows to the individual's supervisor for approval. Once fully approved, the requisition becomes a purchase order and is sent to the supplier. The approval workflow will follow the supervisor's chain of command (or the next person in line to approve the workflow). Some organizations have dual approval workflows, including the supervisor chain of command plus a budget or cost center owner. This budget owner may not be in the requester's supervisor's chain of command.

If an organizational policy encourages employees to move around the organization every two to three years, employees' roles and the department they work for also change. This could result in a delay in approvals for requisitions/purchase orders. If a supplier does not begin work until a purchase order is received, the delay could result in project delays and costs while the supplier waits for a purchase order. Multiply that outcome by 200 suppliers and the costs can become significant.

The impact of this scenario is related to how the procurement policy is executed. Procurement policies are embedded into an application to facilitate a digital procurement process. The procurement organization should work more closely with the human resources department and IT (information technology) to minimize delays and additional costs. A few months of collaboration to optimize the cycle time from when an employee starts their new role to when the information is updated in the procurement application minimizes those hidden costs. Unfortunately, this is not something that usually occurs. When procurement considers opportunities for savings, this scenario is overlooked, deprioritized, or never considered.

Scenario 2. Another typical scenario is when the company reduces departmental budgets year over year and issues a temporary procurement policy focused on cost cutting as a priority instead of balancing cost, quality, and long-term supplier partnerships. Selecting suppliers based solely on the lowest price does not lead to high-quality products and services. This can increase operating costs (additional rounds of ordering), damage brand reputation (product defects or recalls), and decrease future revenue. The short-term savings realized are small compared to the long-term costs that are not always documented.

WHAT IS A GOOD POLICY?

Effective procurement policies must include the right mix of ingredients and ensure that those ingredients work well together to meet corporate goals. Think of a good policy as a four-legged stool; all four legs work harmoniously to build the proper foundation. Those components are:

- Clearly written
- Clearly understood
- Clearly communicated
- Generates clear consequences

For decades, this has been what many consulting firms would describe as the right balance for developing effective procurement policies. However, the most essential ingredient is missing. There is a fifth leg of the stool that is rarely discussed; it is sometimes considered unnecessary and therefore delayed for a future discussion that never happens. For a policy to be truly effective, it must be *clearly enforced.*

To illustrate this better, a park in West Seattle, WA, posted signs throughout the park and in high-traffic areas near parking lots and other entrances for foot traffic. The signs read, "Obey Poop-Scoop Laws. Violators will receive a $500 fine." (See Figure 4.1.)

- This is clearly written. It is a short phrase someone can quickly read while walking or jogging by.
- This is clearly understood. An individual will understand what is expected of them (i.e., to scoop the poop).
- This is clearly communicated. The signs are posted all over the park area.
- This policy includes clear consequences. An individual (adult) understands that noncompliance will result in a $500 fine.

Another sign reads, "Dogs not allowed in the water. Violators will receive a $500 fine." (See Figure 4.2.)

Figure 4.1 There are clear consequences for your actions

Figure 4.2 Dogs not allowed in the water

These park signs follow the rules of the four-legged stool. However, the challenge here is enforcing these policies (the 5th leg). When talking to many residents who take their dogs to that park, they could not recall ever seeing someone at the park to enforce the signage. In addition, they said they had never known anyone who was reported or had received a fine. There could be several reasons. The park is too large to monitor or is being monitored at nonpeak times. It is also possible there is a staff shortage. Regardless of the cause, it does no good if all of the policy boxes are checked, but there is no enforcement.

Let's assume there is a staff shortage. One idea to combat this problem is for a staff member (wearing a park uniform) to be visible in the park once per week during high-traffic times. Additionally, the staff members can rotate which days of the week they are in the park. The visibility of the staff, in combination with no pattern to when they may appear, will increase compliance and provide a more pleasant experience for the locals and tourists.

The policy doesn't have to be enforced every day or even every week. Sometimes, just knowing the park is monitored is enough to deter people from noncompliance. Consider a police vehicle sitting on the side of the road; when drivers see a police vehicle on the side of the road, it automatically causes them to slow down. This is because even if you have not been pulled over by the police for speeding, you know someone who has *or* you have driven by a car that was pulled over on the side of the road.

Sometimes, in the United States, if you look closely enough as you drive by a parked police vehicle, you will notice no one is in the vehicle. The visibility of the police vehicle is a deterrent on its own. This only works because there is no pattern for when the police vehicle is occupied or empty. Therefore, every time you see a police vehicle, you slow down.

These examples could be applied to the dog park. Just knowing that park personnel are occasionally walking around the park monitoring the policies and that they are willing to hand out fines for noncompliance could be enough to deter potential repeat offenders.

> If the policy is not enforced, is it really a policy?

POLICIES CAN REFLECT THE ORGANIZATIONAL CULTURE

Policies can also reflect and work in parallel with the organization's culture. Culture includes the repetitive actions all employees share that support the organization's values. Not many companies consider creating policies that actively reinforce that culture.

The oil and gas industry is known for its strict safety policies in its plants, distribution channels, oil rigs, etc. Not following safety policies is considered unacceptable and could potentially lead to a loss of life. This culture of safety is also reflected in how people treat each other.

For example, some companies have a policy stating that one person will provide a *safety moment* at the beginning of every meeting. This is usually something this person saw or experienced, and they explain the impact of being unsafe. For example, "I saw someone walking across the street when the pedestrian walk sign was red. This is problematic since drivers may not expect someone to be crossing the street when the traffic light is green, which may cause an accident."

One company I worked for practiced this policy. I could not think of anything to say for the first few weeks and was hopeful I would be skipped. Eventually, it was my turn to volunteer. Earlier that week, during my lunch break, I was sitting at the coffee shop next to the lobby when I noticed three people walking together across the room. The individual on the right turned to talk to the others and didn't notice the glass coffee table. He ran right into it and fell over. He wasn't hurt, and I still don't know how the glass did not break. He was mostly embarrassed, but it could have been much worse. I used this example to communicate the hazards of not paying attention during what most of us would consider routine activities, such as walking and talking, especially in areas you are not familiar with.

When someone communicates their safety moment at the beginning of a meeting, it reminds everyone to be more aware of their surroundings and proactively think about safety. After working at an oil and gas company for several months, I was surprised how much more aware I was of potential risks and more observant than I had been a few months earlier.

The policy was written to enforce safety because it is one of the top corporate values. It reinforces the safety culture in the plants and across all employees, including those in corporate buildings. In reverse, the safety culture reinforces the policy. In addition, it would be difficult for individuals to be noncompliant because the policy is executed at the beginning of every meeting, and each employee takes turns. If employees do not participate, their peers will perceive them as noncompliant. That can be more of a deterrent than showing up on a report to a VP. Incorporating the safety moment at the beginning of every meeting ensures everyone thinks about safety. The story connects their safety, culture, and policies.

FIVE COMPONENTS OF A POLICY (CHECKLIST)

To recap, there are five components of a good policy.

Clearly Written

- Use concise phrasing, avoiding long sentence structures.
- Be direct.
- Be mindful of and limit the use of additional words that do not provide value, such as *that* and *which*. These words are common when speaking but can sometimes lead to misinterpretations in written phrasing.
- Represent realistic conditions or scenarios that the audience will most likely experience in the real world.
- Do not use abbreviations.
- Understand your entire audience. The policy should be able to support employees in all areas of the corporation (i.e., manufacturing, distribution centers, and corporate offices).

Clearly Understood

- Ensure that all employees understand the policy and do not require additional assistance or someone else to explain it.
- Use consistent language throughout. This is a common challenge when multiple people write or modify existing policies throughout the year.
- Use language that will be understood by multigenerational employees or employees of all ages (i.e., baby boomers, Generation X, Generation Y (or millennials), Generation Z, Gen Alpha, etc.).
- Do not use slang.

Clearly Communicated

- Ensure that the policy has been distributed to all employees, and do not forget new hires.
- Ensure that all employees know where the policy lives online.

- Ensure that all employees know how to find the policy.
- Ensure that reminders of the policy and its location are communicated often.

Clear Consequences

- Use realistic consequences (i.e., after *X* noncompliance notifications, the employee will receive a one percent reduction in their next annual bonus).
- Establish consequences that have a relevant meaning for your organization and employees.
- Apply consequences for deterrence. For example, if a policy states the usage of preferred processes and buying channels, an example of deterrence would be additional approval flows. The preferred process should be the easiest and quickest path to follow. Going outside of the policy will have an immediate impact, with more layers of approvals and an increase in the total process cycle time.

Clearly Enforced

- Establish an easy method to identify and understand who is out of compliance; this can be a simple report.
- Establish communication with employees who are out of compliance and ensure they understand what they did wrong.
- Establish a tiered enforcement structure escalating when one individual lacks compliance repeatedly.

The enforcement component is the most difficult to write. No one wants to include language that is acting against an employee. On the other hand, what is the point of writing policies if there is no enforcement? The enforcement section should be written with no bias, have a clear escalating path, and include several options for the employee to understand the policy. The consequences must be visible and available to all employees. The following list contains possible examples of escalating consequences for an employee.

A. **First offense—benefit of the doubt:** Give the employee the benefit of the doubt. Assume they were not aware of the policy or where to locate it. This assumes that all employees do not have a procurement background or the same background related to policies. The first offense response may be an email communicating that they are out of compliance. Include a link to the policy document and a quick reference guide if available.

B. **Second offense—offer education and support:** When the same employee appears on a noncompliance report for the second time, send an email with a link to a mandatory online video. This second email should also include the link to the policy document and specifically reference the section they need to study.
C. **Third offense—mandatory training course:** After further noncompliance, they can be required to participate in a 45-minute lunch-and-learn for a policy refresher. This is often a monthly or bimonthly session for small groups.
D. **Fourth offense—tangible consequences:** Further noncompliance is reflected in their mid-year review and could impact their annual bonus.
E. **Fifth offense—termination:** If employees remain noncompliant, termination from the company may be the final step. This last round of consequences can match the type of policy they have repeatedly ignored. Policies that are not as critical can impact their ability for promotion or can be placed on a performance improvement plan where they educate other departments on the importance of policy compliance.

POLICY FRAMEWORK

A framework is a structure that helps define the shape of something. For example, in a building, the framework is the internal structure of columns and beams that support the final visual view of the building. The internal framework would be different if the building were square rather than circular. The term *policy framework* is used here to outline how policy takes its final shape. Policies may change over time, but the framework is expected to remain constant.

Some policies provide the framework at the beginning of the policy document. In contrast, others will scatter these components throughout.

Those writing the policy will ultimately determine the format, not the company. Consider a framework that contributes to how the policies will be enforced before writing the policies. If the policies have already been written, take a minute to review the following list and see if they have been clearly written and can be clearly understood. A procurement policy framework will address the following questions:

- The purpose or intent of the policy, that is, why is there a procurement policy?
- What is the scope, that is, what is covered in these policies and what is not?
- Who or what areas of the company are not required to comply with this policy?
- How do we manage expectations, in other words, what does the organization expect from its employees?
- How do we handle noncompliance? What happens if the employee does not follow the policy?
- How will policies be communicated and shared with employees?
- When is the employee not required to engage with procurement?
- Who must review a new or revised policy, and what is the approval process?
- Are there roles and responsibilities of policy owners?
- How will policies be monitored, and are specific reports required?
- How and when are employees trained in new and revised policies?
- How will new hires learn procurement policies?

THE PROCUREMENT POLICY

Employees should refer to the procurement policy when they have questions about what and how to purchase goods or services for the company. Policies will vary from company to company, depending on whether it uses an enterprise resource planning (ERP) system or a cloud procurement application for its source-to-pay processes. ERP systems have more limitations than cloud procurement applications, and those limitations are reflected in the purchasing policies.

For example, an ERP cannot effectively monitor purchase orders (POs) against a contract, a capability in most cloud procurement applications. The procurement application's limitations are reflected in the purchasing process and, eventually, in the policies. This means some procurement policies depend on the application's capabilities and limitations and are written afterward.

Procurement policies are living documents that reflect the procurement organization, corporate goals, and strategic direction. Policies can change because the company acquires or sells off a business unit or implements new procurement application software. Policies may also change if the company moves into a different geographic region with contrasting cultural perspectives and government limitations. Finally, policies can change if the company moves in a new direction, altering its original corporate values.

The items covered in the procurement policies may vary depending on the industry sector and subsector of the company. Consider that a professional services company will not include policies unique to a manufacturing company. A cannabis company will have some overlapping policies as a manufacturing company but will also have policies unique to the cannabis subsector. There will also be additional content if the company is global or operates in specific geographic regions. Overall, the foundation of procurement policies will include, but certainly is not limited to, the following:

1. **Introduction/purpose:** Provides a brief overview of why this document was created. This can be a few sentences or a few paragraphs.
2. **Confidentiality:** This section is optional but may be considered depending on the company.
3. **Document control:** This section contains information to communicate that this is a living, digital document, and the procurement department controls all updates.
4. **Values/principles:** Outlines how the procurement activities should be carried out. These core values connect the procurement organization with corporate strategic direction. For example, *transparency*—to facilitate an open procurement process or

fair competition—to support competitive proposals while balancing local suppliers.

5. **Objectives:** Provides a list of the goals and outcomes expected for procurement. For example, cost efficiency and value of the company dollars spent on fostering supplier diversity and promoting sustainability. For a manufacturing company, an objective may include ensuring consistent supply and supporting continuity.
6. **Scope:** Provides an overview of what is in and out of scope for this department. For example, the procurement department may not handle some categories, such as packaging, corrugated materials, raw materials, logistics, and telecommunications. Additional details would document any departments, geographic regions, or processes not currently covered by the procurement organization.
7. **Engagement with procurement:** Explains when employees should engage with procurement and why they might not. This section may include policies that POs under $25,000 do not require procurement involvement. However, procurement will track all purchases for a supplier, and if the total dollars exceed $250,000 annually, procurement will automatically be engaged.
8. **Process overview:** This may include multiple flow charts covering each stage of the end-to-end procurement process, such as planning, sourcing, supplier selection (prequalification, evaluation, and audits), contracts, and supplier onboarding.
9. **Process (how to buy):** This section will provide detailed processes across a variety of scenarios, such as single-source, sole-source, one-time suppliers, request for proposals (RFPs), supplier performance, emergency audits, preferred suppliers, supplier onboarding, etc.
10. **Approval levels and thresholds:** This section should consist of a few sentences that outline the approval milestones. For example, purchasing orders between $25,000 and $100,000 require approval by the procurement manager. This section would also include whether there were different approval levels for different categories that may be listed as having a higher risk than others.

Additionally, this section would specify when those policies do not apply. For example, a procurement application can be configured to automatically approve POs for the category of office supplies under $75. This category and spend threshold are considered low risk and have a high transaction volume. The effort to approve a requisition did not add value or reduce risk.

11. **Supplier relationship management:** This section will outline supplier segmentation (i.e., strategic, critical) and guidelines for how often they should be evaluated. For example, the company may care more about the top 100 suppliers based on spending. Depending on the segmentation, the evaluation process may be annual, biannual, or quarterly.
12. **Conflicts of interest:** What is a conflict of interest, and how is it identified? One example is if the procurement manager evaluates a proposal for a supplier they also have a 25 percent ownership in, or if the procurement manager used to work for that supplier before joining the company.
13. **Ethics:** This section should include policies on bribery, corruption, and nondiscrimination.
14. **Roles and responsibilities:** This section contains a chart that outlines the responsibilities of each level within the procurement organization, such as the procurement officer, directors, suppliers, and employees. It may also document the responsibilities of various committees, such as an audit or supplier diversity committee.
15. **Organizational chart:** This section includes a diagram showing the roles within the procurement department and what procurement area is covered. The goal is to assist employees who have questions but may not know whom to contact.
16. **Documentation/retention:** Based on government and legal regularities, this section will include the number of years that documentation has to be physically stored and the requirement for access by government auditors. For example, a country in Europe, the Middle East, or Africa may require purchases of items considered capital improvements (defined by that country) to

be stored for 15 years. Another example is that all invoices must be stored on a server in the United States for seven years.

17. **Quality control:** This section may only be applicable to manufacturing companies. It will provide policies for the inspection and rejection of materials.
18. **Risk management:** This section includes guidelines for a supplier risk assessment and when these occur in the supplier's life cycle with the company. For example, an initial assessment may be completed during the RFP phase, and a more comprehensive risk assessment may be completed after an award. However, risk management should not stop there. Additional times to reevaluate risk are at the time of contract renewal or if the supplier changes certain information on their supplier profile.
19. **Delegation of authority:** This section explains how and when to delegate purchasing authority. For example, a VP cannot delegate authority to someone with a lower purchasing authority.
20. **Monitoring/auditing:** This section will outline policies on the frequency of reporting and auditing. For example, contracts over two million dollars are subject to an audit of the process, or once a quarter, three sourcing events will be selected for auditing.
21. **Compliance/consequence:** This section outlines what noncompliance is and the consequences of repeated noncompliance.
22. **Reviews/amendments:** This section details the review policy for the procurement policy document. For example, policies will be reviewed every two years or in the event of acquisitions, company-wide projects, or the inclusion of new geographic regions. In addition, changes to the policy will be drafted by the policy manager, reviewed by the procurement VP, and approved by the procurement officer.
23. **Appendices:**

    - *Definitions*: No two companies have an exact understanding of standard terms and terminology. Including a definitions table should be considered mandatory.
    - *Approval thresholds and limits*: This includes the details behind the previously outlined policy; for example, a table that

outlines the approval limits across employee roles (or titles). If the company allows for cost-center approval, there would be a separate table for the level of financial approvals.

- *Proposal evaluation criteria and scorecard*: This is a table outlining the standard criteria for measuring all procurement proposals and when a deviation from those standards should occur; for example, price, financial stability, supplier diversity, innovation, capability to meet requirements, technology capabilities, geographic considerations, corporate social responsibilities, etc.
- *Conflict of interest declaration form*: When a conflict of interest is identified, this form is completed and stored. This will provide evidence of a formal recusal of procurement team members in case of a supplier appeal.
- *Supplier code of conduct*: This is a standard document to be shared with all suppliers. This may include specific details; for example, all supplier representatives may not wear shirts, pants, or clothing with graphics, illustrations, or words beyond the suppliers' logo and slogans.
- *Gifts*: This should include details supporting the gift policy under the conflicts of interest section, such as a list of what gifts are acceptable, in which situations receipts should be documented, when gifts are not acceptable, and how to respond.
- *Sustainability guidelines for suppliers*: These are standard guidelines distributed to suppliers supporting the company's sustainability goals. This section may also include guidance for when a supplier cannot accommodate all of the sustainability guidelines in this section.

CHAPTER 5

AUTOMATION AND PROCESS IMPROVEMENTS

Process improvements are steps taken to change or modify an existing process to improve results; at least, that is what we hope. Unlike a transformation, a process does not need to be fully transformed to make a difference. It is possible to make a single change or to modify one step of a process to gain significant advantages such as reducing the overall process cycle time (from start to finish), increasing savings, reducing cost, and improving relationships between procurement and the stakeholder.

Process automation can often strengthen the perceptions of internal stakeholders by improving their experience. For example, automating the requisition approval process reduces errors and ensures consistency. This operational efficiency can provide faster turnaround times and increase confidence. This, in turn, boosts the perception that the organization is prioritizing responsiveness and builds trust in the application's reliability.

Successful process changes can increase the procurement organization's value and free up procurement professionals for more strategic activities. Procurement can directly impact operational efficiencies instead of focusing on administrative activities like reviewing purchase orders (POs) to determine compliance. Instead of being perceived as primarily cost-center-focused, procurement can directly impact profitability. Automation enables procurement to focus on market research and more advanced sourcing strategies. Therefore, stakeholders begin to view procurement as a valuable contributor to supporting their goals and objectives.

The introduction of cloud procurement provided a great leap forward since it allowed for the possibility of automating manual and repeatable tasks. However, gaps remain when you fast forward to the present day, and many repeatable tail-end processes continue to be done manually. These types of processes make up about 20 percent of total process steps and are usually the last remaining steps in a process life cycle.

It was initially thought that these smaller, tail-end steps could not be automated. Around 2015, applying an agile mindset to the procurement organization was the attempted solution to automate a process fully. Several years later, CPOs (chief procurement officers) recognized that creating a more agile process did not resolve the existing manual steps in the process. Procurement organizations pushed back on the application providers who developed the cloud-based enterprise suites of applications. Even with a cloud-based procurement application, some process steps still required the end user to click the same button every time. For example, when a contract was fully executed, the user was still required to log back into the contract application, open the contract, and click a button to publish it. It was the same button every time, regardless of whether the contract was a master service agreement, a statement of work, or an amendment. This was a perfect opportunity to automate, and it would have been even better if the application provider could fix this within their applications. However, providers did not want to make the effort to automate a few steps inside one application when there were other more prominent features to focus on that could provide more perceived value.

PROCESS IMPROVEMENT DONE RIGHT

Improvements often lead to cost reduction, cost avoidance, and minimizing the number of errors that occur within the process. When a process is *done right*, the changes within the end-to-end process cycle create a result that improves one or more of the following areas:

- Process simplification: How the user interacts with the process and how many steps are required to complete the process
- Efficiency: The reduction in process cycle time and how long it takes to complete the process

- Resource reduction: How many internal and/or external resources are required to complete the process

Improvements within the process should have a lasting, positive impact on the organization. This is the most important consideration and the most overlooked. Changing a process only because specific changes were previously included in the scope of a larger project will always yield unproductive results. Changing just one part of the process is also not favorable. It is essential to follow the process to the end, no matter where it leads or how many departments a process touches. Yet both of these concerns continue in almost every transformation initiative and are another variable leading to why transformation initiatives are labeled failures in less than two years.

Figure 5.1 shows a great example of a real-world internal process improvement that positively impacts all areas: process simplification, efficiency, and resource reduction. It displays an internal process improved by deploying a cloud-procurement application, shown in the future state illustration as (cloud eProcurement or CeP), plus cleaning up the manual steps occurring outside of CeP.

This organization utilizes an in-house Print Production team that can support most requests and works with third-party suppliers as needed for more custom requirements. This was more cost-effective than outsourcing or working with multiple suppliers for every request. In the current state, the business units collaborate with a department that documents the requirements and translates them into a *Job Jacket* the Print Production team can work with. The Print Production team can support most of the requirements but also requires a third-party supplier to execute a portion.

The process diagram shows many internal and external stakeholders and multiple systems needed to support one request. As a result of the current state process, the Finance team was also included because of the intercompany transfer of funds across the departments and their responsibility for manually reclassifying those funds. As more steps are required, there are more opportunities for errors, more oversight is needed, and more delays occur from when the request was made to when the order was started.

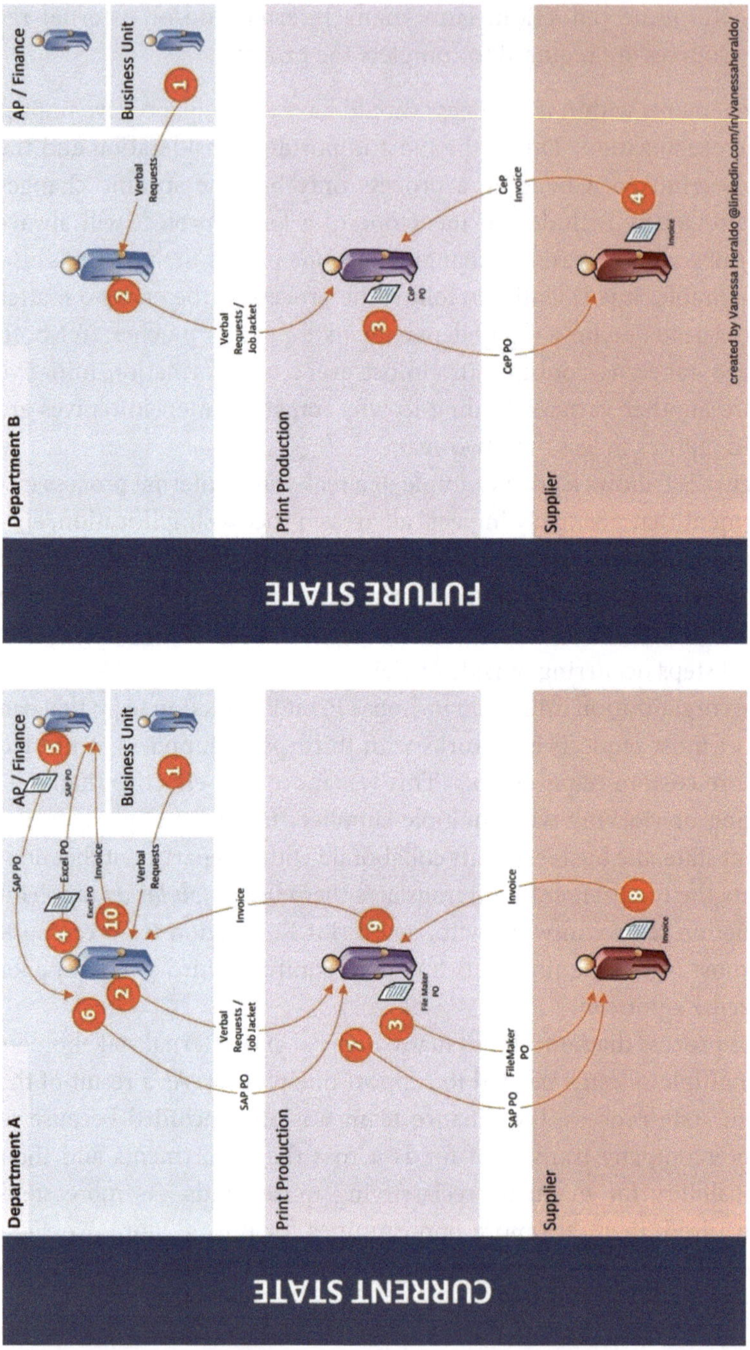

Figure 5.1 Process simplification, efficiency, and resource allocation

In the future state, Figure 5.1 shows an optimized process with four steps and one system instead of 10 steps and three systems. The cloud procurement application used to transform processes with external suppliers was also leveraged across the entire process, including the processes between departments. Excel spreadsheets no longer needed to be sent to the Finance team because a single PO was required instead of multiple orders for the same request. This PO documented the correct accounting string and sent that information directly to the financial system.

When you look at this diagram more closely, the most significant impact was not the Print Production team working with the external supplier but all the steps before that between the Business Unit and the Print Production team. The project team took extra time to document the current state from start to finish. Because of that, they could identify how to enact real change and generate real value that would continue long after the project was completed.

This phase of the transformation initiative was completed in 14 months and included all global regions except Asia-Pacific. The goal of the transformation was due to a change in the strategic growth of the company. For 60+ years, this company had grown organically but recognized it had to change to remain competitive. This meant the company needed to grow through acquisitions. Since this had never been a part of its corporate strategy, the processes and systems could not support this. To achieve this new goal, leadership was willing to prioritize resources and funding. The desire was to *transform* once by developing a solid foundation with the understanding that minor changes (a few resources and a few months) would be needed in the future to support changes in consumer demands.

Ensuring lasting success meant focusing on the 28 departments that had the most significant impact on the company's core competencies or had a large amount of spending. This meant the project team met with each of the 28 departments identified, talked to them about what they buy and how they buy it, and documented the current state process. In two meetings, for a total of six hours, the project team had enough information to translate *what they buy* into a handful of commodity codes to support future automation in the requisition-to-order process. The team also created detailed process flows highlighting which internal and external groups were involved at each step from start to finish.

All the information captured in those department meetings was used multiple times to support change management (people and adoption readiness), automation through a cloud procurement deployment, and process efficiencies not supported by technology. The company completed its first acquisition as planned and, two years later, successfully absorbed a second acquisition. If the company had decided to deploy procurement technology *only* or decided *not* to create detailed current-state processes, it would not have been as successful.

OVERCOMPLICATING AN AUTOMATED PROCESS

Overcomplicating a process can occur when a manual process is automated, and the results usually have a negative impact on the user. A negative impact can be defined as *when more resources are required in the automated process than in the manual version* or *when the total process cycle time ends up being longer in the automated process compared to the manual version*. Unfortunately, this happens often. Many times, a process is automated simply because it can or theoretically should be, but with little thought given to the final design.

The best example to illustrate this is the automation of approvals in workflows. These are the most revisited and corrected processes after completing a transformation initiative. The challenges and solutions found here can be applied to most other processes when considering automation. These challenges are the most overlooked because the company associates the definition of agile with *hurry, hurry* to have something in a production environment for the end user. The following mistakes are the most common and consistently occur when considering process automation:

- **The purpose of the workflow was incorrectly translated:** Documenting the business requirement may only require a couple of sentences. However, translating that into the scripted language needed to configure the workflow may look like an *if-then-else* statement with tiered levels of approvers based on the delegation of authority, dollar amount, and/or exceptions. This is normal.

Often, the scripted version becomes so loopy (yep, that is a technical term) that the automated version is longer and more complicated compared to the original manual version.

- **The manual workflow was not properly dissected:** Consider this scenario—step one of a workflow requires the finance department to approve solely based on the amount of money evaluated in the workflow. The finance department may not want to approve until the cost center owner has approved, which would confirm if there was enough budget to cover the requested amount. At this point in the discovery phase, the discussion may have ended. However, in the manual version of this workflow, the cost center owner verbally provides updates to another business group owner. This could have been missed entirely since it was not a physical step in the manual version of the workflow. This would have gone unnoticed until a few months after a live environment when the business group complained they no longer had visibility into the process.
- **The workflows were not all considered simultaneously:** Some consulting firms may recommend breaking workflows into phases and automating the simpler or shorter workflows first. Initially, this may sound like a logical and reasonable idea, but what sounds great in theory often does not always work well in practice. For example, a different workflow may exist in the current state for the same process across two business units. Only after both workflows are documented and reviewed simultaneously would the similarities be uncovered, i.e., having the same steps or touching the same group of approvers. What was initially considered as two different workflows was really the same workflow in two different business units. Unfortunately, in this real-world scenario, the company did not evaluate the workflows simultaneously and created the same workflow for each department. It wasn't discovered until after go-live.
- **The application may have specific limited capabilities:** The resources configuring the workflows may not fully know all the existing application capabilities and limitations. While this is not ideal, cloud-based applications are updated quarterly, and it can

be challenging to stay on top of new features and functionality. This can lead to a modification of the scripted version of the workflow due to application constraints. It is also possible that these limitations can create unknown problems, forcing workflows to be separated or merged or causing reconsideration of the business policies. For example, a "cost center approver" sounds simple in the manual version and can easily be translated into the scripted format. However, the automated version may require additional data that is not readily available to support the cost center budget owner. In this real-world scenario, leadership had to evaluate the time needed to create the formatted data along with its impact on the timeline.

PAYMENT TERMS—A DATA AND PROCESS EXAMPLE

Process and data are often intertwined, and the impact of not considering both simultaneously can be costly. Considering payment terms and where those payment terms are integrated into the process is usually an afterthought and another common barrier to a successful process. Most transformation processes either neglect the payment terms process completely, shift it into a future phase, or try to mimic an enterprise resource planning (ERP)-like process.

In the ERP system, the payment term and the supplier are most often linked. When shifting to a procurement technology, one faulty procedure is documenting a standard payment term at the supplier level during the supplier registration process. This only works if the company has only one payment term or scenario across that individual supplier; this is highly unlikely.

Another assumption is that payment arrangements are discussed during contract negotiations and populated in the payment-term field in the contract management module. However, what is missing is how the negotiated payment term is made available to the system issuing the supplier payments. The missing piece is where the payment terms are stored—or the source of truth—and how the payment terms will be available to the system paying the supplier.

Let's step back for a moment to look at the larger picture. After a contract is negotiated with payment terms of net 45 (45 days after the invoice date), eventually, an invoice will be received against the work outlined in the contract. When the supplier invoice is approved, details of the invoice, such as supplier name, invoice amount, etc., are pushed to the ERP system (for this scenario, we will assume the ERP is the same system issuing supplier payments). This is referred to as the okay-to-pay file. This information will sit in the ERP system until the payment terms come to fruition, and only then will money be distributed to the supplier.

There may still be a gap between the negotiated payment term and the payment term in the ERP system. This gap could exist for a few reasons:

- **Scenario *A*:** The company cleaned up all master data, including suppliers, and populated the payment-term field in the ERP supplier table as net 60 days across all suppliers.
- **Scenario *B*:** A generic payment term was created at the time the supplier onboarded and was automatically sent to the ERP during the supplier integration sync.

One option to resolve this is to work with the integration team to send the payment terms from the contract to the ERP system. At first glance, this sounds like a great idea. But recall, the procurement professional is negotiating at the supplier-contract level, not at the supplier level. The ERP supplier master data table stores data at the supplier level, not the supplier-contract level. This approach will not work because one supplier can have many contracts, each with different payment terms. The result of this approach is that the payment terms data will continue to overwrite what is in the ERP system for that supplier. For example, in scenario *A*:

- When supplier *A* was onboarded for the first time in 2017, the ERP was populated with payment terms of net 90 days.
- When contract *ABC* was negotiated in 2017, the payment terms were negotiated to reflect net 60 days for a 24-month contract. The ERP system was updated with this latest information; net 60 overwriting the original terms of net 90 days.

- Then, in 2018, supplier *A* negotiated a second contract (contract *XYZ*). This was a short-term six-month contract to backfill an immediate issue with another business unit. Supplier *A* now has two active contracts with the company. As part of the negotiation, it was agreed that supplier *A* would receive a payment term of net 45 days for this contract only. The ERP system was updated with this latest information (net 45 days), overwriting the previous net 60 days.

This approach would allow the ERP system to reflect a net 45 for this supplier. All future invoices from that supplier will also receive net 45 payment terms. This may be great for the supplier, but is not something the company wants to support. The payment term process is a notable example of following all the scenarios and asking a lot of questions:

- Is the negotiated payment term automatically flowing to the associated invoice?
- Is the payment term from the invoice flowing into the ERP?
- Are there middleware applications or staging tables between the invoice application and the ERP that have changed the payment term field or are not pushing the payment term field through to the ERP?
- Which payment term field is used to calculate supplier payments? Do not assume that because the payment terms were associated with the invoice, the ERP is using that field to calculate the payment.
- How is the payment term from a PO updating on the invoice?
- How are the payment terms handled when creating an invoice without a contract or PO?

Since applications are bolted on at different time frames, the craziest things can occur. For example, one company had the right idea, but the execution was poorly thought through. The payment term was indeed on the invoice and was sent to the ERP, and the invoice payment term was "correctly" used to calculate the payment date for the supplier. After two years of supplier complaints, the research concluded the payment term on the invoice was automatically updated from the contract module, which was automatically updated from the payment term documented at the same time the supplier was first onboarded with the company. The payment term negotiated at the time of the contract was never captured.

This exercise shows the importance of following the process from one end to the other. Another consideration is discussing with your IT (information technology) team how the ERP system stores and uses payment terms. For example, if the ERP system is SAP, it can store payment terms at different master data levels, like the supplier master table, the supplier master table plus purchasing organization, or the supplier master table plus company code. This also depends on which modules are used in SAP and how invoices are created and stored. Having all of the information straightened out will help smooth supplier payments.

Dynamic Discounting and Working Capital

It is worth discussing the option of deploying a payable or working capital application that includes dynamic discounting capabilities. This application bypasses the ERP and sits on top of the invoice module. The supplier interfaces with the payable application and receives payments from one of the participating banks from which the supplier has agreed to receive funds.

The benefit of the payables application is that it is linked to the company's cash flow and working capital. For example, for supplier *A*, contract *XYZ*, the payment terms are net 45 days. When using dynamic discounting, the supplier is allowed to change the payment terms in the middle of the contract but at a cost to the supplier. For example, supplier *A* may need to be paid sooner than net 45 days, and is willing to offer a discount (i.e., net 30 days; 2%) for that earlier payment. If the supplier accepts this arrangement, the company will reduce the invoice amount by two percent, but the supplier will receive their money for that invoice in 30 days instead of 45.

Again, this appears to simply allow the supplier to be paid earlier than the negotiated terms but at a lower cost than was previously committed. Remember, this exercise is to follow the process from end to end, which also includes considering our stakeholders. Payment terms have a direct impact on the company's cash flow. Cash flow is the net balance between the money that moves in and out of the company at any given point in time. Payment terms allow for a more positive cash flow. The money is moved out of the organizational bank account as a supplier is paid. If the company is late in paying the supplier, the money remains in the company bank account longer, thereby drawing interest. In theory, the company would prefer longer payment terms, such as net 90, while the supplier also manages their cash flow and prefers lower payment terms, such as net 30.

There are professionals in the finance and treasury departments who think about this all the time. Optimizing the payment terms process is a perfect example of what may sound simple on the surface. Still, many variables must be considered regarding data, processes, technology, and policies. There are treasury departments that block the use of payables and working capital solutions because it reduces the amount of money that is earning interest. Balancing the amount of money lost from potential earned interest compared to the amount of money saved by paying suppliers early is crucial. That is a part of the business case that procurement would want to consider if dynamic discounting is a potential option for the future.

AUTOMATING TAIL-END PROCESSES

Like tail-end suppliers, which are a group of unmanaged suppliers that generate a combined 20 percent of the company's spending, tail-end processes are defined in a comparable way. These are the 20 percent of processes that were not automated when leveraging the technology of an enterprise suite of applications or by purchasing a one-off application module. We care about tail-end processes because this is one of the areas holding back procurement and supply chain resources from fully stepping away from tactical tasks to focus on more strategic activities. These strategic activities carry more value and impact the organization at a higher level.

A complete solution for automating tail-end processes was unavailable until a few years ago when artificial intelligence (AI) technologies emerged. RPA (robotic process automation) supports process automation under the umbrella of AI technologies. Wikipedia provides a good definition of how the use of AI technologies has enabled RPA to become the leading method of repeatable task automation:

> *"In traditional workflow automation tools, a software developer produces a list of actions to automate a task and interface to the back-end system using internal application programming interfaces (APIs) or dedicated scripting language. In contrast, RPA systems develop the action list by watching the user perform that task in the application's graphical user interface (GUI), and then perform the automation by repeating those tasks directly in the GUI. This can lower the barrier to using automation in products that might not otherwise feature APIs for this purpose."*

The next step to automation is selecting the first use case, perhaps talking with other CPOs and companies or checking out the responses to ChatGPT-4 (the latest version of OpenAI's artificial intelligence chatbot, released in October 2023). The question was, "What are the most common use cases in procurement for RPA?" The following list includes eight of the responses received from ChatGPT-4:

1. PO processing
2. Invoice processing
3. Vendor onboarding and management
4. Supplier communication
5. Contract management
6. Compliance monitoring
7. Requisition processing
8. Catalog maintenance

This is a good start, but ChatGPT will not include all the possibilities. There are many more granular use cases beyond what is listed here, and the potential is much larger than realized. Any task with one or more repeating steps, regardless of the scenario, is an opportunity. Let's explore examples in the requisition-to-order process:

- **A sourcing event to create a requisition:** Data from a completed sourcing event can be extracted to automate the creation of the requisition. This automation can pull the details of the sourcing line items, such as description, quantity, and price, to auto-populate a requisition.

- **PO change requests:** Once the PO is open, a form can be visible for the user to answer a few questions. Information from the form can be used to automatically create the PO change order, auto-populate the correct fields, and initiate the approval workflow.
- **PO compliance monitoring:** This is a monthly review of PO line-item pricing against contract pricing and policies. A report can also be generated that identifies discrepancies and prioritizes where to focus research efforts.
- **New catalog creation:** Catalogs simplify the users' purchase process, but analyzing spend data is a very time-consuming activity. Automation can generate reports to review purchasing data and identify the best opportunities for catalogs.
- **Existing catalog updates:** Reviewing off-catalog purchasing to determine whether items should be included in an existing supplier catalog is another time-consuming activity where automation can create immediate benefits.
- **PO force-close:** This is a specific example of a process conducted by the system administrator to force-close a PO that remains open with no activity against it. In many companies, the system administrator generates a report of open POs with no activity after six months. They will manually open each of the POs, click a few buttons, and force-close those POs. These steps are always the same, and therefore, this is another opportunity for automation.

Procurement organizations should consider two or three resources trained in process automation and development to truly leverage the potential of automation; this can be within a procurement center of excellence or reside under a director of procurement operations. Instead of reducing headcount to save a quick dollar, consider reallocating those resources to value-added activities that will provide a long-lasting impact.

ONGOING HEALTH CHECKS

Updating, redesigning, optimizing, or simplifying processes is not completed once and then forgotten. Periodic health checks are a way to plan and build in time for the minor but necessary adjustments to remain effective and continue to add value. When implementing an enterprise application suite, it is not realistic to expect 100 percent of all the company processes to be redesigned and automated, nor should it be assumed that because you implemented business requirements for a requisition approval process, there is no need for adjustments. While this sounds counterintuitive to the purpose of the project you just completed, a realistic perspective allows for a slight drift between what was implemented (or deployed to the end users) and how the end users are using the system and interacting with the automated process.

It should be mandatory to have a health check around three to four months after processes have been automated and deployed to the end user. This is different from the term *hypercare*, which is post go-live support and is when the consulting firm provides resources two to four weeks after go-live to ensure the system is technically working, the integrations are indeed working as expected, and data is moving to where it needs to go. A health check, on the other hand, validates the processes are working as expected and allows for minor process adjustments as needed.

Items that tend to bubble up in the first health check are highlighted mainly by the most vocal end users who use the system and processes the most. That is good and should be encouraged. By listening to the more active users who do hold influence over others, we improve user adoption and strengthen the relationship between procurement and business-unit stakeholders. Examples of modifications during the first health check may include:

- Making a document available inside the application instead of having the end user leave the application to find it
- Changing a step in a process from mandatory to optional
- Adding a user group into the project folder because it was discovered this user group is being added manually to every project
- Changing the field type from a radial button to a drop-down

The next health check milestone occurs around 12 months after automated processes have been deployed to the end user. During this health check, application updates are reviewed to determine if they have a significant positive impact. For example, the procurement operations department should keep track of stakeholder feedback and suggestions for improvements. When compared to the application's list of potential new features and capabilities, there may be an opportunity to resolve stakeholder feedback by enabling a new feature. As a result, this new feature is enabled, tested, approved, and made available in the production environment. The documentation is updated and communicated to end users.

The most important health check to discuss is the one that almost never happens. This health check milestone should occur approximately 24 months after the initial go-live and should review anything that could have happened within and to the business that impacts primary and/or ancillary processes. These changes can result from the CEO shifting the company's core competencies, acquisitions, the inclusion of new technologies, the discontinuation of old or legacy technologies, or existing processes no longer being as efficient as they once were.

Also, around this time, the procurement organization should assess how to gain more value from their technology solutions and/or evaluate how to leverage the existing technology solution to support a revenue-generating organization. Other activities that typically occur around this time frame include integrating and mitigating risk into the entire supplier life cycle from sourcing to onboarding through contract renewals—none of which would have been possible two years prior. However, this is certainly a possibility now with two years of data being captured.

The two-year milestone is not simply looking at a few key processes that should have been included in the scope of the 12-month health check, but rather it is a review of all processes end to end. This is an important distinction. At the 24-month health check, processes are viewed across their life cycle, along with how the steps of intersecting processes impact them. Decisions made in one process should be evaluated to determine how each decision will affect that same process further down the line and how that decision will impact other processes that intersect it. Adding this two-year checkup as part of a continuous improvement process fosters opportunities to track process performance, identify inefficiencies, and remove them. More important, integrating regular health checks will establish and strengthen a continuous improvement culture within the procurement organization.

CHAPTER 6

REQUEST FOR PROPOSALS

A request for proposal (RFP) is not just a document. It is a crucial tool that solicits proposals from suppliers to address specific needs. It is the cornerstone of the procurement process, the very reason the procurement organization exists. The RFP process is instrumental in helping organizations identify the right supplier, one who can deliver products and services that align with a set of required variables, such as cost, timeline, quality, diversity, and skills, along with an approach and solution that meets the intended needs.

Over the past 100 years or so, the RFP process has not deviated much from its original methods, yet some perceive it as being worse today than ever. Both statements can be factual because they point to a result that no longer provides much value. As the procurement organization has evolved alongside changes in technology and consumer demand, the RFP process has added layers on top of layers over procedures to remain relevant. The outcome is ineffective but has become more arduous and time-consuming for the organization and the supplier, placing a significant burden on the procurement team.

LENGTHY QUESTIONNAIRES WITH NO VALUE

Lengthy RFPs with 300 to 400 or more questions may feel comprehensive. Some may think that the more questions asked, the better. More is not always best in this scenario. Longer RFPs extend the total time from start to finish; it requires more time to draft, more time for the supplier to complete, and more time for the procurement team to evaluate. A lengthy RFP does not always result in a differentiation across suppliers.

Often, supplier responses are quite similar, so the supplier scorecard does not show a significant difference. When this happens, the procurement team has no choice but to draft and distribute another RFP. Round two may have a smaller subset of existing questions (100–200) to clarify supplier responses or be a complete overhaul.

If the current RFP does not provide answers to easily evaluate the supplier's differences, it is crucial to stop and reflect. Take a pause and gauge whether the RFP is doing its job correctly. Asking more questions without understanding whether they are the right questions leads to misunderstandings, which may not be visible until contract negotiations.

> If your RFP does not help you understand the differences among suppliers, then you have been asking the wrong questions.

> ***Real-world scenario:*** *A supplier responded to an RFP and checked a box in an Excel spreadsheet showing that free training was included. Partly because of this, the supplier was awarded the business. During contract negotiations, the procurement team discovered that the free training was for one individual only. The supplier did provide supplemental attachments outlining the training options, but the procurement team did not read the fine print. The supplier had checked a box on the RFP spreadsheet stating that training would be provided but did not clarify how many users could participate in that training. At the same time, the RFP spreadsheet did not allocate a specific column for comments. When the supplier tried to modify the Excel document, the additional columns added by the supplier were not uploaded back into the original procurement application.*

This situation can cause friction between the business stakeholders, the procurement team, and the supplier. Stakeholders look to the procurement team to formulate good questions on the RFP and then provide expertise in evaluating the responses. The procurement team believes the supplier is not forthcoming or honest. The supplier believes it truthfully answered the question in the RFP, and the RFP was to blame for not allowing comments in that section. To help avoid this type of sticky situation, here are a few questions to ask before drafting an RFP.

- Are you reusing an RFP:
    - Issued *two or more* years ago?
    - From another category or service that must be modified?
    - With more than 50 questions?
- Is your RFP Excel only?
- Is your RFP drafted without input from stakeholders?
- Is your RFP drafted in less than seven business days?

You have increased the chance of failure if you answered yes to one or more of these questions. It is better to take a few days to reevaluate your RFP-creation process instead of rushing to meet a short-term deadline. Creating a thoughtful RFP will reduce the total RFP cycle time. It will result in selecting a supplier who is the best fit to work with your company to meet each stakeholder's business goals.

The RFP can be written to provide more value-driven responses with fewer questions. Focusing on key areas such as the number of business challenges that can be solved with this RFP, the level of process improvement to be expected, and how to gauge the level of success is vital. Consider the following:

- **What is driving the need to create an RFP?** Is the company looking to optimize and automate internal processes, support an acquisition strategy, achieve cost savings, realize cost avoidance, support regulatory requirements, initiate changes to internal controls, minimize risk, or promote more self-service to the general user? The underlying reason for the RFP is a set of guardrails. Each question in the RFP should match up with one or more of the guardrails. If they do not, then perhaps the right questions are not being asked.
- **Who will be using the product or service?** Determine whether the procurement team or the general user will utilize this product or service the most and how much of it each stakeholder group

will use. For example, when evaluating an enterprise application with multiple modules, determine which type of user is the primary one for each module.

- **What is the level of risk for this product or service compared to the amount of spending?** This could potentially gauge who has the buying power—your organization or the supplier. Understanding this can potentially change how you ask some of the questions in the RFP.
- **Beyond the award criteria, what are the requirements for success?** When the project is completed, how will you and your stakeholders know if it was successful? Mapping out a few ideas with the stakeholders may lead to questions initially missed on the RFP.

Understanding the answers to these questions strengthens the RFP and will generate better responses from the supplier. If there is no clear reason why the RFP is required, it should not hurt anyone's feelings to ask. For example, understanding the purpose of the RFP and which stakeholder(s) has the most to gain or lose could be the key to selecting the right supplier. The answer to this question may change depending on which executives you ask. For example, the CTO (chief technology officer), CPO (chief procurement officer), and CFO (chief financial officer) will each have a different lens they use to establish the definition of success. Understanding who to ask is just as important as asking the question.

> ***Real-world scenario:*** *Before developing an RFP, a senior executive asked, "What is the purpose of the RFP?" The company needed the right supplier to align with a larger corporate objective. Another executive responded, "The purpose in selecting the right supplier is to not only automate the process but, more importantly, to provide a competitive edge in our industry that will increase market share, improve customer service, and give us access to information unavailable today."*

This response is very different from wanting to evaluate suppliers at the lowest cost or finding a supplier with experience in one domain over another. Understanding the purpose resulted in an RFP questionnaire that differed greatly from a traditional list of questions about cost and value.

When drafting an RFP, ensure the question provides a response that:

- Assists in understanding the difference between one supplier and another
- Can be directly linked to a business process or business challenge the internal stakeholder is trying to solve
- Provides clarity on how the supplier will solve the business problem
- Supports the purpose and intent of the RFP

Consider an RFP to evaluate enterprise cloud procurement technology providers such as Coupa, Ariba, Ivalua, Determine, and Jaggaer; these companies are mature within their space. Creating a comprehensive spreadsheet with a list of application features may not be the best use of time for you or the supplier. An RFP with over 200 questions about features and capabilities tends to have the same results. Each supplier answers, "Yes, we have this" or "Yes, all of these features are out-of-the-box or configurable."

- The term *out-of-the-box* is defined as a feature that is included and available after the application is installed and no other intervention is required. For example, the ability to flip a requisition into a purchase order once all approvals are received is out-of-the-box or a standard feature.
- The term *configurable* refers to a feature that the company or a third-party consultant can configure without needing a resource from the application provider. For example, for requisition approval, the application will allow approval rules to be created by a general user (or a consulting firm acting on behalf of the user) with no development experience. Configuration often requires users to drag and drop fields or search and select a field from a list.

This is a prime example of questions that were more relevant ten years ago when application providers were at different stages of their maturity, both in the industry and with their technology. Yet, these same 200 or more capability questions remain a part of the process inside the procurement organization today. Instead of understanding market and supply base changes, the same list of questions is used repeatedly.

To differentiate between application providers, consider the following questions—which do not focus on what they already have available but rather on what is not available, along with the level of effort necessary to extend or add to the existing footprint—as a starting point:

- What is not configurable in the application for the user?
- Are there scenarios that require the application provider to be involved in the configuration? Are these resources part of the implementation cost, or is there an additional cost? Is there a limit on the number of weeks the application provider resources are available before additional fees are required?
- Is there a limit to the number of fields that can be added to the application? Is there an additional cost to adding more fields if there is a limit?
- Is there training included in the license fees? What is the number of users supported in the license fee with no additional cost?
- What scenarios require the application provider to be involved post-implementation?
- What integrations are not available?
- What data sources are configurable or are available through application programming interfaces?
- What integrations are one-way versus two-way?
- Can the application support a specific architectural landscape?
- Can the application be integrated into an architecture supporting many enterprise resource planning (ERP) systems?

The current architectural landscape is another piece of information that must be included in an RFP. This information is often left out of the RFP because:

1. It was thought to be unnecessary
2. The information does not exist or has never been documented
3. No one wanted to work with the IT (information technology) department to document
4. No one wanted to take the time

Right-sizing the RFP is about balancing why we want to buy, what the supplier needs to respond to, and what information we need for evaluation.

When the procurement professional understands how to balance these three elements, the RFP is exactly where it needs to be: concise but comprehensive.

This approach minimizes misunderstandings and eliminates the blame game. It also reduces the need to extend deadlines, which causes project delays and cost overruns. It will reinforce the selection of the right supplier and, more important, eliminate the need to rewrite and redistribute the RFP a second time.

For example, one requirement may be the need to integrate with four ERP instances of Oracle or two ERP instances of SAP and two instances of JD Edwards. This information can profoundly affect the responses from the application providers. Additionally, not every cloud procurement application can integrate with multiple systems or many different ERPs. Providing a list of systems required for integration and asking about integration capabilities is one question that can lead to eliminating most suppliers, resulting in a much shorter list to evaluate:

> ***Real-world scenario:*** *When I worked in consulting, my team was short-listed as a potential supplier. At this stage of the RFP process, we were invited to a workshop to review our proposal and allow both sides to ask clarifying questions. About 30 minutes into this meeting, we discovered the company had over 120 global ERPs and other systems that would require integration. None of this was included in the RFP, so we did not provide the proper timelines or costs to support this requirement. The company decided to extend the RFP deadlines to allow all the suppliers to resubmit responses. The project's start date was delayed because the RFP responses were delayed. This led to company resources moving to another internal project, causing more delays. Our team communicated we did not want to guarantee the revised estimates if the project start date was delayed more than three months; in other words, our estimates would expire after three months. This allowed us (the supplier) flexibility to adjust the timeline and cost based on holidays and resource availability. To conclude, the project start date was delayed 12 months beyond the original RFP estimate. This could have been mitigated with a better RFP.*

RFP questions provide a solid foundation, but the real value is how suppliers respond to real-world use cases. Use cases can be specific business challenges/situations or represent existing processes that will be optimized using a procurement application. Seeing how an application responds will give the organization more valuable information than a list of 200 or more questions. An RFP question cannot address how the application is configured to support future changes, the effort to integrate new systems, or the ability to provide self-service access to multiple stakeholder groups.

For example, instead of asking 60 questions about the features of an eInvoicing solution, ask the provider to demonstrate how the eInvoicing application would work with different ERP systems or support invoicing solutions in other countries. Additional examples could include calculating the withholding tax or determining how the invoice application can reduce the workload of accounts payable resources. If the RFP focuses on a service rather than a product, it is valuable to ask suppliers to outline how they plan to solve a problem and explain their approach. It is necessary to understand how flexible the supplier plans to be when it comes to accommodating changes and whether they will be able to outline improvement opportunities throughout. A dialogue will always provide more comprehensive results than a list of questions on an RFP.

FORGETTING ABOUT YOUR STAKEHOLDERS

When we think about the procurement organization, the procurement team connects the external stakeholder (supplier) with the needs of the internal stakeholder (business user). The procurement organization is like an internal consulting group supporting its internal customers. The procurement team acts on behalf of their stakeholders during an RFP process to ensure the right supplier is selected to meet the stakeholder's goal. The results can be detrimental if the internal or external stakeholder is ignored during this process.

> If there is no method for internal stakeholder feedback, how does the procurement team know what their stakeholders need?

> ***Real-world scenario:*** *I was asked to provide input into an RFP process for application selection and implementation. Since the application would be used mainly by users outside of the procurement team, we discussed the importance of understanding their needs. I scheduled two to three hours to talk with stakeholders who used the process the most, especially those who have been more vocal about their pain points in the recent past. I also spoke with representative stakeholders who had the most complex processes.*
>
> *After 30 minutes of talking with the procurement team, someone mentioned that the RFP had already been distributed, and they had yet to speak with any business stakeholders before writing or sending the RFP. They commented that they had never spoken with their stakeholders in the past and did not understand why they needed to. They developed an RFP based on the requirements the end users would think were most important. The procurement team was making decisions about an application they were not expected to use. I politely asked several follow-up questions, hoping their responses would help them understand the importance of talking with their internal customer.*

This procurement team often stumbled throughout the process, pointing fingers between the technology provider, the RFP process, the internal stakeholder, and the individuals who drafted the RFP. The timeline and cost increased, leadership was unhappy, and budgets were impacted the following year. Other projects were delayed as procurement was still focused on this RFP evaluation. There was no clear methodology for evaluating supplier responses. Six months after distributing the RFP, they still had not selected a supplier and now felt pressured to "just choose one."

The impact of this supplier selection process was multifaceted and had long-term negative results. The pressure to just select a supplier doesn't provide much confidence that they chose the right one that best fits the company's goals. The internal stakeholders did not see value in working with a procurement organization that did not want to talk with them. This pushes the internal user further away from procurement and into doing things independently. The supplier does not have much faith that the procurement organization can commit to what they signed up for in the RFP if selected. This will lead to change orders requesting more funds to support delays. Suppliers have been known to decline an award because they believe the company does not know what they want, or the supplier thinks it will be more painful to work with this company and decide it is not worth it.

The best approach for the procurement team members would have been to pause the RFP process midway to reevaluate. Pausing for two weeks would have allowed the procurement team to change directions enough to resolve the immediate issues and avoid unnecessary delays and long-term negative impacts. This is another example of setting up for failure. The procurement team either did not have the skill sets to evaluate these suppliers properly, or their managers did not have the skill sets to provide the right coaching.

NEGOTIATING DURING THE RFP EVALUATION

Frequently, procurement will ask the supplier to review and redline company terms and conditions (T&Cs) as part of the RFP process. Depending on how many suppliers you have invited to the RFP, this could elongate the RFP timeline. Suppliers require their legal teams to review company T&Cs and provide initial feedback about any disagreement. When I asked why this process is necessary or what the purpose of this is during the RFP phase, the responses fell into one of these three buckets:

1. I am not sure why this process exists.
    a. This is what I was told to do when I was hired or when I started working in the procurement organization.
    b. This is how we have always done this.
2. It speeds up the total RFP cycle time.
    a. If all the suppliers redline the T&Cs now, we will already have a copy of their redlines when we award business to a supplier and can more quickly get through the contract negotiation process.

   b. We noticed that the time frame for asking for T&Cs after selecting the supplier is much longer than during the RFP phase when a specific deadline is included.

3. The number of redlines can hurt a supplier in an award evaluation.

   a. We consider the supplier's redlining as another variable in evaluating it. In other words, we do not want to work with a supplier with many redlines on the T&Cs.

For clarification, the term *redline* refers to a process whereby a supplier manually marks up a paper contract in red pen to highlight areas where the supplier is not in agreement with the company.

In the first bucket of responses above, a new procurement team member was brought into the procurement organization and taught something they did not fully understand. However, they continued the process anyway. If they did question the process, the response was usually, "This is how I was taught when I was hired." It is perplexing why the conversation stops there. How long ago was *that* person hired, and how long has the procurement team been doing the same activity the same way?

With regard to the second bucket of responses above, the request is for the suppliers' legal team to review the T&Cs during the RFP timeline. The thought being if the supplier can respond with preliminary redlines, this will reduce the time it takes to draft and execute a contract. Personally, this has never produced any valuable results. The legal team never has time to review the content sufficiently during the two or three RFP timelines. The legal team will not want to dedicate resources to redlining a master services agreement if they are not short-listed as a potential supplier.

Instead, the legal team will redline a few items that immediately appear as potential conflicts but not spend more than a couple of hours doing so. They will always include a disclaimer in the RFP response that the T&Cs will be reviewed in more detail upon award selection. This means additional redlines may result. The request for a legal review and redline as part of the RFP does not significantly impact the overall RFP and contract cycle time. The terms and conditions would still require further review from the supplier's legal team upon award.

The third response (including redlines in the supplier evaluation) has always surprised me. I first encountered this in 2015 with a procurement team in the financial service sector. More perplexing is that this still occurs today, and this process is not specific to one industry or another. A few times when I came across this process, there was a deeper discussion about the value of requesting this during the RFP. The reply I heard the most was, "If the supplier has many redlines, it tells us they will be more time-consuming during the contract phase," or "It tells us whether the supplier is going to be difficult to work with."

What is most surprising is when there is a line item in the supplier scorecard where points are deducted for how much redlining is done by the supplier. The input from the supplier's legal team is about mitigating risk in a contract; they are not responsible for the implementation, success, or failure of the product or service. Asking all the suppliers to review T&Cs wastes their time; it adds more time to the RFP evaluation process and does not provide real value to understanding if the supplier can meet the RFP's needs. To include redlining as part of the supplier scorecard creates a skewed result that may incorrectly point to a supplier who is not the right fit for the RFP requirements but has very little redlining.

THREE BIDS AND A BUY—IS THIS STILL RELEVANT?

The *three-bids-and-a-buy* policy makes it mandatory to invite three suppliers to respond to an RFP. This policy was developed in the early 1900s to ensure more than one supplier was receiving the RFP and to improve competition. This policy was created to remove the perception of favoritism toward one supplier over another. When only one supplier is invited to bid, that supplier will automatically receive the award. There was a concern that procurement resources would invite only one supplier they had a relationship with outside the company or perhaps were receiving monetary incentives for inviting one supplier over another.

Fast forward to the present day, this policy has remained the same in the procurement and supply management organization. While the original concept was valid in the early 1900s, the interpretation of the policy has been translated to define a minimum standard. In some companies, this has also evolved to measure the performance of procurement professionals: "For all the RFPs completed this year, did you invite at least three suppliers to each?"

When inviting three suppliers, one of those will be the incumbent (or the current supplier who has the contract); this leaves two new suppliers invited to bid. Most of the time, those two additional suppliers already do business with the company. Evaluating three suppliers already working with the company is easier than inviting suppliers who still need to complete supplier onboarding and risk assessments. The challenge with this approach is that there is no opportunity for diverse responses. There is no opportunity to evaluate suppliers the company is already doing business with against new ones. By inviting new suppliers to the RFP, the company can:

- **Have visibility into current industry pricing:** If the industry lowers pricing due to increased competition, the company may never know and may pay more for products and services than it needs to.
- **Compare available products and services:** It is beneficial to compare new suppliers with what the company is already receiving. Depending on how long the company has been working with its suppliers, it is probable that new suppliers may offer new or expanded services for the exact price the company is paying today. Also, if the company does not want to change suppliers, this information can be used to renegotiate with current suppliers.

Unfortunately, most procurement professionals only invite up to three suppliers. There is no incentive to do more than the minimum requirement. Even if senior management directs procurement to support diversity efforts across the business, the procurement professional is still measured by the minimum three-bid policy.

THE FUTURE OF THE RFP

The traditional RFP method typically does not meet the company's underlying needs or provide real value. Keep in mind that this is another process created more than 100 years ago. What the RFP was intended for and how it was used then are different in our current world. Yes, a process is still required to evaluate suppliers, but is the current RFP method the right way to pursue this?

The traditional approach for an RFP is to tell the supplier what the company needs, outline a list of requirements, and receive input from multiple suppliers about how they can provide that need. The list of requirements is the procurement organization's interpretation of what they believe the stakeholder (or the company) wants.

It is human nature to want to communicate a solution. It is also easier to jump to a conclusion than to dig deeper to understand the underlying challenge or the real problem that needs to be solved. Even worse is when the business unit submits a request to the procurement organization asking them to create an RFP to evaluate suppliers against what the business unit thinks it needs. The RFP has become a list of requirements, asking a supplier to develop a solution against those requirements and hoping those requirements will solve the problem.

Perhaps a better option is for the internal stakeholder to complete a brief questionnaire for the procurement team that may include questions such as:

1. What is the need, issue, or concern?
2. Why is this not working as expected?
3. What is the current process for solving this need, issue, or concern, if applicable?
4. How would you like to see this change?
5. What do you need to perform your job effectively?
6. Is there an immediate need for this request?

An ideal future state would have the procurement team review the answers to these questions and determine how to solve the problem. This could be training, a system configuration, or a process change requiring no purchases. There could be an existing project addressing these needs that has not reached this stakeholder. It could also lead to an RFP to evaluate suppliers. If an RFP is required, the suppliers must understand the problem, and it is their responsibility to outline a solution. This changes the nature of the procurement organization, requiring it to become a problem solver instead of acting as a pass-through between the company and the supplier. The procurement organization becomes a strategic ally to the business, adding value across business units and departments.

CHAPTER 7

CONTRACTS

A contract is a legally binding document between two parties that confirms their alignment on various items such as scope of work, pricing, payments, schedule, and service level agreements. The purpose is to ensure value to the organization through formal documentation that solidifies a verbal agreement between the supplier and the organization. The procurement team, a key player in this process, invests significant time in negotiating the business terms of a contract, including scope, deliverables, caps and collars, rebates, key performance indicators, volume and tiered discounts, and much more. Thoughtful consideration is given to an escalation process for conflict resolution while establishing roles and responsibilities for each party. Ultimately, the contract provides documentation of the organization's initial expectations and how the supplier will meet those expectations.

Contract management is often overlooked before and during a transformation program, even though it is an integral part of the effort. *Contract transformation* is more than uploading completed contracts into a new technology for storage, it is about leveraging that technology to automate workflow, drive compliance, and improve efficiencies. It enables sharing the visibility of contracts with global users to leverage existing contracts instead of negotiating new contracts with the same supplier. It allows having the capabilities to search for specific clauses impacted by regulatory changes and having more control of the contract from negotiation to termination. The impact is the same whether the scope is domestic or across multiple geographic regions.

The most significant impact to the user is *during* the program when the contract process is affected the most; when a paper contract with a manual process now becomes an electronic contract with an electronic process. Additionally, new technology capabilities can also create changes in existing procurement policies. Some of those policies may no longer be relevant or will require updating to reflect decisions in automation, delegation of authority, and separation of duties.

Before we can talk about transforming the contract management process, we must first start at the beginning when procurement is negotiating the contract with the application provider who offered, for example, a five-year license agreement for its cloud procurement and supply chain application.

NEGOTIATING THE APPLICATION PROVIDER CONTRACT

Before signing (or executing) a contract with a service implementation partner or an application provider, it is crucial to consider a few key aspects. Next are some examples of what can be overlooked or directly cause delays during a project:

1. **Scope:** This outline covers technologies, processes, business units, geographic areas, and internal and external users. This is important because the scope may include Europe, the Middle East, and Africa (EMEA) and EMEA users, but the scope of processes and contracts may carry over into other areas where the suppliers are located. Also, consider documenting what is not in scope. At first glance, this may appear trivial because of the list of in-scope items, but this exercise has two benefits. The company usually discovers more items to include or exclude. If there is a question six months later, the contract sets the boundaries to avoid pursuing activities outside the agreement.
2. **Roles and responsibilities:** Edmond Sheehan created the *responsible, accountable, consulted, and informed* (RACI) matrix in the 1950s to facilitate more robust communication. This model worked well for many decades, but in modern organizations with cross-functional collaboration, there are many challenges

with the traditional RACI model because there is no clear role for a *decider*. In the traditional RACI model, decision making is delegated to the resources assigned to the *responsible* role, which are the resources performing the activities. These resources tend to be more junior and uncomfortable with making decisions that can significantly impact the outcome. The traditional RACI model facilitates a silo approach where the resource *responsible* for performing the activities is not the same person held *accountable*. Many believe the person performing the activity should also be held accountable for their work. A common workaround is to add multiple people into each RACI role, which was not the original intention of the model. Companies are now using a variety of alternative frameworks. It is recommended to determine which aligns with your organizational culture:

- RASCI: This is the RACI model with the addition of the *S* to include *supportive*
- DACI: driver, approver, consulted, and informed
- RAPID: recommend, agree, perform, input, and decide
- DARE: deciders, advisors, recommenders, and executors

3. **Risks:** This section outlines what happens during various scenarios, such as project delays, technology failures, technology upgrades during the project, cost overruns, etc. Your company and the supplier have internal investments linked to this project, and delays impact the timeline. This means more costs are incurred each week, as resources may not be working. This section is similar to contingency planning when things do not go as planned and risk mitigation strategies have failed.

   Additional costs may be incurred on long-term engagements as supplier resources are promoted, which carries a higher bill rate. These can be hidden fees that some suppliers will not pass through to a current program. However, not all suppliers are the same.
4. **Resources:** Resource allocation usually becomes an issue six months into a transformation program. Resources on the supplier side can leave in the middle of a project because they no

longer work with the supplier or they were swapped to another project that needed their expertise. It is common for the supplier to find anyone available to replace that resource who may not have the same level of knowledge or limited experience in customer-facing projects. This creates project delays due to onboarding, training, and the time it takes to understand the project's history. If that resource is not the right fit, the supplier may be asked to find another replacement. To mitigate this, include a 30-day notice before the resource rolls off the project and request to interview the replacement. Consider financial compensation when a 30-day notice cannot be followed. This could be monetary credit or extra weeks of post-implementation support at no additional costs.

5. **Data privacy:** Digital transformations deal with large volumes of data, and the contract should outline compliance with various data privacy laws and regulations. Take time to consider other countries where supplier resources are located. For example, in some countries, an individual can walk out of their office with stolen client data, and the laws may not be sufficient in that country to support data protection or legal recourse to retrieve that data. Consider where the company data is stored, who will access it, and where the supplier's resources are physically located. Additionally, discuss encryption, transferring large files, access to enterprise resource planning tables, and responses to potential data breaches where applicable. Finally, review the contract for how your data can be used by the supplier (or the application provider). Most likely there will be a clause about their use of your data stored in their cloud application, but it should include language about how that data is to be used and how that data will be sanitized. For example, customer data may be used to gauge which features are used the most to prioritize research and development on future features. What you do not want to see is the opportunity for your data to be sanitized and sold externally.
6. **Intellectual property (IP) rights:** Depending on the scope, complexity, and deployment schedule, a transformation program

can span multiple years. It is impossible to predict what will be developed in that time frame. For example, leveraging mathematical algorithms (or AI technologies) to automate repetitive tasks may not have been considered or in scope when the contract was signed. It is becoming more common for suppliers to identify these opportunities. It is essential to understand whether a developed algorithm is your intellectual property after you agree on added scope and costs. If there is no reference to IP in the contract, the supplier may argue they own the IP for that algorithm and will use it elsewhere as an added selling feature to generate revenue.

7. **Regulatory:** Program changes occur frequently during transformations. For example, suppose an EMEA country has been approved to move forward with electronic invoicing, which must now be included in the scope of an existing contract. In that case, the company and supplier must consider how they will approach this *before* the contract is signed, *not after*.
8. **Knowledge transfer:** This is rarely included in contract negotiations but should be considered just as important. Once the program is complete, the supplier will walk away with much of the company's knowledge. A knowledge transfer clause ensures that information and supplemental documentation are properly transferred back to company employees or never leave the company's province.
9. **Post support (hypercare):** Post-transformation support is critical for user adoption and suppliers must allocate resources to remain after go-live. Specific items related to scope, resources, and training must be documented in detail. The goal is to understand the number of resources supporting hypercare, whether part-time or full-time, where they are physically located, and whether they are functional or technical.
10. **Escalation:** Most contracts will only document the first line of the escalation process or the first person you will contact if things are not going as planned. It is common for this individual to be a project manager, a customer support advocate, or a customer success manager. Do not focus too much on the title

but more on what this person has the authority to do. Suppose you require a point person to navigate the supplier organization. That person may be entirely different if you want that someone also to be able to make decisions. Use this clause to document multiple escalation layers. The company may never have to escalate, but if there is a reason to escalate, the expectations are documented. This one addition can easily avoid a delay of two to three weeks.

PRIORITIZING CONTRACTS FOR TRANSFORMATION

In a transformation project, a separate workstream should focus on an *open-transaction strategy*. Open transactions are the open purchase orders (POs), contracts, or invoices that are live with stakeholders while a transformation is ongoing. For example, an invoice was received via email on March 15, but on April 1, a new application is now available. What happens to that invoice? How will the invoice be approved and paid if it is still under the old process on April 1. An open-transaction strategy will review all potential open transactions and documents at different stages within the order-to-pay cycle. The goal is to determine the best approach to handle various situations before and after the go-live date.

The strategy will help define what exactly will be in scope and guide alignment on the number of POs, contracts, and invoices impacted. Contracts may have a more complex approach because a contract can have multiple POs and invoices against it. For example, at the time of the April 1 go-live, a contract is three months into a 12-month term. How will financial allocations be calculated if there are three POs against that contract, but only one invoice has been paid and another invoice was received by email on March 20? Every scenario will have key factors that must be discussed, pros and cons to that organization that must be understood, and important decisions that must be made (hopefully, correctly).

Every organization has contracts but understanding which contracts will be impacted the most and which contracts will impact the users the most at go-live is sometimes not so easy. For example, if the project team decides that only active suppliers within the last 18 months should be prioritized, make sure the definition of active includes contracts and not just POs and invoices. Not all POs are associated with a contract. Also, contracts can have varied lengths and sometimes auto renew, meaning a contract can be active for 10+ years.

The open-transaction workflow strategy should follow a three-step process:

1. Determine scope
2. Prioritize
3. Align on key decisions

The first step is the most critical in setting up this workstream for success—determining which contracts should *not* be included in the scope of the transformation. Examples of contracts that do not require attention are:

- Statements of work (SOWs) that have already expired before the go-live date
- SOWs that will expire within three months after the planned go-live date
- SOWs for a one-year term and require a one-time payment (e.g., software license)
- Contracts stored in another application
- Self-service invoicing
    - This is commonly seen in insurance carriers where the company automatically creates a monthly invoice based on the negotiated rate per employee. Each month, the company calculates the invoice amount, generates a report (number of employees multiplied by the negotiated rate), and then creates a payment based on that calculation.

The second step is prioritizing which contracts will be reviewed first. After step one, hundreds of contracts may be in scope. It is recommended that a phased approach be developed, grouping contracts into manageable segments focusing on higher-priority contracts. Each company will have a different meaning of priority, the project team will determine its definition. The following variables can be used to assist in that prioritization activity.

- **Dollar threshold:** This is the total dollar amount over the entire contract.
- **Department/business unit:** Some business units may take priority over others; for example, HR (human resources) contracts may have priority over facilities contracts.
- **Commodity/category:** This taxonomy is used to classify contracts into buckets, such as professional services, media, or marketing.
- **Supplier capabilities:** Critical or strategic suppliers may be segmented, or some may be identified as a higher priority. Another category to consider would be if the supplier was sole-sourced, which refers to this supplier as the only supplier with the capabilities used by the company.
- **Number of invoices:** In reviewing the payment schedule, some contracts may receive invoices against the contract once per month, while others would be more frequent.
- **Accessibility:** Can the team locate and receive a physical or digital copy of the contract?
- **Geographic region:** North America, EMEA, Asia-Pacific, etc.
- **Country:** A subset of geographic regions—some countries may have priority over other countries in the same area. This is primarily due to the location of manufacturing plants and administrative sites.

Decisions can impact contract management processes and compliance in many instances. The most common example is implementing a digital contract management application that provides features and capabilities the procurement department can leverage. Key decisions can translate into procurement contract policies and may be required to be included in future contracts as standard terms. There are also examples where a decision in the contract workstream can significantly impact the requisition-to-invoice process.

The third step is aligning on key business decisions. The following list contains a few examples of issues that can be reviewed and potentially updated in future contracts during and after transformation:

- **Invoice exception—number of days for change:** How many days after the contract end date will the business be allowed to receive and complete the invoice exception? This scenario would occur after the contract has expired, but there is still one last invoice to be received. The number of days should be included in future agreements to inform the supplier not to delay sending the last invoice and allow time for processing and approval. For example, if the number of days is 7 and the contract expires on May 30, the supplier must submit their final invoice no more than seven calendar days after May 30.
- **Contracts with variable quantities but not pricing:** A great example is parking garage contracts. The parking garage will allocate spaces to the company at $200 per month for employees or $15 per day. Each month, the company will receive an invoice where the quantity (or the number of spaces used that month) varies while the negotiated amount does not change. For example, for October, the company received an invoice for 50 employees at $200 per month + 62 parking spaces at $15.00. The following month, the number of parking spaces may change, but the negotiated prices will remain unchanged.
- **Backdating invoices against a contract:** This is a feature in many electronic contracts. There are scenarios where an invoice against a contract is received considerably late due to technological issues. The invoice may be dated two weeks before the company receives it. The supplier may consider the date on the invoice to be the date entered into the system, and since payments are calculated based on the invoice date, there could be an assumption that the invoice date will be backdated in the system.
- **No-PO/no-pay policy:** Before digital contract management application tools were available, contracts were typically tied to no-PO/no-pay policies. This type of policy existed because of

the limited capabilities of enterprise resource planning (ERP) systems, which could only link so many invoices to a PO. There was no way to link POs or invoices to contracts, which could eliminate the no-PO/no-pay policy.

Cloud procurement applications can allow a direct contract-to-invoice process with a two-way match. A 3-way match can be simulated in the contract-to-invoice process by allowing users to sign off or approve when contract milestones are complete. Milestones are defined in the work statement and indicate how much work is to be completed by a specific milestone date. These milestones act as a receipt for the services, similar to a receipt on a PO. For example, suppose a contract milestone was due May 30, and the supplier sent their invoice on May 30. The contract owner can reject the milestone if the services for that milestone were not yet completed. If there is a delay, the milestone date can be changed to June 15. The invoice will be paused in the process. Once the milestone is achieved, the invoice is released for processing and approved.

COMPLIANCE IMPACT ON SAVINGS

Compliance with the contract means end users can purchase products or services outlined at the prices and discounts negotiated. Most of the time, procurement teams negotiate strong business terms with clear benefits to the organization but with little consideration for:

- Whether anything in the contract is enforceable
- Whether the procurement organization can monitor the contract post-signature
- Whether users have the capability to purchase products/services at the negotiated terms

For example, if the contract includes a table with volume and tiered discounts, it is an expectation that when the items purchased reach a certain level (as outlined in the contract), the cost of the item is reduced. To illustrate, I bought 100 widgets on March 15 at $1.00 each. Per the contract, this meets the requirements of the first tier, meaning the next time someone purchases widgets against this contract, the price for those widgets will be less than $1.00 each. If the procurement organization has no tracking method that reports this information, all widgets purchased will remain $1.00 each. This example is simplistic, but when considering a contract with a high volume of purchases in multiple tiers, each with an expected price reduction, the potential of savings lost can be in the millions (see Table 7.1).

Table 7.1 Percentage discount tier structure

Tier	Description	Discount
1	$0.00–$2M	0%
2	$2M–$4M	2%
3	$4M–$7M	3%
4	$7M–$10M	4%

Furthermore, it is not the supplier's responsibility to manage a contract's compliance on behalf of the organization. This means the supplier is not responsible for validating the pricing on purchases over time by end users at the prices negotiated in the contract. This responsibility falls onto the resources of the procurement department. A contract manager or a group within the procurement organization is commonly responsible for monitoring all executed contracts and ensuring that key compliance dates, conditions, and negotiated pricing are observed.

Consider what the consequences would be if there were no monitoring or if reports were unavailable to highlight discrepancies. In 2019, ContractSafe.com estimated that large companies maintained as many as 40,000 active contracts. For this exercise, let's assume a smaller number of 10,000 active contracts, which brings many more mid-sized companies into this calculation:

- Start with 10,000 contracts
- Assume 10 percent of the 10,000 contracts have an average contract worth $250,000
- Multiply the $250,000 contract value by these 1,000 contracts, and that gives you a total value for these contracts of $250 million dollars

- Assume a 5% loss on each contract for noncompliance (this is a conservative number in my experience), and that means $12.5 million in savings is potentially lost over the life of those contracts

This is a real and sizable figure, so monitoring, tracking, and enforcing your contracts is vital.

There are generally four main types of savings areas: planned, sourced, negotiated, and actual (or realized) (see Table 7.2). Most organizations today track the first two—planned and sourced. Most will also include documentation tracking the savings after the contract is negotiated. The following three stages are completed before the contract is executed:

- **Planned:** This is the expected amount of savings available before a sourcing event. This dollar amount or percentage is often based on the procurement manager's experience with researching changes in the market, supply base, and other global economic factors. At this stage, the confidence in achieving the estimated savings is around 50–70%.
- **Sourced:** After the sourcing event, the planned savings are adjusted to reflect the feedback and information gained during the sourcing process. At the end of this stage, the confidence in achieving the estimated savings is updated to 70–80%.
- **Negotiated:** During this stage, the conversation between the supplier and the organization often leads to minor changes impacting the total cost of the contract. At the end of this stage, the confidence in achieving the estimated savings is updated once more as 80–90%.

Table 7.2 Types of savings

Savings Type	Description
Planned	Expected savings before starting the sourcing process
Sourced	Revised savings estimated upon supplier selection because of the RFP response
Negotiated	Revised savings estimated upon execution of contract
Actual (or realized)	Revised savings estimated from a comparison between negotiated savings with actual purchase of product or service

The concern with the aforementioned definitions is the rise in confidence levels in achieving the estimated savings. As the procurement organization moves through the stages, the confidence level rises. These confidence levels have little value in the real world if no method validates those proposed confidence percentages. Most organizations never look beyond the negotiated stage. They fail to track the actual (or realized) savings. The two primary reasons for this are:

- The belief that the organization is saving money by not dedicating a full-time resource to monitor post-contract compliance
- The belief that once a contract is negotiated, the savings are guaranteed

The realized savings validate what was promised in the contract compared to what the organization bought the product or services for. It is only at this stage that the confidence level is 100%.

REAL-WORLD SCENARIO 1: COMPLIANCE IS THE COMPANY'S RESPONSIBILITY

> ***Real-world scenario:*** *A consulting firm was hired to analyze all contracts, invoices, and other supplemental information over the past three to five years to validate compliance. For example, one contract included a discount structure based on spending volumes. There was a table in the contract that outlined the tiered structure. When the organization met the requirements of tier 1, a discount of two percent was applied to all purchases. When the organization met the requirements of tier 2, a three percent discount was applied to all purchases, etc.*

The procurement team did a good job negotiating this discount structure. Yet, this company did not have a real-time method to track compliance. The procurement team's efforts did not make a difference to the bottom line because there was no way to track when purchases hit those individual tiers.

When the analysis was completed on this contract, it was estimated that $1.5 million in savings was never obtained but should have been.

The procurement team first contacted the supplier, sharing the analysis and requesting a credit of $1.5 million. The supplier declined to provide the credit and responded that the company paid the invoices and the checks were already deposited. After months of back and forth involving the legal departments of both sides, it was determined the supplier was not legally required to provide the credit.

REAL-WORLD SCENARIO 2: LACK OF CONTRACT TRACEABILITY

> ***Real-world scenario:*** *A contract was negotiated for paper directly with a paper manufacturer. The contract included caps around price increases during the life of the contract since the prices of many commodities can fluctuate annually. The contract stated that the company would only pay for a price increase if documentation showed three of the four major U.S. paper manufacturers were also raising their rates and correspondingly showed the percentage of those increases.*

The procurement team did an excellent job negotiating this contract. The contract stated that if rates were to increase, there would be a cap (or limit) on the percentage of the increase during a 12-month period. Another cap was added to ensure prices did not continue to increase by more than a certain percentage every year. The challenge was that the company could not track this contract after the negotiation. The supplier sent a letter increasing their pricing. No one at the company knew the details of this specific contract or that there was an internal process they had to follow before accepting the price increase. No one had visibility. The same contract was renewed for another two years, and this process continued until someone finally started asking questions.

Some might question why the contract was not revisited or reviewed before renewal. Perhaps the contract owner would have known the details, but resources change constantly in these settings. Often, a new resource will take over existing contracts and, more often than not, will not take the time to read through all the contract details. Would the use of a digital contract management tool solve this problem? This depends on how many of the capabilities are implemented. Unfortunately, most companies that purchase digital contract management tools never exceed the contract repository capabilities of uploading and storing the executed PDF. If the full capabilities of contract authoring or clause libraries are not fully implemented, it falls back on the contract owner to read through every contract they inherited and document notes about the action required. Contract authoring is the ability to create contracts electronically by adding and removing contract clauses. This capability will auto-populate information from the sourcing application, such as the supplier information and the line items awarded in the RFP (request for proposal). Clause libraries are a list of clauses approved by legal. This allows more control by the contract owner to create contracts and swap out clauses with alternative pre-approved language without going to legal for every change. When contract owners inherit contracts, they can quickly run a report for specific clauses like reasons for termination, penalties, and renewal options.

REAL-WORLD SCENARIO 3: CONTRACT INCONSISTENCY

> ***Real-world scenario:*** *During an assessment of contract processes within an organization, it was discovered that contracts were negotiated very differently among the five negotiators in the professional services category. The team members were brought together in one room where they discussed the different terms in their contracts. As each team member discussed their perspective on essential business terms to negotiate, other team members were surprised: "That is a great idea. I will include that next time."*

Even with cloud procurement applications and numerous available contract templates, this scenario occurs more often than you may think. Most commonly, this results from multiple reductions in headcount at the request to save money. In the past, larger organizations had two groups: those focused on strategic sourcing and those focused on contracts. Each group had the opportunity to maintain specific skills within their group in order to be more effective. For example, those in the contracts group would receive training in writing effective contracts, negotiation skills, and contractual risks. In contrast, those in the strategic sourcing group would learn how to evaluate supplier, category, and market risks to develop a plan that would best meet the organization's needs.

When resources were reduced, the two groups merged. One resource was now being asked to outline a strategy, run an event, negotiate the contract, and, in some organizations, also manage the supplier's performance. One person will never be truly effective in splitting their time amongst these tasks across the entire supplier life cycle. This can lead to resources who may feel confident in their ability but are not educated in knowing all the potential things to look out for, to ask about, or to negotiate. Also, be mindful of the sales folks on the other side of the procurement negotiations table. They are receiving annual, recurring training and other educational opportunities to improve the skills dedicated to their roles. It is no wonder the negotiations may often feel one-sided. When there is a lack of consistency in the negotiated business terms of contracts across the organization, the impacts can be extensive:

- There is an increase in the lack of visibility in contract risks when a supplier has multiple contracts across different procurement categories that are managed by other teams
- There is an increase in the financial risk where similar contracts are negotiated with inconsistent standards
- There is a decrease in efficiency as resources are not consistent in their contract negotiations
- There is an increase in potential mistakes leading to fees and penalties

REAL-WORLD SCENARIO 4: PRESIDENTIAL EXECUTIVE ORDER

Real-world scenario: *In 2019, during the Trump administration, the minimum salary that companies had to pay H-1B visa holders* *increased. An H-1B visa allows U.S. companies to sponsor non-immigrant visas to temporarily employ foreign workers with at least a bachelor's degree in specialty areas such as engineering, computer programming, science, health care, and education. This policy change had a negative financial impact on the organizations working with existing H-1B contractors. For context, the Department of Labor uses four levels to calculate the prevailing wage for a particular position or occupation: Level I (entry-level), II (qualified), III (experienced), and IV (fully competent). Each wage level has been based on the wage percentiles of the Bureau of Labor Statistics database of occupational employment statistics for the occupation in which the proposed H-1B position lies. The changes are to the percentile calculation for each wage level, increasing the lowest salary amount a company must pay. This means a contractor with an H-1B visa is now more expensive. Table 7.3 illustrates the final percentage change of each wage level after the executive order. Another way to think about this is that if a Level 2 H-1B contractor made $70,000 per year, they would now be able to receive a 19% increase or $83,300 per year.*

Table 7.3 2019 H-1B Percentage salary increases

Qualification level	Salary change increase
Level 1 (entry-level)	17%
Level 2 (qualified)	19%
Level 3 (experienced)	22%
Level 4 (fully competent)	23%

Sources:

https://www.gray-robinson.com/insights/post/2761/immigration-e-lert-new-h-1b-rules-salary-increases-for-h-1b-workers-but-fewer-will-qualify

https://news.bloomberglaw.com/daily-labor-report/dols-sudden-mandatory-pay-increase-rocks-h-1b-worker-employers

https://www.shrm.org/topics-tools/news/talent-acquisition/dol-increases-h-1b-wage-minimums

Once the policy change was announced, many companies did not have the data insights to know the exact number of existing contracts this impacted. There were no details about the financial impacts or if their existing contractual language covered this kind of federal mandate. A small change in U.S. policy had a huge impact on existing contracts in the United States. Companies had difficulty identifying the impacts and went about the discovery phase in various ways. Let's look at two examples:

1. **Company A (no contract technology):** This company allocated three full-time resources to manually review existing contracts in order to identify which ones utilized H-1B visa contractors. Then, each contract was read more carefully to determine if the company had any liability. The results of this assessment identified that some contracts had additional clauses that protected the company until the contract expired, while other agreements did not have this clause. Without this protection, Company A was forced to increase salaries that year, plus any future years, until their contract expired. The total financial impact was just over three million dollars. The additional funds were pulled from the department budgets that owned the contracts and impacted those departmental budgets in 2019 and beyond, depending on the length of the contracts. With no contract technology, the assessment was completed in six months and thought only to uncover approximately 70% of the contracts. For Company A, the total additional financial impacts were still yet to be uncovered.
2. **Company B (using contract technology):** Company B allocated one full-time resource to run queries and review existing contracts online. Their contract repository provided a high confidence level that all existing contracts were covered and offered the capability of reviewing contracts electronically by searching keywords. It did not, however, provide the details needed to search for contractor types or, more specifically, if the contract included H-1B visa holders. The company then allocated three full-time, more experienced resources to perform a manual review of existing contracts, just like Company A. The total time

required to complete the assessment was less than 60 days. Still, the total financial impact was just under seven million dollars, with similar impacts to departmental budgets.

Even though Company B used contract technology, that only served to run the assessment more quickly and feel more confident all the contracts were reviewed. Also, despite this technology, most of the procurement resources in Company B did not include clauses to keep prices firm during the contract period. Only a few more experienced resources who had been through something similar in their past included additional language. Ultimately, this example shows that implementing contract management technology does not replace better contract negotiation processes and resource training.

CHAPTER 8

TECHNOLOGY

OVERVIEW OF PROCUREMENT TECHNOLOGY

The procurement architecture journey (see Figure 8.1) truly began in 2007 as cloud technology became more accessible. Before 2007, procurement and supply chain applications were either on-premise or applications were installed behind an organization's firewall. The advancement and accessibility of cloud technologies opened the door for application providers to push updates to the customer instead of the customer pulling updates from the provider. This opportunity to receive updates directly from the application provider allowed information technology (IT) and procurement teams to review which updates had the most value and enable (or turn on) those features. Other benefits included the immediate receipt of software fixes, improved security, and opportunities to receive new functionality more than once a year, as cloud technologies eliminated many process blockers.

The most significant change to developer resources was the realization that customizations and configurations require *different* resources. For example, customization requires IT resources and has longer cycle times. This is in comparison to application configurations that a procurement professional could own. The time between when a requirement was approved and the point in time when the configurations were available in production should only be a matter of a few weeks compared to customization, which could take three to five months. More than any other cloud-related topic, this culture shift from an IT resource to a procurement resource for application changes led to many internal

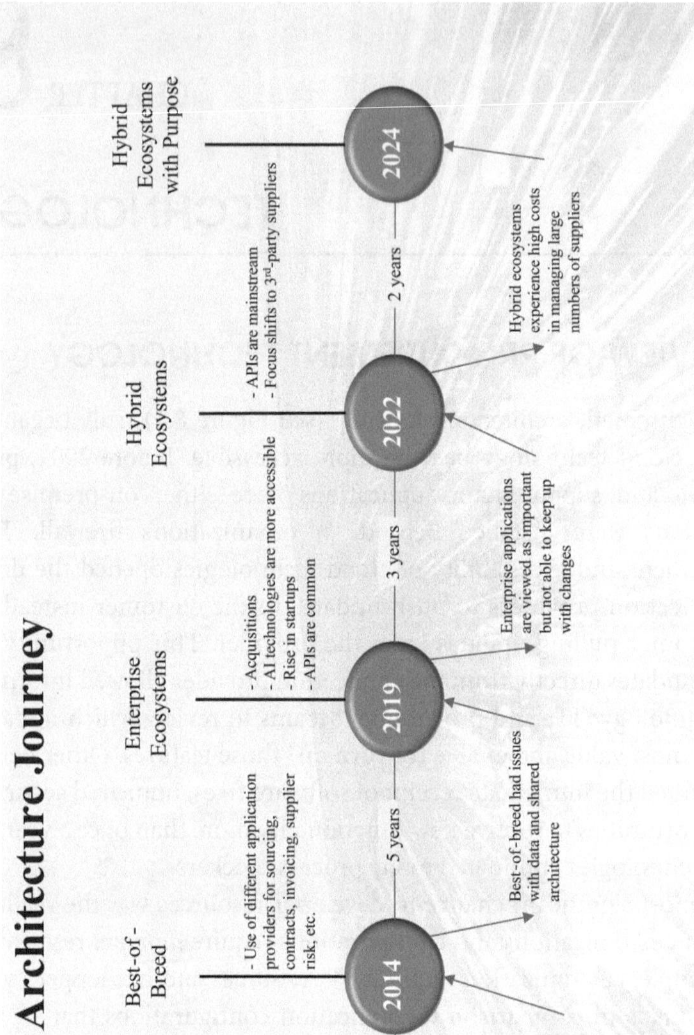

Figure 8.1 Procurement architecture journey

political conversations around funding, application ownership, and where the configuration resources would sit. Eventually, around 2009, the shift to a cloud-based procurement application was more accepted, and customers began to see the advantages of strictly cloud-based over on-premise.

Shifting to the cloud also allowed the customer to consider buying multiple applications simultaneously instead of one at a time. This created the start of what is known as the end-to-end (enterprise) suite of applications focused on indirect spending across sourcing, contracts, projects, purchases, invoices, and basic supplier capabilities. The value was stringing the processes across multiple modules to enable improvement in the automation of data between each process; that is, the data in the purchasing module was closely connected to and shared data with the invoicing module.

However, it took only a short time before customers realized the high-level connectivity of an integrated suite of applications was not meeting their expectations. Around 2014, a shift began in the market where some organizations advocated changing their IT strategy and selecting better process modules than those in the integrated suite. For example, the sourcing modules from application provider A were perceived as better than the same application module from application provider B.

Before companies understood the impact of their decisions, a public debate between *integrated suites* and *best-of-breed* became the main topic at conferences during that time. Some companies went so far as to purchase applications from different suppliers, creating a patchwork effect like a quilt. Just as quickly as the debate started, organizations soon experienced integration and data-sharing challenges. While the best-of-breed approach did provide more features and capabilities within a specific module (i.e., sourcing), this approach could not connect to the other applications purchased from other suppliers. Companies were not too keen to return to an integrated suite primarily due to the cost, which was still relatively high and time-consuming to implement.

To capitalize on this emerging trend, application providers began advertising the upstream and downstream processes as alternative approaches. The term *upstream* represented sourcing, contracts, and supplier performance, and the term *downstream* represented the requisition to receipt and invoicing for transactional processes. The upstream modules could be self-contained, while the downstream modules had to integrate with enterprise resource planning (ERP) software. This alternative approach opened the market for other competitors who had not previously been able to compete with a fully integrated suite of applications.

It also provided a good compromise between best-of-breed versus integrated suites. Companies could now choose to implement one provider for the upstream processes and a second provider for the downstream processes. The procurement organization was managing two suppliers instead of six. If integration was required to share a limited amount of information between the upstream and downstream applications, the use of an application programming interface (API) could make this request achievable.

Ah, but the customer is forever fickle. How the suppliers structured their databases and tables made it significantly challenging to share master data such as cost centers, locations, and suppliers between upstream and downstream applications and the ERP systems. Additionally, IT resources had to develop and maintain multiple custom integrations, which became costly and time-consuming. The end user slowly realized their user experience, data sharing, and automation were application limitations that could not be resolved.

Around 2019, the market slowly drifted back to the enterprise (or fully integrated) suite of applications. Technology had leveled out, and application modules had existed long enough to be perceived as stable. Third-party consultants could no longer charge a premium for implementation services. Application providers now had more competition in the market and could no longer overcharge for software licenses. That combination made it easier for Fortune 100 companies to pay the switching costs to move from one application provider to another.

It also supported a more favorable price point for Fortune 250 companies to enter the integrated suite of procurement applications by purchasing a procurement application for the first time. These smaller companies, referred to as the mid-market, typically have annual revenues of around one billion dollars. Before 2018, the mid-market had a small handful of applications to select from. Those application providers were merging, acquiring, and divesting every few years; the volatility made it simpler and safer for mid-market companies to retain email, XLS, and MS Word purchase orders (POs).

In parallel, application companies quickly purchased smaller software companies to add capabilities to their portfolio to avoid the lengthy development cycle of a brand-new product; Coupa expanded into inventory and direct materials, while Ariba expanded into risk management. The larger integrated suites updated their backend table structure to allow for better data sharing across existing modules and to absorb new acquisitions quickly. Improvements in integration technology allowed cloud-to-ERP integration to bypass the need for middleware or staging tables required initially for data to travel from point A to point B. This capability to plug and play into an ERP system reduced the implementation timeline by reducing the number of developers required.

Around the same time, companies like Ariba prioritized the *partner-model concept*. While some application providers had started to shift in this direction, it was now perceived as critical to remain competitive. The partner-model concept is when one primary provider partners with one or more secondary companies that can dedicate their resources to sales and support. The primary provider gains an expanded salesforce and implementation resources. These implementation partners focus on selling software and services for the primary provider. They also help the end customer with certifications, training, and communicating application updates. The primary provider concentrates their resources on development, testing, and some customer support. For companies like Ariba, which had already been in operation for a few decades, this was a change in their business model. Companies like Coupa, who were new to the industry, started their business model with the partner-model concept.

As you have observed, every shift in the market has positive and negative results. Application providers were now laser-focused on acquisition strategies, developing a partner business model, and strengthening the user experience. The application partner could dedicate resources to building more capabilities based on customer feedback and pushing these to customers more frequently, eventually three to four times per year. Yet, many customers were more interested in automating the smaller repeatable tasks still buried within each module than all the new features and capabilities. While an integrated suite was great, and there were significant advantages to an integrated suite, lingering manual tail-end processes remained. This is where the user clicks the same buttons every time, regardless of the scenario, to execute a step in a process. When application providers leveraged the partner business model, they eventually announced that these partners would be responsible for this type of automation. Some partners were large consulting firms that could develop in-house RPA (robotic process automation) teams to assess automation opportunities. Other consulting firms developed RPA libraries to support major applications and folded this into their request for proposal (RFP) responses as accelerators and differentiators against their competitors.

Shifting to a partner business model increased the number of implementation partners customers could select. This benefited the customer by giving them more options and the potential to work with new, smaller implementation partners instead of larger consulting companies, such as Deloitte and Accenture, which had worked in this domain for many years. While this successfully brought down the price point, it unexpectedly created a significant price gap between the larger and smaller firms. At first glance, this was considered favorable; however, it generated RFP responses with such a vast price difference that procurement resources thought either the larger, more experienced consulting firms were overcharging or the smaller consulting firms were missing something in their response. These RFP responses meant already-thin procurement departments had to spend more time investigating these bids to select the one that could best benefit the business.

The lower price point and shorter implementation time frame ushered in the *lift-n-shift* approach, which became standard for a time. Companies were led to believe the lift-n-shift was a good starting point for automating basic processes and showing progress to end users. This approach reduced the implementation timeline to approximately nine months for a full source-to-pay suite. This was a good approach in most scenarios, but it was frustrating due to a disconnect in expectations from the business. Customers did not understand that a lift-n-shift would not include project management, change management, process improvements, or complex configurations to meet internal policies. The customers that understood and managed this expectation internally with the end user adequately planned for future funding cycles in more phases. Others were disappointed and vocal in expressing negativity about the implementation supplier.

While all this was happening, a niche market was beginning to open. It was the opportunity to develop capabilities the large enterprise-integrated suites had communicated they would no longer prioritize. Companies that were not implementation partners entered this domain. The best example is Fairmarkit. It leveraged an opportunity to develop an enhancement for customers using Ariba applications. In the Ariba Buying module or the requisition to receipt process, there is a capability to support requisition collaboration, sometimes called ad hoc purchasing. The concept provided the ability to quickly send a purchase request with line items, quantity, and shipping information to existing suppliers already approved to do business with the company. This process was based on requisitions with low dollar amounts, such as under $10,000. The requisition was sent to three to five suppliers with a quick turnaround time. Each supplier would enter the price per line item. The procurement team would most often select the lowest bid and immediately flip to a PO that was ready for approval.

This capability automated the three-bids-and-a-buy process, commonly supported in a manual, paper-based procurement process. However, customers wanted to expand this capability to include already approved suppliers and invite a few new suppliers outside the application. The point was to drive more competition against the suppliers already approved and have an opportunity to check out new suppliers with a small purchasing requirement.

The challenge was a combination of some application limitations, company policies, and perhaps an overly complicated onboarding process including, but certainly not limited to, supplier risk analysis, banking information, and often a separate team performing data entry to set up suppliers in the ERP(s). This is where Fairmarkit came in. It developed a solution with an API that connected directly to the Ariba Buying module. This enabled the end user to compare internal and external suppliers.

This example is one of many where nonapplication partners saw a huge opportunity. Suppliers would develop one-off solutions that could often be packaged and uploaded to the application's online library. Customers could pay, download, and click install. These features would seamlessly integrate with the application and support specific one-off customer requests. It was a perfect model where the enterprise-integrated application providers prioritized enhancement requests that covered 80 percent of their customer base while other suppliers supported the rest.

All of this would not be possible if artificial intelligence (AI) technologies had not become more accessible. Either the technology did not exist to support the development of a specific solution, or the technology did not allow the supplier to scale their solution to where it could be commercialized.

ACCESSIBILITY OF AI TECHNOLOGIES

AI technology is a broad term that encompasses many things. Figure 8.2 outlines the subsets or subfields under the umbrella of AI technologies. When applications use AI technologies, they could be one or more of the technologies listed in the figure. These technologies use AI models created with mathematical algorithms to analyze large amounts of data to address a specific question.

The concept of AI technologies has been around for a long time, and perhaps you were using some form of AI technology but did not know it. Labeled as expert systems or knowledge engineering, this process

Technology	Definition	Examples
Machine Learning	Increases accuracy of predicting outcomes. Machine learning algorithms use historical (retrospective) data as input to predict new output values.	- Patient diagnosis (Healthcare Industries) - Supplier portal (Linkana)
Deep Learning (Subset of Machine Learning)	Imitates how humans collect and synthesize data to create meaningful information. From digital images, videos, and other visual inputs, it supports actions or makes recommendations based on the information collected.	- Driverless Taxi (Zoox) - Facial Recognition (iPhone) - Speech (Alexa) - Language translations (Google) - Customer recommendations (Netflix) - Efficiency in logistics (Cainiao)
Natural Language Processing	Understands, interprets, and manipulates human language. Communicates information and meaning using semantic cues such as words, signs, or images.	- Spend analytics (Creactives) - Speech (Alexa) and language translations (Google) - Contracts (Seal) - Supplier portal (Linkana)
Neural Networks	Recognize relationships in a set of data that mimics the way the human brain operates (e.g., data patterns, clustering data, learning, and improving).	- Predictive sourcing (Arkestro) - Spend analytics (Creactives) - Driverless taxi (Zoox)
Robotic Processing Automation (RPA)	Performs tasks done traditionally by human beings. Robots are widely used in such industries as automobile manufacturing to perform simple, repetitive tasks.	- Auto force closing of an open PO after X months - Automating tail-end processes
Computer Vision	Gains meaningful information from digital images, videos, and other visual inputs and take actions or make recommendations based on that information.	- Detect defects on assembly line (manufacturing) - Detect apples are ready for harvest (Chooch) - Driverless taxi (Zoox) - Early detection of fires (multiple)

https://www.linkedin.com/in/melissa-drew/

Figure 8.2 Examples of AI technologies

leverages an individual's knowledge. Then, it automates it into a centralized application so that more than one person can leverage that expertise.

For example, around 2004, I was hired by a company called Softface in Walnut Creek, California, to leverage my expertise in cleaning and classifying procurement spend data. Before that, I worked with Kearney as their data management organization. One of the activities we supported was *strategic sourcing opportunity assessments*, a quick review of all spending data to document the sourcing opportunities that should be prioritized, the expected percentage of savings in the current market, and a phased approach for future categories.

To deliver those results, the company data had to be normalized, cleansed, enriched, and classified to the United Nations Standard Product and Services Code, a global taxonomy for categories of products and services. Sometimes, my job required manually sifting through millions of rows of data across credit cards, invoices, POs, etc. Over time, I developed a methodology to help me move through the data more quickly and consistently to establish those results. Even with my methods, an MS Access Database, and SQL scripts, completing an assessment would still take me nine weeks at 70 hours a week.

Softface was developing an automated version of what I was doing manually. My contribution was working with software developers and mathematicians to recreate how I made decisions when reviewing a single line of information with multiple variables such as a general ledger account, cost center, supplier name, and PO description. I walked them through every decision, why I made those decisions, and the step-by-step thought process before getting my final answer. The result was an inference engine.

Once that was complete, I shifted to developing AI models using patented grammar-based, natural language processing and machine learning technologies. My role expanded to how the AI models could be better leveraged across different industry sectors, leading to greater customer success and increased adoption. The product was made available to companies and other consulting firms. Within a short time, Ariba purchased this application, which has been the primary engine supporting their spend visibility solution ever since. AI development was used to automate a specific activity or process to provide higher confidence in the results and to support better decisions. It is the same concept still in use today.

The constant improvement of IBM's silicon chip enabled many suppliers to leverage the process. AI technologies sit on top of data. Creating and consuming more data yearly increases the amount needed to make business decisions. Just as humans have limitations in how much their brains can process, those limitations also exist in the silicon chips that process information in every computer, phone, and electronic device.

The silicon chip has always been something that could be improved upon. According to a 2021 article on IBM's website, "Since 2015, IBM has consistently improved the performance of AI chips, boosting power performance 2.5 times yearly. We've been creating algorithmic techniques that enable training and inference without losing prediction accuracy . . . and we've been creating a software stack that renders the hardware transparent to the application developer and compatible across hybrid cloud infrastructure, from cloud to edge."

IBM created a chip that could process more data more accurately and was more affordable for cloud architecture. This is why AI technologies were more accessible to all suppliers, not just the large ones like IBM, Accenture, and PwC. This contributed to the explosion of suppliers capable of creating products to address specific business challenges, which led to the same explosion in the number of new technology start-ups.

THE HYBRID APPROACH

The hybrid approach is another compromise between best-of-breed and integrated application suites. The concept is to blend the best of both worlds, keeping the capabilities of shared data favored with the integrated source-to-pay applications while also having applications for solutions to business challenges. Leveraging API-integrated suites can pull in additional data to complement what is already available in the integrated suite. For example, a risk module may need to provide comprehensive data on sustainability initiatives for direct (or manufacturing) suppliers.

Data intelligence is more than having the right data at the right time. It is about having data at a time that is the most impactful to the decisions made in the organization. We have always tried to achieve this but have yet to succeed. The hybrid approach enables companies to leap forward and have the data available at the correct time to improve the confidence level in decision making.

Connecting to third-party application providers allows access to supplemental data. Combined with existing customer data, the new data improves the data-driven or fact-based decision process for procurement professionals. This approach exploded the application market. It increased the number of start-up providers globally looking to solve specific business challenges and provide customers with a prolific menu of options. Many of these existing business challenges were simply waiting for a solution. However, this technology also springboarded a number of new business challenges. Companies were now hungry to automate wherever possible. This need was driven by changes in consumer demand, exiting the COVID pandemic, and performing at the same level with fewer employees. In November 2023, Market Research Industry News published an article predicting the procurement software market to be worth around 17.6 billion dollars by 2032, up from 7.8 billion dollars in 2022 and growing at a compound annual growth rate of 8.7 percent during the forecast period from 2022 to 2032 (see Figure 8.3).

LIMITATIONS OF THE HYBRID APPROACH

The hybrid approach shifted responsibility and effort to the company, which was now forced to take the lead—or act as the general contractor—to figure things out. Resources were required to search through an ocean of small, medium, and large enterprise providers that could compete at the same level. Companies no longer had the luxury of sending requests to a third-party consultant who figured it out or solved it on their behalf.

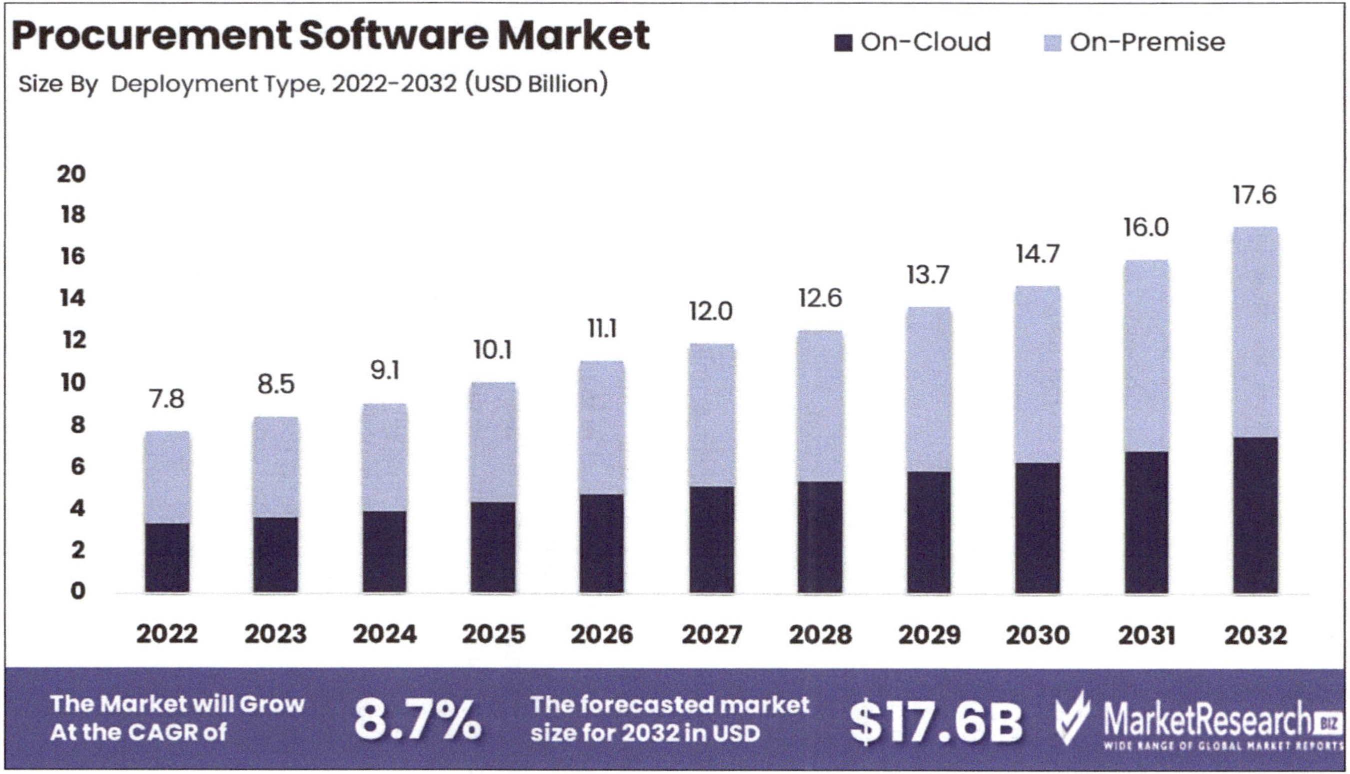

Figure 8.3 Forecasted growth of the procurement software market

This additional effort is time-consuming—at a time when procurement organizations are already stretched thin. The following questions have been more challenging to answer for those looking for procurement technology providers. They are all reasonable questions with no clear answers:

- How do I know when to stop looking?
- If I had problems finding diverse-owned suppliers before, how could I expect to find a small start-up in London that could solve my business challenge?
- What if I think I found the right supplier but then realize six months later that a better one is available?

The spider map, published by Dr. Eloise Epstein on LinkedIn, is a good visual representation of the evolution of procurement technology; each version is larger than the previous one. Figure 8.4 represents a version from 2017, while Figure 8.5 represents a version from 2020.

Where we once saw a handful of enterprise applications (or what used to be the middle of these spider maps), we now see hundreds of supplier applications often positioned in a niche market. In the upper left corner of Figure 8.5, you will notice a dotted box around the risk suppliers' domain. Compare that to the spider chart published in 2023 (see Figure 8.6), which reflects the latest developments in the modern procurement platform stack. The risk domain has grown so large that it could easily have its own map. The number of risk suppliers is rapidly increasing, and each supplier within that domain focuses on a different risk area, such as financial risk, compliance risk, and cyber risk.

Even within the same domain of expertise, suppliers specialize in different areas. The categorization of suppliers is narrowing and becoming more fragmented. For example, there are suppliers for commodity insights compared to commodity indexes. There are suppliers for curated

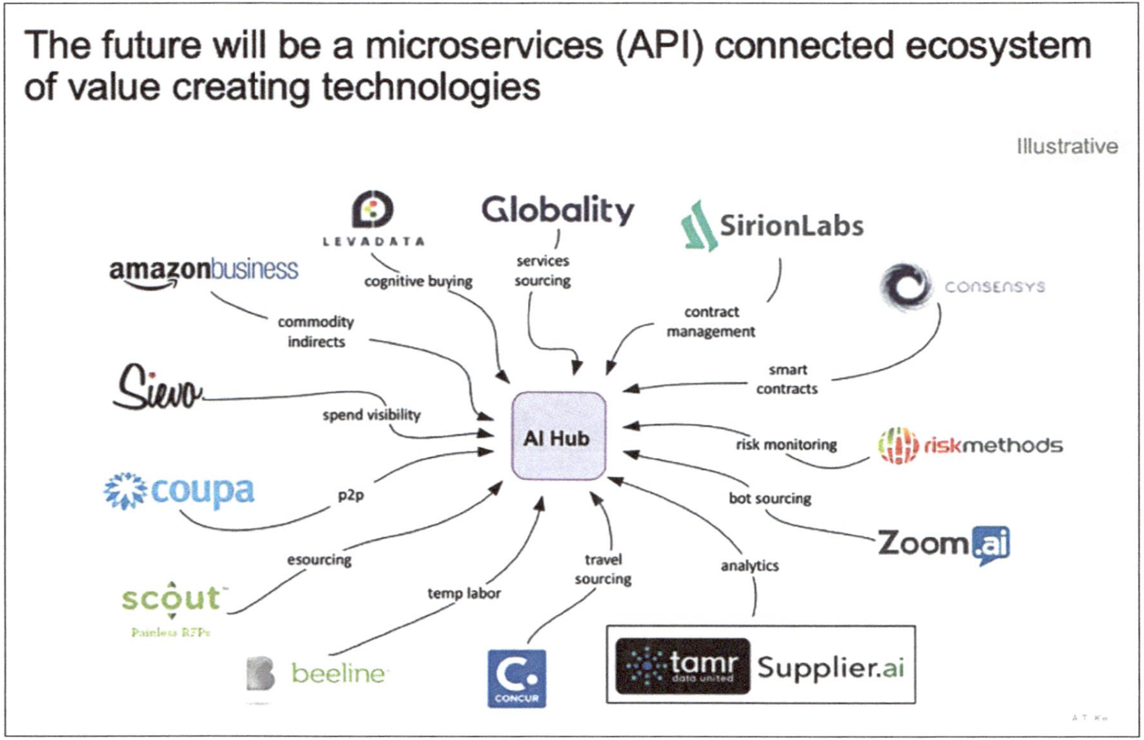

Figure 8.4 Emergence of API in the procurement technology landscape (2017)

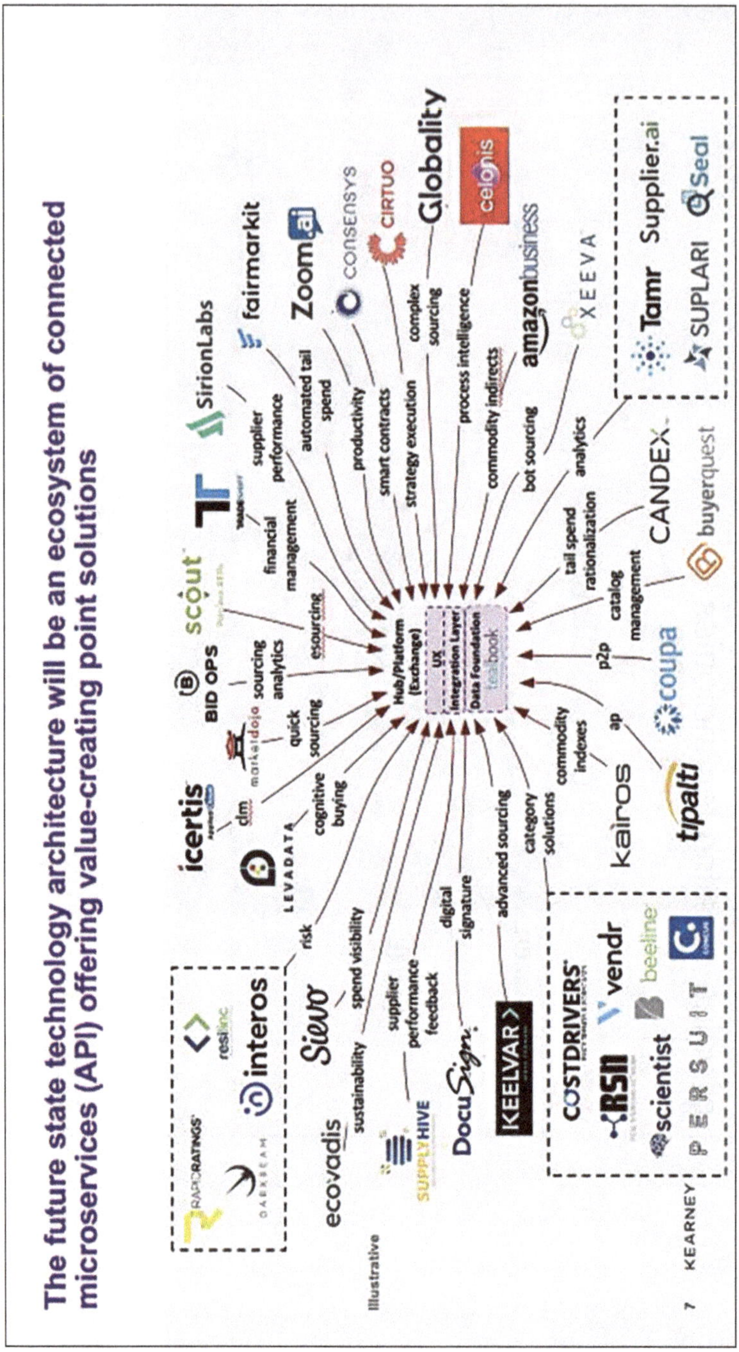

Figure 8.5 Expansion of API in the procurement technology landscape (2020)

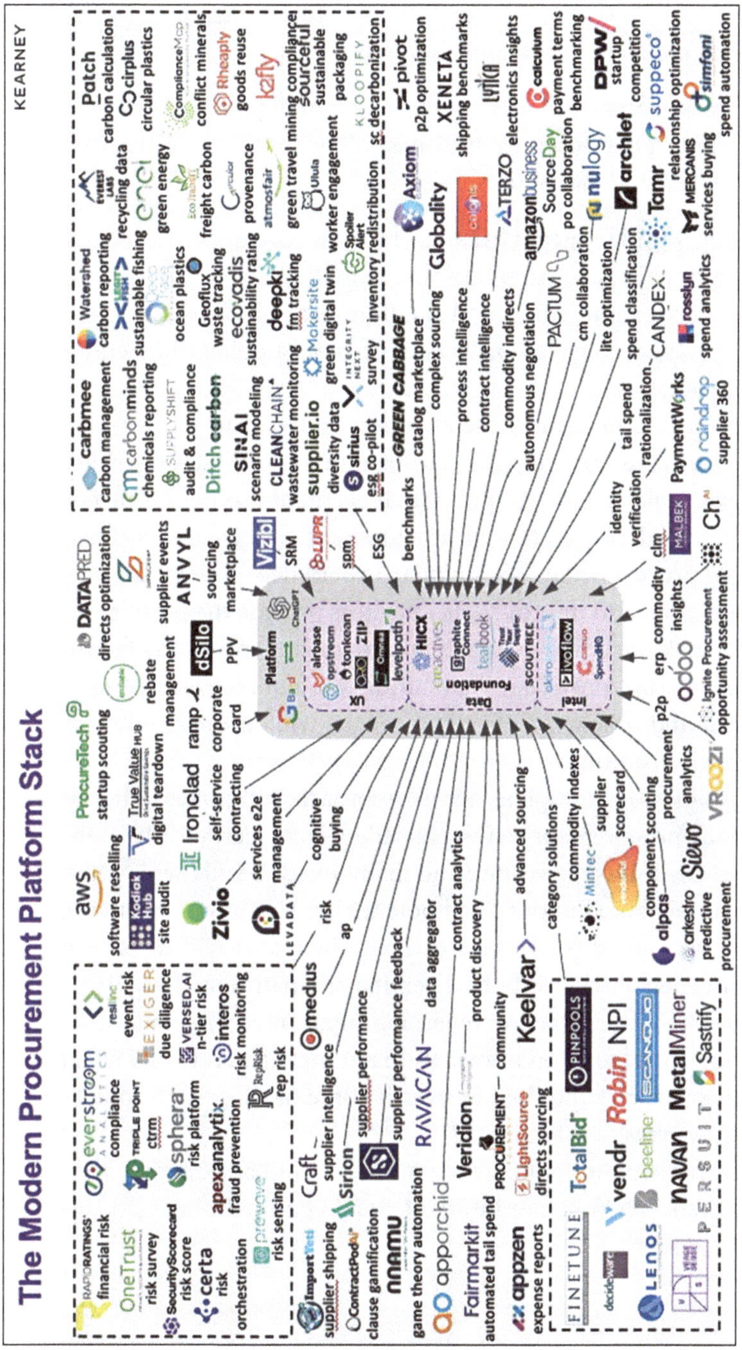

Figure 8.6 A rapid growth in the procurement technology landscape (2023)

data compared to data aggregators. All this tremendous growth and competition creates two significant issues:

1. Companies will work with more new suppliers than ever before
2. Enterprise applications suites will no longer solve every business challenge that pops up

In talking with IT category managers, they have documented a 40 percent increase in new suppliers between 2022 and 2023. As more and more start-ups and small and medium-sized businesses leverage AI technologies, a considerable influx of new suppliers has entered the marketplace.

Challenges similar to those experienced ten years earlier will be experienced in the coming years. The integrated suite has lingering limitations, particularly in the supplier management modules. The company needs updated corporate and procurement policies and a flexible onboarding process while continuing to experience resource shortages that are not expected to improve. These factors provide the perfect combination to block the ability to make minor adjustments in the face of more frequent disruptions. Like maintaining an automobile, in the absence of proper and timely maintenance, repairs will become more expensive and time-consuming.

Shifting into a complete hybrid approach will increase the number of various procurement requests needed each year and the number of contracts that must be written and maintained. It will increase the number of suppliers to onboard and potentially the number of suppliers required to monitor performance. These increases will directly require more time, resources, or both. Even if a company could highly leverage automation with AI technologies, a human must understand the context, evaluate it based on information not included in the AI results, and perhaps overwrite the final answer if some of those decisions fall into those gray areas (see Figure 8.7).

Effective supplier onboarding processes and associated policies will be required to handle the influx of small and medium-sized suppliers.

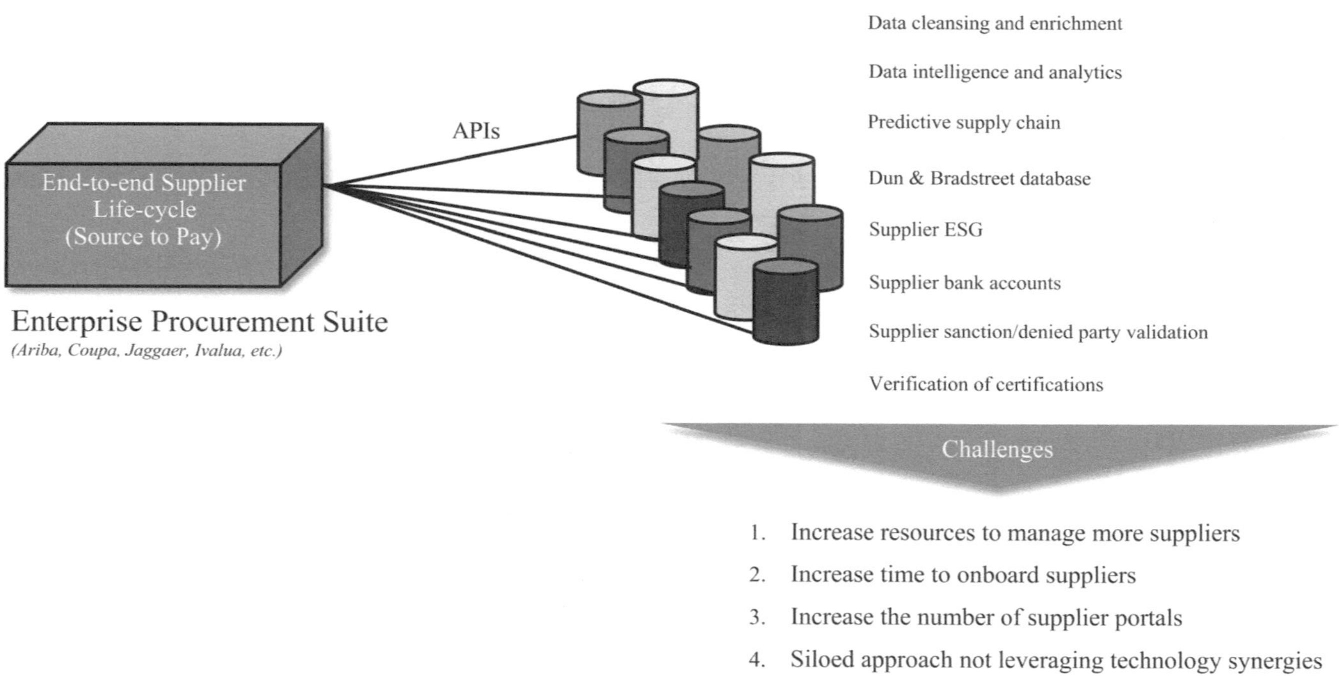

Figure 8.7 Initial challenges with the API technology landscape

The current supplier management process in most integrated suites was mainly designed to support large suppliers that are high risk and have a global footprint. Larger suppliers have more operational, regulatory, and reputational risks. The onboarding process is designed to evaluate a supplier from a legal, financial, and compliance perspective to mitigate company risk. This equates to more lengthy and time-consuming processes with a workflow interacting with 6–10 internal groups depending on the level of risk identified in various categories and the escalation process. Mid-market suppliers don't carry the same kind of risks as larger suppliers, but the current supplier management processes force companies to follow this comprehensive workflow to evaluate them. It does not provide the flexibility to engage with suppliers on a one-time need.

The hybrid landscape already feels packed and will likely get more crowded in the next few years. More suppliers solving more specific and unique business challenges will require more API connections between the integrated suite and third-party suppliers. Most suppliers will need to work closely with the integrated suites to develop new APIs. At the same time, some suppliers will have to rebuild API conduits between their databases and integrated solutions. This will increase the complexity of these systems and will make them more challenging to manage.

Consider this scenario: your company has a license with a third-party application for environmental, social, and governmental (ESG) supplier data. The license may provide 25 fields of information, but the integrated suite only has room for 20 fields on the supplier risk dashboard. The integrated suite does not bring over all the available data. This is something to be mindful of and manage. Are those five missing fields relevant to company decision making? Should another third party be brought in to add those five missing fields to the dashboard? What will this cost and is it worth it? It is easy to see how increasing the number of hybrid options opens up a Pandora's box of questions that need to be answered successfully to receive maximum value from these applications.

THE HYBRID APPROACH AND THE SUPPLIER PORTAL

The crowded hybrid landscape will only magnify one of the largest existing challenges in our current landscape: the supplier portal. This is a portal or opening into the companies' procurement suite of applications. When suppliers want to engage with a company, the supplier portal is the primary method to generate requests for proposals, POs, and invoices. It is where a supplier will update their company and payment information, what goods and services they provide, and what geographic locations they operate in, as well as upload documents such as certifications and tax information. The challenge is that not all companies use the same supplier portal application. Companies can choose to use the supplier portal embedded with the procurement suite of applications or purchase a third-party option. This means a supplier may have to engage with 30+ application systems to do business with all their customers.

From the company's perspective, the supplier portal was not designed to support all the information it needs to evaluate the supplier fully. Therefore, more software applications were developed to fill in the information gaps. This means the company must link to external databases and systems to, for example:

- Validate bank account information to reduce fraud
- Validate sanctioned suppliers who are listed as a high threat by the U.S. government
- Verify industry certifications
- Conduct risk management
- Acquire financial and credit scores (Dun & Bradstreet, Experian, etc.)
- Validate supplier diversity and ESG scorecards

Companies are also linking to more third-party (external) applications and databases to cleanse their internal supplier list and acquire purchasing information to understand whether a supplier is working with other business units. This creates visibility for the company in terms of how much the company is spending on the goods and services that match what a supplier is willing to offer. There are still more applications and databases not listed here to support complex strategic sourcing categories, contract management, supply chain management, etc.

This is not a sustainable solution. Instead of connecting to multiple suppliers and dozens of systems and databases, procurement needs a centralized portal that can funnel supplier-related capabilities into one single point of entry. This will automate and streamline supplier interactions, leading to fewer contracts and fewer suppliers to manage. It also frees up organizational resources to focus on more value-added activities, such as fostering strategic partnerships and supplier relationships.

This approach provides consistency in supplier interactions. That consistency has benefits such as improved transparency in the supply chain and reduced supplier risk. The organization is no longer the general contractor; this responsibility shifts to the centralized supplier portal with centralized resources. The approval workflow is simplified as supplier information is consolidated into one area. This reduces overall end-to-end supplier cycle time. Suppliers know what to expect and are sheltered from organizational changes. When changes occur, the impact is on the centralized supplier portal, not the individual connections to hundreds of hybrid suppliers, systems, and databases.

CHAPTER 9

ENVIRONMENTAL, SOCIAL, AND GOVERNANCE (ESG) CRITERIA IN THE PROCUREMENT ORGANIZATION

ESG is a framework designed to be embedded into an organization's strategy to evaluate and manage its (E) environmental impact, (S) social responsibilities, and (G) governance practices and policies. This requires procurement professionals to modify the traditional approach and processes in procurement. The goal is to confirm that supplier and organizational decisions positively impact the sustainability and social goals outlined at the executive level (see Figure 9.1).

- **Environment:** How does the company view impacts on the environment when making decisions? This may include evaluating suppliers who reduce carbon emissions and waste or use renewable resources. Examples may include suppliers with certifications from the Forest Stewardship Council or in International Organization for Standards (ISO) 14001 (environmental management).
- **Social:** How does the company view and manage internal and external stakeholders and their impact on the community in which it operates? This may include evaluating suppliers that prioritize fair labor practices, emphasizing a safe and ethical work environment, or promoting diversity. Other examples could be evaluating suppliers with programs supporting their local community or taking steps to eliminate child or forced labor in the supply chain.

- **Governance:** How does the company operate or govern itself through policies and influence in state and federal legislation? This includes evaluating suppliers who provide corporate transparency, integrity, and ethical behavior. Other examples could be transparent procurement processes and governance in supplier selection and performance monitoring. This may also ensure suppliers are in compliance with in-country and international regulations, especially anti-bribery and anti-corruption.

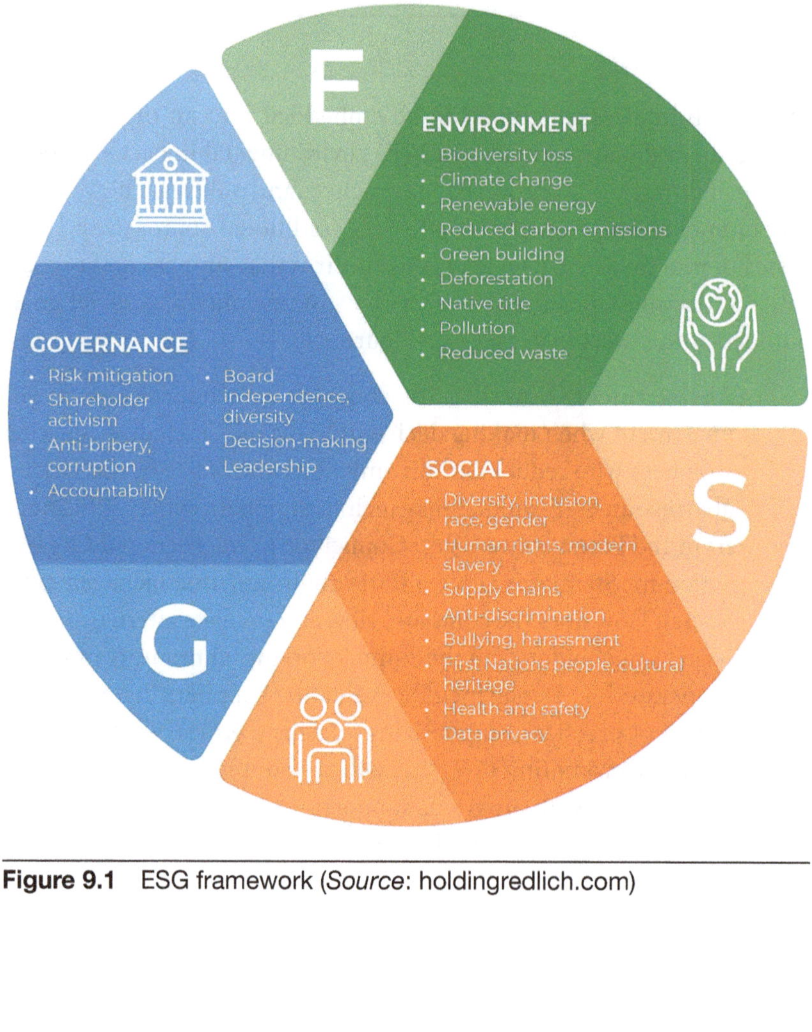

Figure 9.1 ESG framework (*Source*: holdingredlich.com)

In its current state, ESG has become a standard that socially aware consumers and investors use to evaluate how and if a company is performing against current social guidelines. As more companies show their commitment to sustainability, procurement's role is critical because it is the only organizational group that evaluates and manages suppliers closely before and after doing business with the company. An effective ESG procurement strategy can improve brand reputation.

EVOLUTION OF ESG

ESG began in the 1960s as an investment strategy where stocks would be excluded from some portfolios; for example, if a company did business with South Africa's apartheid regime, that company's stock would be removed from the portfolio. It was not until 2004 that the United Nations used the phrase ESG in their Who Cares Wins report. It was the first time ESG criteria were to be used in the financial evaluation of companies. At the time, 63 global investment companies worth 6.5 trillion dollars agreed to fold this into financial reviews to develop a more sustainable investing method.

The United Nations created 17 Sustainable Development Goals (SDGs) (see Figure 9.2) based on the ESG framework: "The 2030 Agenda for Sustainable Development, adopted by all United Nations member states in 2015, provides a shared blueprint for peace and prosperity for people and the planet, now and into the future. The 17 SDGs are at its heart, an urgent call for action by all developed and developing countries in a global partnership. They recognize that ending poverty and other deprivations must go together with strategies that improve health and education, reduce inequality, and spur economic growth—all while tackling climate change and working to preserve our oceans and forests."

ESG mainly remained under the radar until 2017 when State Street Global Advisors (SSGA) voted against the reelection of directors at 400 companies, which SSGA said failed to make any significant effort to appoint women to their all-male boards. This decision was on the heels of a survey published by Business Wire, which found 68 percent of its

Figure 9.2 ESG sustainable development goals (*Source:* https://sdgs.un.org/goals)

respondents said that implementation of ESG criteria aided in improved returns, along with 77 percent of respondents that said they invested in ESG strategies due to its impact on a public company's financial performance. Also, in 2017, 62 percent of ExxonMobil shareholders went against management's recommendations by voting to require the world's largest oil and gas company to report on the impacts of climate change on its business. This was an increase of 38 percent of the vote from the previous year.

WHY DO WE CARE?

The short and more cynical answer to this question is that we care because ESG has hit the mainstream, and everyone is talking about it now. The longer response to this question, and the response I would hope is more accurate, is that we care because every time a consumer purchases a product or pays for a service, the consumer is essentially voting for that company. Each vote makes up the market share that the company currently maintains. The more market share, the more revenue, the more employees, and the more profit. Some consumers are *brand loyal*, meaning there is not much a company can do to push that consumer away, but for the most part, consumers are fickle. They are more informed, more educated, and can connect with other consumers globally for nearly real-time information about what a company is doing or not doing.

As a consumer, I choose a food product to purchase for my daughter based first on whether it is nutritious. What if there are two products on the market that my daughter likes, and both have healthy ingredients? My next decision variable may be about the company's supply chain choices. Does the company have operations in the United States, and does it hire local resources? The closer the value chain is to the end user, the better for the environment in many cases. These ESG metrics could be used to change my mind about purchasing a product from company *A* versus company *B* if other variables were equal. The consumer has more purchasing power today than ever before.

In 2020 in Davos, Switzerland. The World Economic Forum (WEF) and the WEF International Business Council (IBC), under the chairmanship of Brian Moynihan (CEO of Bank of America), in partnership with the Big Four accounting firms (Deloitte, PwC, KPMG, and Ernst & Young) moved ESG forward by developing a set of standardized metrics supporting ESG transformation. In addition, these metrics were supported by a structured framework in which companies would report on their results. Over 120 multinational financial and nonfinancial companies agreed to use these metrics to demonstrate long-term value to investors.

For a multinational organization to formally adopt the ESG metrics, it must also position its company more favorably to investors and individuals looking to buy stocks and funds where their company was included. It also placed the company in a more favorable position with consumers who wanted to purchase products and/or services from a company with similar beliefs. Before 2020, ESG was a tool used by a handful of investors to prioritize where to spend their money. After 2020, ESG became more mainstream. This is illustrated best in Figure 9.3, showing that Google search trends in the United States have jumped since 2020.

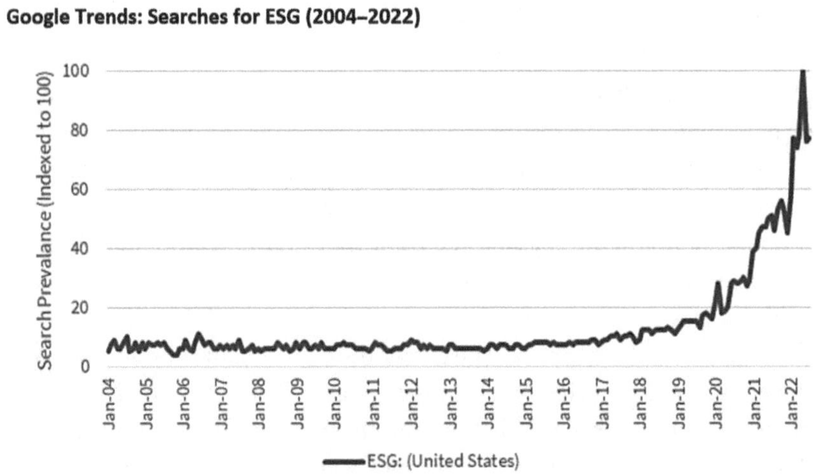

Figure 9.3 Google ESG search trends (2004–2022)

The ESG metrics formalized in the 2020 WEF annual meeting centered around four key areas: Principles of Governance (led by Deloitte), Planet (led by PwC), People (led by KPMG), and Prosperity (led by Ernst & Young) (see Figure 9.4).

With a global set of standards in place, there needed to be a way to gauge or report how companies performed against those metrics, and in came the ratings firms. While companies with ESG-related measurements are not new (RepRisk, a pioneer in ESG data science, started in 1998), there are now over 140 ratings agencies worldwide. A ratings agency may be specific to one aspect of the ESG platform, such as carbon footprints or supplier diversity, while others may provide a more holistic view.

These third-party ESG ratings firms have evolved to provide ESG information to the public. As with any information-as-a-service, these reports provide a better understanding of ESG parity between what the company is doing and the variables it is measured against. Compare this to taking your car into a shop that offers a free 20-point inspection. The 20 points are the variables your vehicle is measured against, and the report you receive shows how well your car performed against those variables.

In a hypothetical scenario, suppose my 20-point inspection showed a gap between the current state of my brakes and where they should be for safety. The recommendation was that nothing needed to be done today, but the brakes should be replaced no more than six months from now. This time frame helps me assess the level of risk I am willing to accept. For example, there is a potential risk for me, my family, and others on the road if the brakes are not replaced. In this scenario, I would not have passed 100 percent on the item for brakes; however, I did not fail either.

A similar comparison is completed between a list of ESG metrics and how well the company is doing against those metrics (see Figure 9.5). In some areas, the company may be doing well—even 100 percent—while in other places, it may need to improve.

As someone who has been working with data since 1995, I do not accept any report at face value. It is the analyst's responsibility to understand the sources of data, whether the data was changed or altered in any way, what assumptions were used in collecting the data, how the ratings were calculated, whether an inference or other kinds of weighting

Principles of Governance	Planet	People	Prosperity
The definition of governance is evolving as organizations are increasingly expected to define and embed their purpose at the centre of their business. But the principles of agency, accountability and stewardship continue to be vital for truly "good governance."	An ambition to protect the planet from degradation, including through sustainable consumption and production, sustainably managing its natural resources and taking urgent action on climate change, so that it can support the needs of the present and future generations.	An ambition to end poverty and hunger, in all their forms and dimensions, and to ensure that all human beings can fulfil their potential in dignity and equality and in a healthy environment.	An ambition to ensure that all human beings can enjoy prosperous and fulfilling lives and that economic, social and technological progress occurs in harmony with nature.

Figure 9.4 The four pillars of sustainable development (*Source*: World Economic Forum and Big Four analysis. Definitions taken from the UN's 2030 Agenda for Sustainable Development)

Figure 9.5 EcoVadis ESG Dashboard

were used in the final scorecard results, etc. Be mindful that one ESG ratings report is not the same as another. There will be variances when attempting to compare one against the other.

HYPE OR REALITY?

ESG started as and continues to be primarily an investment tool. In August 2022, in the state of Texas, the state comptroller claimed that ten energy companies and 350 investment funds had boycotted fossil fuel companies in Texas. More specifically, those funds were advancing agendas that threatened the energy industry in Texas. The state comptroller said the focus on ESG standards in finance had become a proxy for political agenda-setting. "The environmental, social and corporate governance movement has produced an opaque and perverse system in which some financial companies no longer make decisions in the best interest of their shareholders or their clients, but instead use their financial clout to push a social and political agenda shrouded in secrecy," said Glenn Hegar, the Texas State Comptroller at the time. As a result, Texas has ordered some state government funds, such as state pension funds, to divest from shares in the companies listed in Texas divestment statutes. The point here is that the more visible ESG is to the public, the more it will be discussed in the news, and the more criticism it will receive from those with an agenda other than the UN ESG goals.

What about outside the United States? According to a 2022 PwC ESG Trends study, Australia had more climate change litigation per capita that year than anywhere else globally. Australia is emerging as the precedent for litigation in this field, and if companies consider slowing down their focus on ESG as a consumer priority, they could be missing out. A 2022 Kearney study showed Australians were willing to pay between 40 and 80 percent more for leading performance across ESG. Additionally, the survey found between 20 and 35 percent of Australians would be more willing to purchase goods and services where executive leadership is meeting ESG goals.

"Around the world, companies are trying to embrace ESG practices authentically, but still tend to view ESG as a cost to the top line," said Kearney ANZ ESG lead, strategic operations lead, and partner Kate Hart.

"Our data shows that integrating ESG principles into a product's life cycle can give companies the competitive advantage they seek, positioning them favorably in the eyes of consumers and helping their products stand out from the crowd." These are representative examples of two different extremes but highlight the widening gap between the value of ESG to the consumer, the company, politicians, and investors worldwide.

For the procurement organization, is ESG hype or reality? Most procurement organizations still have a reactive approach to the executive agenda. This means they follow what corporate executives have outlined as a priority and work across the business units and stakeholders to execute that goal. When the CEO states ESG initiatives are a priority, the procurement organization pivots to support those initiatives by evaluating suppliers and purchasing policies and measuring how much spending is allocated to ESG initiatives. You may recall reading earlier in this chapter that ESG has many subsets, including supplier diversity, which has maintained a top-five priority over the past 25 years. Supplier diversity remains the conversation in almost all companies in North America and has expanded into parts of Western Europe. It will remain a formal part of the modern future procurement organization.

DEBRIEF ON SUPPLIER DIVERSITY

In 2009, I spoke at a ProcureCon conference in the United States on the topic: *Leveraging Your Supplier Network and Maximizing Your Diversity Spend*. ProcureCon observed this topic had received a lot of traction in the United States in previous years. The presentation aimed to bring this topic forward to a larger group of procurement professionals. My career achievements in this area included improving the existing supplier diversity program for Avon, automating the procurement and supplier diversity program for American Express, outlining the early stages of a diversity strategy for Estee Lauder, and being a founding member of the supplier diversity committee for the Institute of Supply Management (ISM) New York chapter. I was living and breathing procurement, supply management, and supplier diversity. I also volunteered for three years on the Women's President Education Organization NY certification committee in my spare time, validating women-owned suppliers for the Women's Business Enterprise National Council.

My presentation for ProcureCon 2009 concluded, "Developing and/or running a successful supplier diversity program is no simple undertaking. You must implement your formal definitions, define the type of certifications that your organization will accept, and understand how to leverage minority spending across the various categories." Takeaways included:

1. Finding certified diverse-owned companies
2. Tracking and reporting on diversity spend
3. Leveraging your diversity partnerships and alliances

Recently, I reviewed that presentation and compared the content from 2009 to the present day. The number one challenge identified in 2009 was *the lack of finding and accessing diverse-owned supplier data*. Even now, approximately 15 years later, that challenge has not changed. Additionally, the presentation identified the top ten reasons why corporations should work with diverse suppliers in 2009:

1. **Competitive bidding:** Diverse-owned companies tend to lead in patented and patent-pending applications.
2. **Innovation:** Smaller companies can innovate more quickly.
3. **Similar corporate culture**
4. **Better customer service**
5. **Partnership:** The supplier can develop products and services to fit the larger organization's needs better.
6. **Solving a specific business challenge:** With capabilities to innovate more rapidly, specific business solutions may be available more quickly than waiting for an enterprise application provider to agree to add to their roadmap.
7. **Less political:** Ease of navigating.
8. **Spending with local suppliers in the local economy:** Diverse-owned companies tend to be more recognized locally and regionally by their community. Collaboration can raise a larger company's awareness in a new market and enable the larger company to communicate more directly within a regional community.

9. **Contractual requirements:** For instance, diversity clauses mandate *X* percent of diverse spending.
10. **Contractual penalties:** For instance, removal from future request for proposals (RFPs) in the federal sector.

Over the past 15 years, there has not been as much advancement in the supplier diversity space as hoped. However, with artificial intelligence (AI) technologies becoming more accessible for all suppliers, the number of diverse-owned suppliers has been increasing. In 2023, the IT procurement category showed an 18 percent increase in new diverse-owned suppliers invited to RFPs compared to 2022. That percentage accounts only for diverse-owned companies that we are aware of. As a mentor to diverse-owned and technology start-up companies, I have conversed with many professionals on all sides. The following comments help shed some light on the current state of trying to increase supplier diversity:

- From the buy side (or corporate procurement):
  - "We do not attend conferences as much as we used to. Our travel budget was cut during COVID-19 and will not be returned. How do we find more diverse-owned companies?"
  - "Our company policy does not allow suppliers to self-register on our portal. Diverse-owned companies will not be invited to RFPs unless we already know the company exists; yet, we are measured annually in how many diverse-owned companies we include in RFPs."
  - "We just do not have resources who can focus on an internal supplier diversity program."
  - "As a CPO, I was asked to cut funding for three consecutive years. The supplier diversity program was the last one I had to reduce to one person."
  - "We are being asked to do more with less, yet our CEO wants to be the best-in-class for supplier diversity within our industry. The two do not add up."
  - Many newer, diverse-owned companies do not have a business background. They do not know how to talk to the folks (us) they are trying to sell to. It gets exhausting

and frustrating, but it does not impact my willingness to keep listening to diverse-owned companies."

- From the supply side (or the supplier):
    - "I have a patent-pending application that solves a specific business challenge, but I don't have a way to introduce myself to corporate procurement."
    - "I have been working with procurement companies for 16 years and with Fortune 100 brands. The latest procurement professionals do not seem interested in providing referrals or feedback I can leverage for the next RFP. I cannot put my finger on it, but they either do not care or they do not want to get too involved in the success of their suppliers."
    - "Do procurement leaders even talk to each other? It seems each procurement organization is its island."
    - "For the past ten years, I have had to register individually on each company's website. Last year, I was still doing the same thing. There has to be a better way."
    - "It is still a challenge to just get in the door for 15 minutes for an introduction and to outline why a product/service can solve an existing business challenge."
    - "As a supplier, I work with many companies and have recognized challenges and solutions to those challenges the procurement organization may not be aware of. I would have thought that would interest a procurement professional, but it is not a priority. So, what is their priority?"

Tracking Tier 2 suppliers remains essential for many companies who want to track not only diverse suppliers who work directly with the company (Tier 1) but also the diverse suppliers working with the Tier 1 suppliers. The primary challenge is that data is unavailable or, unfortunately, the *correct* data is unavailable because the Tier 2 suppliers are typically smaller companies that may not prioritize diversity or do not have the resources and technology to do so.

In some industries, such as banks, credit card issuers, and other financial organizations, tracking contractors and suppliers used by Tier 1 suppliers is a regulatory requirement. However, even in these scenarios, Tier 1 suppliers do not prioritize tracking the diversity status of their contractors. These companies face the same challenges: a lack of data or, at least, correct data, leading to incomplete or inaccurate reporting.

The recommendations and strategies for increasing supplier diversity have not evolved much over the past 15 years. This includes the use of an internal diversity network and advocate program. This application cleanses existing data to identify diverse-owned suppliers already working with the company and adds a policy that requires a minimum of two diverse-owned suppliers to every procurement request.

It can be difficult for a company to advance supplier diversity if it is internally focused on suppliers it already uses. Making it mandatory to include two diverse-owned suppliers does not matter if no additional details state that the suppliers must be *new* rather than *existing*. Otherwise, procurement professionals will keep dealing with diverse-owned suppliers they already do business with just to check a box. Another idea is not to dictate a minimum number of suppliers but rather have diverse-owned suppliers make up a percentage of total spend. For example, if the total expected spend is $300,000, then include *X* number of diverse-owned suppliers. As the spending increases, so does the number of diverse-owned suppliers.

In September 2022, I discussed this topic in more detail with Tamra Pawloski, Global Director of Indirect Procurement, in her podcast *Teatime with Tamra*. A few of the questions and answers are included here:

- **Question:** Did COVID-19 hinder our ability to engage with more suppliers? Has it created a better path forward?
    - **Answer:** There is a perception that COVID-19 somehow helped the diverse-owned community. While the pandemic did great things to shift business to some mid-market diverse-owned companies, it did not change anything. It was another reactive response, not a proactive one. This means that once COVID-19 was officially over, procurement organizations returned to what was normal for them and, as a result, back to the old policies, culture, and processes before the COVID-19 pandemic.

- **Question:** What techniques have you seen work to ensure companies are aware of diverse suppliers?
    - **Answer:** So far, the best approach to matching diverse-owned companies is what the ISM-NY Diversity Committee started 15 years ago called Diversity Expo. This approach has been proven in the NYC market, and I have seen variations of it in other cities, both in-person and virtual. Virtually, I have seen this as 10-minute breakout sessions or speed dating, but the underlying approach remains the same:
        - Ten corporations that have diversity programs are invited to attend; they each have their own table or breakout room
        - Each corporate member outlines five categories for which they need diverse suppliers
        - The category list is sent to each of the ten corporations who then recommend one to three diverse-owned suppliers for each category requested by the other corporations
        - The attending diverse-owned suppliers are given a list of corporations they should meet based on the requested categories, but they can also introduce themselves to other corporations at the event

      Meeting with corporations who need a category of supplies they support is valuable for diverse-owned suppliers. Meeting with diverse-owned suppliers that have already been vetted and recommended by other companies is valuable for the corporations.
- **Questions:** Is there a path forward to supplier diversity?
    - **Answer:** As a community, we aim to overcome the obstacles from 20 years ago while facing new challenges simultaneously. Baby boomers will soon be entirely out of the market, giving way to a new group of professionals. I mention this because baby boomers were the largest working demographic, and their departure, even with

the emergence of the new generations, will never balance out. This means procurement will continue to feel the pressure of doing more with less. For supplier diversity to remain valuable, many things need to change both internally on the buy side and externally on the supplier side:

- Leadership cannot just verbally commit to supplier diversity as a priority without backing it up with funding and resources
- Procurement leadership needs to push back when asked to cut programs as a primary means to save money and reduce budget
- Suppliers need to think strategically about navigating the corporations instead of listing all the problems they have engaging procurement

GETTING STARTED IN ESG

Consumers are increasingly aware of humans' impact on the world. This has placed an emphasis on how companies produce and buy goods and services and has given the consumer's voice more power to influence change. At the grocery store, consumers have a choice. They decide which product to buy and which company to buy from. Their selection can mean a vote favoring one company over another. Because ESG can be good for business, it has become highly valued by companies looking to:

- Increase brand loyalty: Companies with strong ESG practices and policies tend to have higher consumer loyalty
- Increase internal talent: With many industries experiencing talent shortages, attracting and retaining talent is vital, and workers (especially younger ones) gravitate to companies that share their social-responsibility focus
- Lower supply chain risk: Companies with embedded ESG strategies may be better positioned to identify and mitigate the risk of environmental disasters proactively

- Attract investors: Money from the private sector and government grants are shifting to companies with ESG-focused leadership
- Find a market differentiator: Companies with strong ESG metrics can set themselves apart from their competitors
- Avoid future disasters: Companies already focused on ESG initiatives are evaluating the impacts of climate change, supply chain scarcity, etc., and are considered in a better position to adapt long term to future disruptions
- Increase innovation: The ESG framework can help lead to rethinking existing processes, fostering innovative ideas, improving existing products, and developing new ones

Getting started with ESG in procurement is not an easy task. It requires purposeful intent every year, from the first year of developing ESG goals to each year when the ESG scorecard is reviewed for progress and gaps. It is not a few words on a website or a few lines in an RFP. If the organization wants to move forward with an ESG strategy, it will require a cultural mind shift. A practical roadmap for procurement will encompass the following:

1. Defining ESG goals and aligning them with corporate objectives
2. Assessing the ESG baseline and gaps
3. Establishing policies and processes
4. Engaging with suppliers and internal stakeholders
5. Creating reports, monitoring them, and adjusting as needed
6. Fostering an ESG culture

Defining ESG Goals and Aligning Them with Corporate Objectives

Define what ESG goals align with procurement and the organization's corporate objectives. Confirm that ESG goals are a component that further drives the company's mission and vision statement. For a public company, reading the annual report will offer insights into where the board of directors has communicated specific goals, such as reducing the carbon footprint by 20 percent in 5 years. This alignment will be necessary for continuous, long-term success. Do not consider prioritizing based on the top 20 suppliers (by dollars spent). This approach does not work because these suppliers will create too many goals to be successful.

Assessing ESG Baseline and Gaps

Start with an ESG baseline so you have something to measure against. This will show progression, communicate achievements, and help to refocus the following year in areas that need more attention. An ESG baseline in procurement involves reviewing processes and policies against ESG standards, looking at suppliers and the data available, and documenting what data should be available. Work with relevant teams to assess if the data is available but not visible to procurement. If the data is not available, consider where the data will be derived from and if changes are necessary to existing procurement and supply chain applications. Additionally, determine where ESG standards are obtained for a specific industry or an aggregate across all sectors. Consider monitoring from the same source(s) so the baseline does not become skewed over time. Finally, determine which ESG goals to prioritize. Selecting too many goals or goals that cannot be immediately measured can waste valuable resources and give you nothing to show after the first year of effort.

Establishing Policies and Processes

Include ESG policies that cover selection criteria for supplier evaluations and performance monitoring. Based on the prioritized ESG goals, document what certifications and other materials are required for products and services. If the assessment results recommend focusing on a few commodities or categories for year 1, consider sourcing guidelines and benchmarks for existing suppliers to follow in those areas. Embed ESG language into standard procurement contracts and developed service level agreements to hold suppliers accountable. Work with relevant groups to gain access to available ESG-related data or develop requirements for application changes.

Engaging with Suppliers and Internal Stakeholders

Procurement should engage with and clearly communicate ESG initiatives, priorities, and expectations to suppliers. Emphasize the importance of the initiative in the relationship between the company and the supplier. Do not let this be perceived as an optional exercise. If the company is going to do this, so should suppliers who do business with the company. Depending on the ESG goals and which procurement categories and industries are prioritized, the total number of suppliers impacted in the first year of this program may not be as high as imagined. To maximize this number, do more than send a few emails. Hold a supplier summit, even virtually, for two to three hours to walk them through the program and take time to address their questions. Consider an offer to collaborate on an ESG assessment of their processes that produce goods and services supplied to the company. This will lead to specific recommendations that positively benefit both parties.

Creating Reports, Monitoring Them, and Adjusting as Needed

Leverage existing technology or consider third-party software to supplement ESG initiatives and scorecards. Create an ESG dashboard with key performance indicators updated quarterly and annually. Establish the dashboard at both the supplier and company level, which aggregates across all suppliers. Determine a threshold across each metric to gauge when specific metrics become a concern. This will allow procurement resources to guide suppliers on where to focus their time so they do not have to monitor everything simultaneously. When the metrics fall below the threshold, ensure there are enough details to help identify where to adjust as needed. Stay updated on ESG standards from the same source(s) used in the assessment. Find the right path to stay aware of new ESG regulations or industry standards that may impact suppliers.

Fostering an ESG Culture

Procurement may be necessary to establish, execute, and monitor an ESG program. Still, this initiative will slowly fade without the rest of the organization also engaging in ESG practices. Develop an ESG network with resources identified—in each department or business unit—as ESG advocates. Once these resources are identified, start with procurement-led training to dive deeper into the ESG initiative and provide talking points and FAQs to help them successfully move forward with the message. Create a communication channel and cadence where ESG information is pushed into this network. This channel will also offer visibility into specific challenges and questions across the organization that can be addressed to ensure consistent communication. Finally, virtual training should be provided to all employees to emphasize ESG's importance to the company and the expectations of suppliers in year 1. Keep the internal stakeholders engaged by providing updates at quarterly events. This can be a company-wide or business-unit town hall where ESG advocates provide updates. Don't forget to celebrate success, including small successes that, over time, lead to huge successes. I have witnessed companies recognizing suppliers with the most ESG-related changes yearly, business units that best supported ESG processes, and individuals chosen as the best ESG motivators. Each of these successes was posted internally and externally to underscore the motivation behind the ESG initiatives. External marketing on social media, the company website, and other communication channels strengthened the company as a differentiator among its competitors, attracting new talent and maintaining brand loyalty with its consumers.

CHAPTER 10

PEOPLE AND SKILLS

More is being asked from our procurement and supply management professionals than ever. This often means the same resource owns sourcing strategy, sourcing execution, contract negotiation, and drafting of the statement of work (SOW) with suppliers. These resources are being stretched like never before in procurement's history. Moreover, the skills required for strategic sourcing differ from those required for contract negotiation or writing an SOW. Not only are the resources spread thin, but they may also not be given the time or opportunity to develop the skills needed to master these various roles. This chapter discusses the issues facing today's procurement professionals and the skills necessary to succeed in the modern procurement organization.

RESOURCES WEARING MANY HATS

The idea that procurement professionals are *wearing many hats* really describes the different roles each one plays in the organization. This includes performing many roles in addition to their primary role. For example, in the procurement organization, specifically in the strategic sourcing department, a junior resource may focus on the tactical sourcing components, such as market research and executing proposal requests. A senior resource would have the strategic components of sourcing, such as category plans, supplier strategy, or outlining the best options to reach the goals of the business stakeholder. Once a supplier is selected, the next step is negotiating the business terms of the contract. The senior resource that outlines a category strategy is the same person responsible for negotiating the business terms and conditions of the contract. These resources may have received training in writing requests for various procurement documents (RFXs) and evaluating suppliers. Still, they seldom receive training in the nuisances of contract language or how to determine which service level agreements are best suited for the services and products agreed to in the RFX.

In my experience, there often needs to be more connection between what is in the contract or SOW and the expectations of senior management. This disconnect can lead to extended contracts that stretch 50 pages or more. The theory that more pages will equal a better understanding of what each party expects never works out. Sometimes, more pages mean more confusion in interpreting the contract or results in contradicting statements in other areas of the contract. The language applied to a contract needs to be precise. When the language in a contract is clear, explicit, and unambiguous, there is no need for additional evidence to be considered to determine what the contract means and what the parties intended. That is what makes a good contract.

Contract negotiation can be learned with time and experience. Legal templates are a good start, but providing the skills necessary to minimize risk is essential. Remember, the goal of the contract is to provide the guidelines needed to eliminate confusion between two parties. The supplier will always default to what is in the contract. The approval of their invoices is directly or indirectly linked to what they have accomplished per the contract. When the organization requests actions outside of the contract, also known as scope creep, the contract is supposed to provide clear, explicit, and unambiguous language to settle this confusion.

It does not stop with just contract knowledge. There are many hats required from procurement professionals on any given day. They need to think strategically about category planning and reevaluating the supplier base; play detective to sift through data and identify opportunities for savings; get involved in the optimization processes and understand total cost of ownership; communicate effectively with business stakeholders; possess project management skills to identify and communicate short-term and long-term risks; and have change management skills to better manage the expectations of others. This is certainly not a comprehensive list, but you get the point. How are procurement professionals supposed to be effective at their jobs when they are expected to master such a broad set of roles within the organization?

DOING MORE WITH LESS

Doing more with less is possible if we develop the right foundation of people and skills. Technology is leveraged to automate processes, but the underlying process does not go away, and neither do the people using the process. People and skills are often the last to be considered, removed from the budget, or forgotten completely.

Over the last 15 years, digital transformations have led to a *lift-n-shift* environment with the idea that moving existing processes into a procurement application is necessary to fulfill automation requirements. If we circle back to the definition of transformation given in Chapter One of this book—"transformation is the ability to change from one state to another to end up in a better place than where you were before"—the key phrase is that the goal is *to end up in a better place than where you were before.* Using technology alone will provide some process automation, but it does not position the organization in a better place. If it did, organizations would not voice concerns about not achieving the value they expected 15 months after a technology implementation.

> Technology does not do it alone. People are needed to facilitate the process and provide context to the data, driving better-informed decisions.

Every procurement department has a point where existing processes have reached their threshold. This means existing resources can no longer accommodate the additional workload once that threshold is passed. One of three things can occur:

1. Add more resources
2. Try to do more with existing resources

3. Scale back the number of existing resources available and hope technology (automation) takes care of the rest

The opportunity for organizations "to do more with less" is one of the benefits of a digital transformation—identifying opportunities for automation to increase the productivity of existing resources. Those resources are now able to focus on more value-added activities and outcomes. It is no surprise that industry surveys continue sharing metrics validating that information. For example, the Hackett Group 2019 Purchase-to-Pay (P2P) Performance Study yields the following results for productivity. "By streamlining end-to-end processes and supporting the workforce with digital tools, Top Performers require less than half the full-time equivalents (FTEs) of other organizations and are two and a half times more productive on a per-FTE basis."

When asked to cut costs, the traditional response by management is to reduce headcount. However, jumping to eliminate resources, especially before having an efficient, automated process, will always lead to more issues in the future. Advocating a comprehensive transformation strategy can lead to opportunities for savings and *eliminate* the need to reduce headcount. Consider this scenario that occurs quite often. An organization needs to save $2 million in its annual budget for the following year. It decides to lay off 20 percent of its U.S. resources and shift 45 percent of its procurement responsibilities offshore. This would hinder the ability of the procurement department to be a strategic ally to the business in the future, but it did save $2 million that year. This is often just the tip of the cost-cutting iceberg; two years later, more cuts are required to reduce costs. Eventually, there are not enough resources to perform basic activities, and people leave for fear of layoffs or because they want to avoid working with an organization that sets them up for failure. This is a slippery slope for the organization trying to do more with less. It almost always ends in glaring (and preventable) failure.

CHANGES IN THE WORKFORCE

As an instructor for the Institute of Supply Management for more than 10 years, my role was to create custom full-day Continuing Education Unit-accredited courses. The procurement organizations requested specific topics that supported immediate needs. The following list contains the topics that were requested in order of popularity:

- Spend Management
- Supplier Information Performance Management
- Sourcing 101—Building the Foundation
- Strategic Sourcing Advanced
- Supplier Risk
- Project Management
- Conflict Management
- Effective Communications
- How to Change the Conversation—Leadership for the Modern Organization
- Maximizing Procurement Operations

As the procurement professional's role has evolved, the skills required for that role have changed along with it. What is noticeable in the above list is the request for nonstandard procurement skills such as project management, change management, effective communication, and conflict resolution. Over time, the participants' demographics changed from Generation X to Millennials. In 2015, an earlier course, Sourcing 101—Building the Foundation, reemerged as a reoccurring favorite because a new generation of professionals was entering the workforce.

Resources were no longer dedicating their entire careers to procurement. Gone were the days when it was normal for a workforce to remain at one company throughout their careers. Before 2000, college students were told to expect to work with five different companies and engage in three different career changes. Over the next 20 years, that message changed; the numbers quoted to graduates increased to 10–15 different companies and up to five different careers throughout their lifetimes.

The following list contains examples of how the fluctuation of resource availability and skills impacts the procurement organization:

1. **Cross-functional workforce training:** Some organizations developed workforce training to encourage the shift of resources across different departments in order to gain a better perspective of the larger enterprise. This had some great benefits. The workforce was more loyal to the company, but this also meant experienced professionals moved out of the procurement department every three years with little effort to provide documentation or knowledge transfer to the incoming teams. The negative impact was that resources would spend up to one year learning the ins and outs of the department, and when they began to create real value, it was time for them to shift to another department.
2. **Start-ups:** Several times in the past 15 years, there have been high growth spikes in start-up companies. Most of these companies have not developed formal procurement departments or professionals but have a few resources supporting tactical procurement activities such as supplier evaluations and writing SOWs. If a larger enterprise acquired a start-up, individuals with general operational knowledge were moved into the procurement department to perform transactional activities without understanding procurement or supply management processes.
3. **Baby boomers leaving the workforce:** In 2011, the first baby boomers reached 65 and began leaving the workforce. At the time, this was the largest demographic in the United States. As of 2024, this demographic ranges in age between 60 and 78. According to the Pew Research Center, it is estimated that by 2030, the last of the baby boomer generation will retire from the workforce.
4. **Nonprocurement resources working in procurement:** Resources from other areas, such as the program management office, finance, and marketing, were called upon to meet the demands of the growing procurement organization. These resources

often lacked a background or experience with procurement processes.

5. **Working on their terms—the Millennials:** According to the Pew Research Center, the next largest U.S. generation is the Millennials, born between 1981 and 1996. As of 2024, this group ranges in age from 28 to 43 and has pushed for new working standards since first hitting the job market, focusing on companies that meet their social and environmental awareness. U.S. companies modified employee benefits to offer anywhere from 8 to 40 hours of annual paid time off for volunteering activities to attract new talent. This was on top of their standard yearly paid time off.

   This group of professionals is not known for staying with one company for long periods as prior generations did, and they have been linked to the term Gig Economy, representing a large part of the workforce that is freelance or are flexible working professionals. Watching this generation grow up, I would say they demanded that the term *work-life balance* become a reality and not just another phrase in corporate culture. Their reaction to a traditional company is boredom, just one variable prompting a change to another, trying a new career, or starting their own company.

   In the United States, we are known for *live to work*; in most parts of the world, the phrase is more commonly called *work to live*. This generation reminds me of the latter, working to fulfill their dreams and desires now instead of waiting 50 years for retirement. When I interviewed professionals within this age range, they had a similar perspective: why wait to see the world during retirement when we will be too old to enjoy it? This philosophy and the choice of how they want to live have impacted the ability of organizations to attract and retain talent. Procurement is already experiencing a talent shortage, and there is no expectation of a new workforce large enough to backfill all available positions. It would be wise for procurement organizations to think about adjusting the roles and responsibilities of procurement professionals to put them more in line with Millennial expectations.

6. **Growing up with innovation—Generation Z:** This generation was born between 1996 and 2010. As this book is being written, they are graduating from college, working as interns, or already entering the job market in entry-level positions. This group has grown up experiencing the fast pace of technological changes and innovation. They rely on their mobile phones for more than music and communication; they also pay for products and services. The concept of a wallet is the wallet app on their phone. Growing up digitally also impacts how they see the workplace. Their reaction to a traditional workplace is one of intolerance. If the company cannot keep up with innovation or make genuine attempts to transform, they have no tolerance to stay and hang out. Procurement organizations still working with Excel, managing paper purchase orders, and performing tactical data entry activities may not be the companies that will be able to attract new talent.

DRIVING THE NEED FOR 21ST-CENTURY SKILLS

In the 21st century, technological disruptions, global pandemics, supply chain disturbances, and geological factors are becoming more frequent. The old-school skills of procurement professionals are no longer valid and need to be considered the minimum requirement when evaluating incoming professionals. In interviewing executives for my podcast *Impact of AI (& Data)*, along with numerous informal interviews of chief procurement officers or heads of procurement and supply chains at various conferences and virtual meetings, they all have one thing in common when looking at the future skills needed for their workforce: the concept of a 21st-century set of skills.

21st-century skills are the skills professionals need to acquire to understand the advancements and accessibility of AI (artificial intelligence) and other emerging technologies. These skills will help them evaluate a new group of suppliers leveraging these technologies, adapt to and communicate change, and become trusted advisors to internal stakeholders.

Applied Education Systems (AES) (www.aeseducation.com/blog/what-are-21st-century-skills) has outlined a skill set for those looking to stay competitive in today's changing job market (see Figure 10.1).

Figure 10.1 Summary of the 21st-century skills for the future workforce

These skills will serve as a springboard to the next section when we tailor them for procurement and supply chain professionals in today's job marketplace.

21ST-CENTURY SKILLS (MODIFIED CHECKLIST)

The following six-point checklist is a modified version of the AES 21st-century skills for students (see Figure 10.2). It has been adapted for procurement and supply chain professionals already in the market.

Self-Awareness

Quite simply, developing the ability to evaluate yourself critically to identify your strengths and weaknesses is the most important skill one can have. Honest self-assessment and creating a clear list of opportunities for improvement are critical to preparing yourself for future changes. Strengthen your ability to become more self-aware, and you will always know where to prioritize your efforts throughout your personal and professional career.

Critical Thinking

I will quote Mike Kallet, CEO of HeadScratchers, from his Critical Thinking Training Workshops—"Critical thinking is a tool, a methodology, and a process used during activities such as problem-solving, decision making, innovation, leading, negotiating, influencing, and more." In his example of buying a car, considerations such as the price, the size, the gadgets and features, whether you need four-wheel drive, financing options, gas mileage, and how it feels and rides are variables involved. Critical thinking supports clarity on the objectives and how those objectives match the vehicle's attributes. Using critical thinking evaluates strategic thinking to provide you with a better understanding of how those factors weigh in and whether or not your *thinking* is sound.

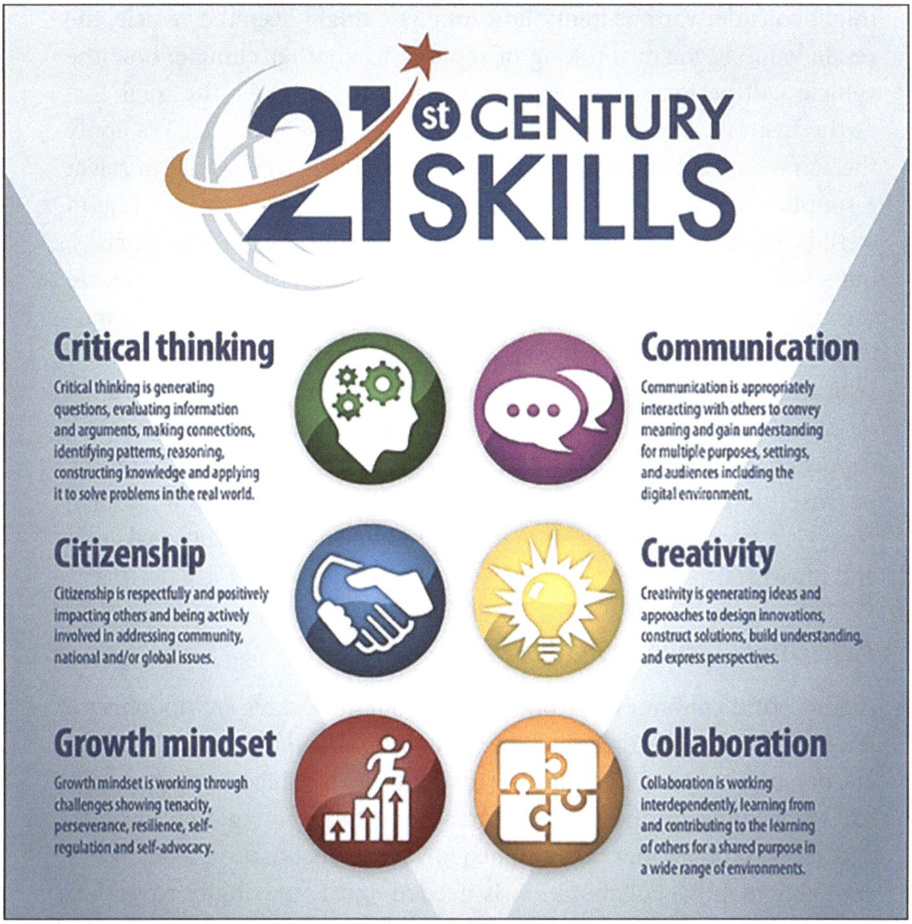

Figure 10.2 21st-century skills prioritized by organizations

Strategic Thinking

Again, quoting Mike Kallet, "Strategic thinking is an activity that involves thinking beyond the specific issue or task at hand." You determine consequences, implications, interdependencies, and indirect impacts in the short and long term. It is an activity where you look beyond the immediate goal or issue and with the context of the world around you, not just the context of the moment. In his example of buying a car, you might consider various items: how long you might keep the vehicle, the resale value if you're thinking of moving to another climate, how the vehicle will perform, the long-term maintenance costs, the total cost of the insurance premiums over the life of the vehicle, etc. We apply the same concepts as a procurement professional who wants to select a supplier to purchase a critical product for the company in a region of the world that is prone to natural disasters. There are known risks, but strategic thinking would help us list all types of risks and evaluate the risk exposure. Based on this analysis, it might be necessary to outline a dual-sourcing strategy to identify alternative suppliers in other regions as a contingency. While dual sourcing may initially cost a *little* more, a cost-benefit analysis may outline a business case where a supply chain disruption may cost *much* more. This is strategic thinking because the procurement professional considers short- and long-term cost, risk, supply chain stability, and alignment with organizational goals and priorities.

Adaptive Collaboration

As the world continues to work virtually, our coworkers are no longer a few time zones away; they can be 12 hours ahead and have a vastly different perspective on accomplishing a similar goal. Collaboration is critical to bringing in diverse ideas, greater visibility to regional insights, and access to a broader talent pool. However, collaboration alone is not enough. Adaptive collaboration is needed and is the ability to understand the kind of person/personality you are compared to the different personalities around you and your ability to adjust or adapt.

For example, suppose you are naturally analytical and are working on an activity or long-term project with a naturally social person. There will be a misalignment in how and what you prioritize when communicating. The analytical person will be straightforward and factual, while the social person will be more expressive. Your working styles will likely be entirely different as an analytical person will tend to focus on the details while a social person will focus on the big picture. These differences can lead to personal conflicts, impact the results you are working toward, and have been known to appear in performance evaluations. Learning how personal styles affect you and your working relationship with others is another skill to add to your tool belt. The end goal is to become aware and adaptable to those around you.

Heather Harper recently updated her top list of personality tests in April 2023. You can read the full details at https://www.workstyle.io/best-personality-test, but the top seven are highlighted here:

1. Truity
2. High5 Test
3. DiSC
4. The 16 Personality Factor Questionnaire (16PF)
5. HEXACO model of personality structure personality inventory
6. Revised NEO Personality Inventory (NEO-PI-R)
7. Myers-Briggs Type Indicator (MBTI)

Use these personality tests to understand yourself and how to work better with others who are and are not like you.

Structured Communication

Communication is critical to a productive conversation. Once in high school, I was asked what was more important: an effective listener or talker. I responded that both were needed to have a productive conversation and provided a few more sentences to explain why I believed the way I did. I was marked negatively for *not answering the question.* I feel just as strongly today as I did then about the importance of both sides. Structured communications include what we learned in middle school English, combined with what is taught in Toastmasters, and layered on top of learnings from Consulting 101. When presenting to an audience, structured communications can be the difference between success and failure. Make sure you recognize the importance of the following:

- **Addressing: What is the point?**—This is not about being concise in delivering the content but rather understanding why this topic is relevant to the audience and how to convey that through the presentation.

- **Answering: Why do I care?**—This is not about why the audience should care about listening to you specifically but, more important, why this topic or content matters.
- **Narrowing down to the key message:** In a slide presentation, what key points should the audience learn before moving to the next slide?

Structured communication can be a game-changer for a procurement professional. It ensures that key stakeholders, such as suppliers, internal teams, and executives, clearly understand procurement decisions, strategies, and needs. For example, when communicating the result of a sourcing decision, try starting with a recommendation and providing the details to support that recommendation, such as cost-benefit analysis, supplier performance, and risk assessment. For more complicated information, begin with the context, outline the problem statement, and conclude with the solution or recommendation. Structured communications is a tool the procurement team can use to tailor a message to the right audience and present information in a clear, logical, and efficient manner, making it easier for that audience to understand, remember, and act on.

Design Thinking

This technique is more than creative problem-solving. Unlike the agile approach, which is a creative way to solve a problem, design thinking is an innovative way to find the problem. It is an iterative process with the end user (customer) prioritized above all else, openly challenging assumptions and continuously redesigning the nature of the business problem. This nonlinear process removes failures before entering a testing phase. It thrives on engagement with a diverse group of thinkers who lead with curiosity and have a high degree of empathy in understanding the end user (customer). This approach is not about taking and improving what is there; it is about wiping away what is already created to avoid unnecessary bias. The result will create a minimally viable solution to expand and build upon in the next iteration (see Figure 10.3).

Applying design thinking in procurement allows for a more user-centered approach, addressing stakeholder needs, enhancing supplier relationships, and improving procurement processes. For example, if there are issues with an existing supplier regarding a process created years ago, instead of making a few adjustments that may provide a

Figure 10.3 Principals of design thinking (*Source*: jetir.org, July 2023, Volume 10, Issue 7)

short-term fix, reconsider the process from end to end to meet current needs. Things are constantly changing; do not assume what worked well years ago will work today. Using design thinking goes beyond cost and efficiency to foster a partnership with suppliers, ensuring long-term value and adaptability.

Section III

Reshaping the Organization

CHAPTER 11

CULTURAL CONSIDERATIONS

IMPORTANCE OF CULTURE

Historically, the most common framework for a successful digital transformation has been the right combination of people, processes, and technology. Around 2015, I added a fourth component—compliance—to emphasize that the three core areas could not bring actual value-based outcomes without compliance. Over time, more elements, such as change management and culture, were added to this framework to strengthen that foundation. Let's use a picture of a chair to illustrate this better. The primary pillars (or legs) holding everything up are people, processes, technology, and compliance. The seat of the chair, which connects the four legs, is change management. And finally, the back of the chair represents culture, which ensures you do not fall backward.

Culture minimizes the chance of returning to past behaviors and reduces the possibility of revisiting the same mistakes. It shapes how we work with each other and provides the guiding principles required to make good decisions in the workplace. Ultimately, culture acts as an influence, and the right culture fosters the right amount of influence and impacts how we make the best decisions for ourselves, our coworkers, the project (or activity) we are currently working on, and the company we work for (see Figure 11.1).

Unlike change management, which did some good in increasing sporadic value, culture has never gained any real visibility or risen to any level of priority in transformation programs for procurement organizations. It is not part of the conversation and is rarely considered a vital part of the effort.

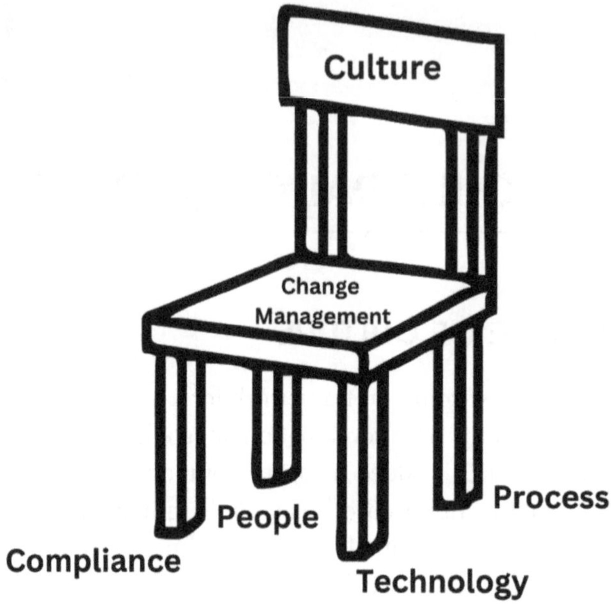

Figure 11.1 Culture supports the organization from falling backward

CULTURAL IMPACT ON THE PROCUREMENT ORGANIZATION

According to Wikipedia, "culture is a word for the *way of life* of groups of people . . . in the way they do things. A culture is passed on to the next generation by learning"; as stated in definitions.net, culture is "the attitudes and behavior that are characteristic of a particular social group or organization"; and as noted by achievers.com, organizational culture is "the collection of values, expectations, and practices that guide and inform the actions of all team members."

Culture is about patterns of behavior that become accepted over time. These patterns may be evident to some, but often, they are unconscious or unnoticeable. Initially, culture may start with written rules or policies, but over time, the organization's culture drifts further away from what was written to reflect more of its current state.

You may recall the example of an oil-and-gas organization from Chapter 4, where the enterprise culture of safety was infused into the organization, with one person volunteering a safety moment at the beginning of each meeting. For new hires, this may seem unusual at first. New hires will take a back seat, listening but not contributing. Over time, they start to notice potential safety moments outside of work and become more comfortable volunteering during a meeting. This level of comfort in accepting the corporate culture is because it is shared across groups and repeated over and over. It is learned through the observance by the next generation or, in this example, by the new hire. This process strengthens the values of the organization by reinforcing them. The same approach can be just as effective for negative behavior that strays away from the original values. Negative behaviors, when left unchecked and allowed to repeat, can have a negative impact on how employees interact with each other, how information moves, and how innovation is fostered throughout the organization.

To assume the procurement organization is part of the larger organizational culture is no longer an accurate assessment. Procurement organizations continue to grow. Some have more resources than the marketing and legal departments combined, while others have grown to include more than 2,300 resources worldwide. To illustrate, the procurement organization for a global consumer and retail company can include all the following but are certainly not limited to:

- Standard indirect categories: temporary services, professional services, capital expenditures, travel, human resources, facilities
- A more unified procurement organization will also cover information technology (IT) and peripherals, utilities, telecom, rents and leases, real estate, plastic cards (credit or gift cards)
- Additionally, procurement organizations are absorbing other categories such as packaging (foam, film, air pillows) and corrugated boxes
- Some chief procurement officers also oversee direct categories, such as chemicals; maintenance, repair, and operations; raw materials; equipment; and items for reselling (pumps, valves, containers)

Regardless of the sourcing categories covered, a procurement organization will also include resources devoted to the following:

- Procurement operations, systems, processes, and governance
- Reporting and analytics
- Change management and communications
- Supplier management (supplier onboarding, supplier performance, supplier diversity)
- Supplier risk

Finally, some modern-day procurement organizations also absorb aspects of the supply chain. For these organizations with a single individual acting as a chief procurement and supply chain officer, 2,000 global resources are no longer an outlier. While this example represents a small percentage, seeing a procurement organization with more than 300 resources is becoming more common.

> The larger the procurement organization, the more culture becomes critical to sustainable success.

Just how impactful is culture? In my experience, developing standard processes enables you to achieve approximately 50 percent of the intended goals of a project or initiative, and leveraging technology will take you to around 80 percent. Change management helps to ensure short-term adoption, but a strong culture will take you over the finish line. In addition, an established culture will keep early achievements in place and allow success well into the future.

> ***Real-world scenario:*** *A major U.S. company was approaching its third transformation in 17 years. As resources were interviewed within the procurement organization and compared to the interviews of resources outside the procurement organization, there was a huge disconnect. It was quite puzzling to hear that the procurement organization was perceived as a silo away from the rest of the enterprise. In other words, the other parts of the*

organization felt the procurement organization and its resources were doing their own thing.

Over the years, it has become common to hear discussions on LinkedIn and at conferences about how the organization is working in silos and the challenges the procurement organization has in navigating these silos. However, it is also very possible that the procurement organization should pause to consider that they may also be contributing to the negative perception of working in silos.

> Where change management supports short-term user adoption, culture leads to sustainable adoption and long-term success.

CONSIDERATIONS FOR THE MODERN PROCUREMENT ORGANIZATION

When resources are allowed to safely consider the *why-not* question, they are empowered to look at existing problems and processes in a new way and have ownership in voicing alternatives. The word *safely* is used here for a specific purpose. Safely considering the why-not question means the organization is comfortable with questions being asked, ideas probed, and open and honest discussions. Over time, when established as a cultural norm, the organization will foster more innovative ideas. Resources will no longer feel it is necessary to follow a 20-year-old process without value to procurement or its stakeholders.

Change to organizational culture does not happen overnight, and your procurement organization may be further along in some areas than others. It is okay to pick one or two concepts with intentional focus rather than trying to deploy all the strategies simultaneously with little or no focus. One option to start this process is to bring the following cultural considerations to your team members and ask them to vote on the top two priorities to launch over the next six months. Be mindful if you have a global team; for example, priorities for U.S. resources may significantly differ from those of your overseas resources.

Be Aggressive in Knowing Your Stakeholder

The stakeholder is the consumer of services and products from the procurement organization. *Knowing* your stakeholders involves listening to what they say and using that information to improve the relationship. This also fosters adjustments in how procurement professionals interact and collaborate with stakeholders in the future. Start small by trying out one or more of these ideas or use these as inspiration to develop your own ideas. The point is to listen only. Do not use this time to propose a solution. Instead, use it to understand their business challenges and why comments are considered pain points. If you walk into this discussion with your predetermined ideas (because sometimes this happens), use this time to ask specific questions that may steer your predefined ideas from one direction to another.

> If you are not obsessing over the stakeholder, you increase the opportunity of failure.

Ultimately, the goal is for the stakeholder, not you, to talk the most:

1. **Virtual open doors (dial-in):** Similar to an open-door policy with your manager, this is a monthly open-door dial-in for anyone who wants to ask questions or provide feedback. This can also be an opportunity to quickly gauge what is working and not working. Additionally, this time can be used to demonstrate an application feature that is already available to resolve their issue. Facilitators can be rotated among procurement resources. The facilitator's responsibility is to slow down the conversation so the issue voiced by the stakeholder can be drilled down into a root cause. If the company is not using a third-party automated note taker (yes, this does exist), then a second resource should also be included to help take notes. The facilitator should not be a junior-level resource but someone who can thoughtfully probe

the initial comments to understand the real business challenge. Of course, no one will attend if they are unaware, so consider contacting corporate communications to see what options are available to market these events.

2. **Online form for ideas:** Not all stakeholders may be comfortable verbally communicating their frustrations or talking about what is not working for them in front of stakeholders they do not know. Having an online form for any stakeholder is also a good method to acquire and indirectly consolidate your stakeholders' feedback. When creating the form, include a space (at minimum) for the stakeholder to capture the problem—the description of the problem and what was happening when the problem occurred—along with their thoughts on how to solve it.
3. **Listening tour:** This is the most time-consuming but will have the most immediate impact. A listening tour (in-person or virtually) is coordinating time across all your stakeholders to genuinely *listen* to them. The best approach is to identify a business unit and invite anywhere from three to six representatives from that business unit to participate as a team in a 90-minute call. It is important to select the business unit resources who may have been the most vocal in the past or are executing specific processes repeatedly. It works favorably when all of them are on the same call, which generates more meaningful discussion as they hear each other's questions and ideas.

Culture—Virtually

Because of the COVID-19 pandemic, the concept of developing culture in the workplace across virtual global resources became more challenging. Yet, culture is even more critical virtually than if the team is meeting in person. The following list includes a few ideas for getting started. Start small by trying out one or more of these ideas or use them for inspiration to develop your own, but always engage your team to get their ideas:

1. **Realign the definition of success:** As the world emerges from the pandemic, leadership has pivoted from *working from home* to *back to the office* to a *hybrid model*. Based on these constraints, employees may have a different definition of what it means to be successful. The question is whether leadership thinks about this as they outline the working relationship between the employee and the company.

   The success of the company is directly related to the employees' success. Now is the best opportunity for a company to rethink what success will look like in one, three, and five years from now. As waves of disruption are expected to occur more frequently, combined with ongoing talent shortages, there will never be a perfect time to think about these things. Take the time now to pause and understand where the company is going. How will the company remain competitive, and how will those core competencies change over time? Once leadership understands this more fully, they can outline what success will look like for their employees and, only then, outline what a working environment looks like.
2. **Refine employee onboarding:** The onboarding process generally begins one to two weeks before the employee's start date. Before 2020, when an employee was hired, they would travel to a nearby city to participate in one or two days of onboarding meetings to learn more about the company and their benefits, pick up a laptop, and work with an IT professional to get everything set up. As of 2023, this process has primarily become fully remote, with access to IT professionals via Slack (after you set up your laptop) and to pages of links to read about benefits, set up an expense profile, and watch videos to create a time sheet. It is unrealistic for a new employee to complete all those tasks virtually, ask questions, understand the answers, and contribute on their first full workday. Executives who believe two days is enough time for successful onboarding are usually the ones who have yet to go through a new hire process since the world went virtual.

For some companies, the future workplace will be a hybrid experience, but the new hire onboarding process remains virtual. The following list includes a few examples of new-hire feedback that would support a smoother onboarding process, reduce stress and anxiety, and, more important, keep your new hire from quitting after week two:

- Set up open Zoom calls for new hires with an IT person. Do not expect the employee to begin setting up their laptop on the weekend or assume they will successfully select the right options.
- Allocate specific times for *onboarding support* so that new hires have daily opportunities to ask questions. Slack is a great way to ask questions, but solving a technical problem in the same format can be challenging.
- Do not expect the new hire to be ready for work in two days. Asking questions via Slack is good, but expecting them to wait three hours for a necessary response before they can move on to the next step in their onboarding process is unrealistic.
- Provide a clear checklist outlining activities to be completed properly with the correct dependencies. For example, if task five needs to be completed before task three, then modify the order of the checklist to minimize rework and further delays. A digital checklist can have links to jump to the right location on the intranet site quickly. Still, it also allows them to check which tasks they have started digitally, are in process, or have been completed, which is extremely helpful. For example, I witnessed a digital checklist with different daily activities over 10 days. If the new hire did not complete a task on Day 1, it was automatically moved and combined with the tasks on Day 2. This continued to occur and resulted in a skewed understanding of task dependencies. The only way this new hire understood what to complete was to wait for an email from HR letting them know they were out of compliance with their new hire task.

3. **Rethink onboarding support personnel:** In some companies, usually between weeks three and eight from the new hire's start date, a new hire is assigned someone to help them become more familiar with the company. It was once known as the buddy system, but that nomenclature was not always accurate, depending on which employee you were assigned to. Sometimes, the assignment was with an employee who understood the company, while other times, the assignment was with an employee who was very chatty but could not provide valuable information about navigating the company virtually. Still, other times, the employee assigned was only there to provide tactical support around time sheets, to provide an overview of department policies, or just to be available when you think you need them. To get real value out of this support system, some thought should go into the level of the new hire, their roles, responsibilities, and what kind of support they need to be successful in the first three months.

    - Ask for volunteers who have gone through the virtual onboarding process but have also been with the company for at least two years. Provide a one-hour kickoff for the onboarding volunteers. Use this time to provide a refresher on company-wide changes that will impact the new hire and, more important, create consistency across new hires.
    - Allocate weekly time to discuss work-related and non-work-related topics. Remember, the new hire is losing some of that social connection they usually experience when working on-site in an office or with a team at a client site.
    - Add new hires from the same geographic region together on a separate Slack channel. This encourages knowledge sharing and provides an instant network for people who share a similar experience. This connection improves a sense of belonging and reduces the feelings of being *left out* or sitting alone in their home office for three hours waiting for IT to reply to their Slack question.

4. **Adjust team-building activities and recognition:**
   - Consider specific Slack channels for different needs, such as *watercooler* channels for random things folks talked about when they were in person, such as when they were in the kitchen getting coffee, or perhaps a *needs and leads* channel where new hires can ask coworkers for advice.
   - Figure out ways to reinvent cultural norms. If your team established a routine of having coffee or doughnuts every other Friday, this can still be accomplished remotely during a Zoom call. Managers can send gift cards to a local coffee or pastry shop. Additionally, block time on calendars for the team to purchase those pastries and then return to a Zoom call for a social visit.
   - Recognition does not have to be a physical award with a high price tag. On a prior engagement, the team created one-of-a-kind certifications and recognitions, showing that we *saw* each other for who we were. For example, I could make a personalized recognition in a few minutes using online certificate templates; one team member received the *Umbrella Award* for always being there for other team members.

Rethink Accountability

Let's start with the statement that the RACI chart is outdated. RACI stands for responsible, accountable, consulted, and informed. It was introduced in the 1950s as the RACI Matrix or Decision Rights Matrix. In the 1970s, the term Responsibility Assignment Matrix was used to reference RACI. A recurring theme in this book is that the older policies and processes introduced decades ago do not work for a modern-day procurement organization or for the procurement organization of the future. That theme certainly applies here, with a responsibility matrix introduced over 70 years ago.

The original intent of RACI was to align responsibilities across multiple departments that were working in silos. RACI requires one person to be identified as accountable for each task or activity. The challenge with RACI is that it:

- Assumes one person is accountable only (i.e., individual accountability) and that decisions are made individually instead of as a collaborative team
- Is super focused on accountability of tasks rather than focusing on outcomes
- Tends to encourage individualism
- Assumes the organization is working in silos and not talking to each other

A high-performing team will take ownership in working together to develop and execute solutions for business challenges rather than focusing on who is doing what task and whether they should be accountable or responsible.

What Is Accountability?

Accountability is taking ownership of the results of one's actions and decisions. Individuals can commit to delivering a desired outcome; they must also be accountable for how their choices and actions (good or bad) affect their ability to meet their commitment. Additionally, suppose the commitment is part of a larger group or process. In that case, individuals must be accountable for their decisions and actions (good or bad) and how they impact their part of the process and potentially other resources (good or bad). Accountability recognizes that some things can be controlled, and some will fall outside their control (see Figure 11.2).

To illustrate, suppose an individual committed to participate as a nonprofit board member. Shortly afterward, this individual experienced a personal health challenge and could no longer continue in that role. Accountability in this scenario occurred when the individual accepted that the health challenge was outside of their control and that remaining on the board would have a negative impact on the other board members. In other words, it was better to leave the board than have others depend on this individual who would fail to meet the commitment.

Figure 11.2 The weight of accountability

Look at that example in reverse. What if the individual decided to remain but missed multiple meetings, could not meet deadlines, and consistently communicated excuses? This ultimately hurts the commitments of other board members to achieve their obligations. In this scenario, it is reasonable to think the board members were sympathetic to the individual's health challenges and provided some flexibility. However, if the situation does not change, at some point, it will lead to friction. The individual would most likely be asked to take some time off, and if that did not happen, they would probably be voted out.

Accountability in the Office

Henry Evans, the author of *Winning with Accountability*, says accountability is "clear commitments that, in the eyes of others, have been kept." As mentioned previously, part of being accountable includes how the individual communicates with others about their accountability. For accountability to be effective:

1. Clear roles and responsibilities must be outlined and understood by all.
2. Communicating commitment to other team members is essential. Saying it aloud to yourself and other team members makes the commitment more real.
3. Creating opportunities to review updates, including successes and where help is needed, is important.
4. Remember to lead by example. Take opportunities for team members to hear examples of how others held themselves accountable.
5. Clear expectations must be managed. Avoid using terms that may mean different things to different team members. Do not assume everyone is on the same page. For example, the phrase *agile mindset* may have a different meaning to you than someone else on your team and may even be defined completely differently in another department or business unit.

Cultivate Talent with Purpose

Funding for education, training, and opportunities to attend conferences has decreased yearly. In some organizations, funding is no longer available. Employees must pay their own travel expenses and conference registration fees. Other companies expect employees to use their vacation days when attending in-person conferences. Yet, one of the top five challenges for today's organizations is around talent—either a lack of finding skilled talent or a lack of providing skills to existing talent.

> If upskilling users is critical to the organization, why are education and training not higher priorities.

Cultivating talent with purpose means pausing to understand where your company is going, how your organization will support the larger enterprise goal, and what skills are required to meet those goals; that is, the skills needed today and an understanding of the skills needed for the future. To succeed, the organization requires the right talent at the right time with the rights skill set. Perfecting the timing of these factors so they all come together for the greatest impact is not an easy task. Primary skills can be divided into two major groups: what is needed now and what is needed in the future. These skills may include understanding AI technologies, data literacy, giving presentations, public speaking, etc. For example, paying for courses in change management is a great idea. Unfortunately, the content may be forgotten if the resource does not use these newly acquired skills within two to three months of completing the course. It will not provide substantial value to the resource or the procurement organization.

Before you can determine what skills are needed in the future, a detailed understanding of current skills is essential and should be updated yearly. Once you have a clear outline of the current state and current organization, compare that against the future view of the organization, which will highlight the gaps in skills you need to fill on your team.

One method to collecting skill-gap information starts with creating a spreadsheet of the required skill types. This may include strategic sourcing, category expertise, supplier performance, supplier management, reporting, data and analytics, or contracts. Add a level for each area, such as beginner, proficient, competent, and advanced. Providing a clear definition of each level will improve the quality of the data collected. For example:

- **Beginner/novice:** An individual who has no knowledge or who took a course in this subject over six months ago.
- **Proficient:** An individual who may have some experience demonstrating the skills in question and has less than two years of hands-on experience and/or has worked on *X* number of projects. This individual requires support from another to complete the work required.
- **Competent:** An individual with more than two years of experience and/or worked on *X* number of projects. This individual does not need support from another to complete the required work.
- **Advanced:** An individual who is comfortable teaching or has taught this skill to others.

Topic	Coaching	Mentoring
Timeframe	Relationship is more likely to be *short term* (up to 6 months or 1 year) with a specific outcome in mind. However, some coaching relationships can last longer, depending on the goals achieved.	Relationship tends to be more *long term*, lasting a year or two, and even longer.
Focus	Coaching is more *performance-driven and* designed to improve the professional's on-the-job performance.	Mentoring is more *development-driven,* looking not just at the professional's current job function but beyond, taking a more holistic approach to career development.
Structure	Traditionally more *structured,* with regularly scheduled meetings, like weekly, bi-weekly, or monthly.	Generally, meetings tend to be more informal, on an as-needed basis, required by the mentee.
Expertise	Coaches are hired for their *expertise* in a given area, one in which the coachee desires improvement. Examples: Presentation skills, leadership, interpersonal communication, sales.	Within organization mentoring programs, mentors have more *seniority and expertise* in a specific area than mentees. The mentee learns from and is inspired by the mentor's experience.
Agenda	The coaching agenda is *co-created by the coach and the coachee* to meet the specific needs of the coachee.	The mentoring agenda is *set by the mentee*. The mentor supports that agenda.
Questioning	*Asking thought-provoking questions is a top tool for the coach, as it helps the coachee make important decisions, recognize behavioral changes,* and take action.	In the mentoring relationship, *the mentee is more likely to ask more questions*, tapping into the mentor's expertise.
Outcomes	Outcomes from a coaching agreement are *specific and measurable,* showing signs of improvement or positive change in the desired performance area.	Outcomes from a mentoring relationship can shift and change over time. There is less interest in specific, measurable results or changed behavior and *more interest in the overall development of the mentee.*

Figure 11.3 Comparison: coaching versus mentoring (*Credit*: Christine W. Zust, M.A.)

Adding a resource's role with the organization will strengthen the results. For example, the survey may show that many resources are lacking in project management when only a few of those resources are required to have project management skills in their current roles. Once the information is collected, creating reports and charts will provide the first step to understanding what types of skills should receive priority. Remember, cultivating talent is more than just learning a new skill; it should also be supported in other ways, such as allyship programs, mentoring, and coaching (see Figure 11.3).

CHAPTER 12

VALUE IN PROCUREMENT

WHAT IS VALUE?

The definition of value can differ across industries and organizations and often across each business group in the same organization. It just depends on which lens you are looking through. For example, Thomas Burola wrote an article in June 2023 for the digital magazine *Medium* stating that: "Value for money in procurement means achieving a desired outcome at the best possible price, based on a balanced judgment of financial and non-financial factors. It also means not overpaying beyond what an informed participant would agree is an economically fair price for the supplier."

Consider this variation of that definition: "Value for the procurement organization is about more than price. It is not about minimizing cost or finding the cheapest supplier; it is about what provides the most significant benefit for the organization." This is a balancing act of the outcomes of purchasing goods and services. Depending on the organization, this may include but is not limited to, the quality of the goods or services, working with an innovative supplier, reducing risk, and increasing capabilities concerning sustainability. Ultimately, this means coupling procurement actions against short- and long-term corporate strategic goals.

Aavenir, a source-to-pay application provider founded in 2019, shares on its website that "procurement value in purely economic terms is about more bang for the buck, where *bang* is the utility the business gets from supplier products/services, divided by the dollars (i.e., spend), which then decomposes to activity versus cost, and then cost decomposes again down to price and nonprice costs."

The French procurement software application provider Ivalua, founded in 2000, says on its website that "procurement value, in economic terms, is a metric that assesses the efficiency and effectiveness of the resources invested in acquiring goods or services. This concept is broken down into several components, starting with the utility derived from supplier products or services and divided by the overall expenditure."

Another definition is illustrated by KPMG's website, which references value in a case study: ". . . the integrated company needed a way to embed controls, improve compliance, increase spend visibility, and drive savings globally. The focus was on unlocking overlooked value within indirect procurement in a controlled manner, without disrupting day-to-day operations."

After reviewing websites, talking with chief procurement officers (CPOs) and executive leadership, reading studies, and analyzing my experiences in procurement, I realized that they have one thing in common: value is defined when something has greater weight than something else for that company. The definition of value will differ for suppliers, consulting firms, and companies. There can also be differences in how value is defined between executive leadership and employees of the same company.

A company may define value by expanding its market share into Brazil or deciding to deploy an existing application to its internal users in Asia Pacific. The definition of value can differ when working with innovative suppliers or improving customer experience. This is balanced by evaluating the effort needed to achieve a desired outcome and whether it was worth it. The results of that evaluation show why the definition of value has different meanings across different companies and various projects in the same company. Translating that to the procurement organization, value will need to align with the company's larger goals. Value is an outcome that delivers measurable and actionable benefits, aligns with the short- and long-term strategic corporate goals, and is sustainable. This means that value can be defined in various ways, both tangible and intangible. In the 1950s, value was determined mainly by how much an item cost compared to how much we paid. If the item was one dollar but we ended up paying 95 cents, the value was defined as saving five cents.

Today, value has evolved into more than strictly cost savings. Studies have documented, and companies have proven, that cost alone is not the only factor supporting real value. It can also include utilizing alternative sources in supply, mitigating supply chain risks, building strategic partnerships with suppliers to reduce product packaging, and working with manufacturers to find a way to reduce product costs. These can directly align with the company's strategic goals, primarily driven by what is defined as valuable. There is a clear cause and effect between the role of procurement and corporate strategic goals.

Value has also expanded to include process improvements and efficiencies that, when executed correctly, give employees more time to focus on the direct activities listed in the previous paragraph. For example, if processes improve, employees will have more time to focus on alternative sources of supply, which directly supports the goals outlined by executive leadership to expand market share, improve profitability, and remain competitive within a specific industry.

When considering metrics and actions that lead to increased value, exceptional procurement organizations consistently focus on two common items: total cost of ownership (TCO) and supplier relationship management (SRM).

Total Cost of Ownership

TCO is the comprehensive assessment of all (total) costs associated with purchasing, operating, and maintaining a product or service over its entire life cycle, not just considering the cost at the point when the purchase is made. The phrase *life cycle* starts from the point in time someone (also known as a supplier) wants to buy a product or service to the point in time when the contract or the relationship with that supplier has ended and, where applicable, items are correctly disposed of, recycled, or a final decision is made to no longer engage with that supplier.

Most organizations are adamant about following this approach. For example, they consider all costs associated with purchasing an item, including the price of the item, along with tax, tariffs, shipping, fees, penalties, switching, etc. This narrow definition stops once the item is purchased. What about the cost of maintenance fees or the time it may take to customize or develop an application to meet future requirements? Also, it may not consider the expenses required to dispose of an item correctly.

Organizations can make better decisions that reduce long-term expenses by considering *all* cost variables and future scenarios. Often overlooked is evaluating the company's long-term goals and integrating them into TCO. For example, suppose the company wants to focus on acquisitions to gain market share more quickly or prioritize collaboration and innovation with suppliers. Each of these scenarios will change how TCO is evaluated and the types of questions that should be asked when evaluating TCO. Consider a company that purchases a cloud-based procurement application to be deployed globally. The company determines that improving the internal user experience is more valuable than improving the external supplier's experience, giving more weight to the user experience than the supplier experience. This decision directly impacts the outcomes of the key decisions required during the application project's design phase. Specifically, the answers to the design decisions will change because the internal user experience has been given more value over the external supplier experience.

One example is the supplier registration onboarding process. The project team will face many decisions regarding how to simplify/automate this process. The results of those decisions can favor the internal users over the supplier. This could mean the supplier has more steps to complete, reducing the overall effort for the internal user.

Supplier Relationship Management

SRM strategically manages the interactions with suppliers who provide goods and services to an organization to achieve greater value. Strong relationships with suppliers can lead to better pricing, improved quality, increased innovation, and reduced risk. This allows organizations to collaborate more effectively with suppliers, which is critical to ensuring supply chain reliability and securing long-term value.

As much as companies claim they are doing this by pointing to a dedicated supplier management team or sharing "a robust and comprehensive annual plan for their top 30 global suppliers," this has become another box to check. A closer look at this robust plan is a meeting with suppliers every six or 12 months to review how they managed against the key performance indicators in the contract. The meeting may include feedback on an internal scorecard and outline the company's issues with the supplier. The scorecard may consist of quantitative and qualitative inputs. Still, it rarely provides real insights to improve the supplier relationship, or the insights are outdated, and the opportunity to make a difference was several months before the annual review.

If the supplier is an application provider, there will be a discussion about the product roadmap and how well it meets the company's enhancement requests. The supplier may use this time to provide an update on their plans to open a location near one of the company's plants. Some companies document action items to consider before the next supplier meeting, but these items often go unchallenged, meaning there is no enforcement of consequences.

The actual value of effective SRM is limited because of fragmented communications, the inability to effectively harness suppliers for valuable insights, the prioritization of short-term gains over long-term partnerships, and the delays in waiting for a specific time to talk about the value each could bring to the other. SRM is not about checking in with suppliers once every six to 12 months; it is important to understand whether that supplier is continuing to meet or exceed the match between what the company sees as value and how that supplier is helping to support it.

SRM must include the company's values to be effective. For example, if the company values minimizing disruption to external customers, it doesn't matter if the project team determines that the supplier delivered the design documentation on time. That has no overall value to the company. What matters is what the supplier is doing to ensure future disruptions have minimal impacts on the company. Discussions with the supplier should include how value is defined for the company, how the supplier can assist the company in achieving value, and actionable steps the supplier can take until the next review.

Value-Based Outcomes

It is important to tie *value* (saving money, improving processes, etc.) with the *values* (being first to market, innovation, lowering product costs, improving sustainability, etc.) a company wants to achieve. This is often accomplished through the support of a procurement department that is in lockstep with the values of the overall organization:

1. **Cost optimization:** This differs from finding the lowest-cost supplier and focuses more on the TCO across the entire supplier life cycle. A well-known example is Toyota's use of the just-in-time methodology, which aims to reduce inventory holding costs and ensure that production components are delivered where they need to be when they are required. When introduced in the 1970s, it revolutionized the automobile industry by minimizing inventory and increasing efficiency.
2. **Innovation:** Innovation between the company and the supplier must continue. Apple's partnership with its chip manufacturers to develop custom silicon chips to improve product performance and gain a technological advantage is a terrific example. Not all companies value innovation heavily, while others cannot remain competitive unless they constantly innovate.
3. **Risk:** While it is essential to identify risk, how and what actions to take when that risk is identified are often more critical. An excellent example is how companies pivoted during the COVID-19 pandemic, which was unprecedented in magnitude and presented a delicate situation regarding the global supply chain footprint. Beyond understanding risk thresholds, it was necessary to develop a playbook detailing the actions to find alternate suppliers and reduce overall supply risk.
4. **Sustainability and ethical sourcing:** While this has been important for many years, it has only recently become more valuable for companies as they look to keep or regain customer loyalty. Achieving these value-based outcomes did not usually originate internally with executive leadership. They were driven by consumer demand and what consumers believed to be valuable. A good example is Ikea, which has been vocal in its commitment to sourcing 100 percent of cotton and wood from sustainable sources. This means the wood used in their products is not from a tree that took 50 years to mature but rather from forests that grow quickly.

5. **Agility or flexibility:** If a company values its ability to pivot and respond quickly to the demands of its customers, then flexibility will be its focus with the procurement organization in support. Collaborating with suppliers who can match this value will be a priority. However, this is not easy to accomplish. Internally, this requires harmonizing technology, culture, leadership, and process. Externally, this requires suppliers with the same value to prioritize their investments to ensure they match. One great example is Avon, a cosmetics company that relies on an agile supply chain. Their digital catalogs update every two weeks to add and subtract items. This cannot be achieved without a procurement department that can respond to customer preferences while minimizing overstock.
6. **Supplier diversity:** Supplier diversity means spending company dollars with organizations predominantly owned by women or minorities. Some companies have expanded the definition to include businesses that are owned by veterans and people in the LGBTQ+ community. In the United States, supplier diversity, similar to ethical sourcing, is a company value driven externally by the customers they aim to serve. Most customers prefer to do business with companies that work with and buy from diverse suppliers. However, there is a chance that the company only mimics the values of its customers and does not truly believe in them. In that case, it will never prioritize those values. It will end up with a supplier diversity program in name only with policies that require the invitation of one diverse supplier per request for proposal regardless of whether they qualify. Some great companies that truly believe in the value of supplier diversity are part of the Billion Dollar Roundtable (BDR). This is an exclusive group of firms that spend one billion dollars annually with diverse suppliers. In 2023, $122 billion was spent with diverse suppliers across BDR members. By August 2024, 11 more companies had been inducted into its membership, totaling 43 companies.
7. **Compliance and regulatory values:** Companies that value compliance with laws and regulations to reduce legal and financial

risk are in this category. Financial institutions, chemical producers, and healthcare providers most often value compliance over everything else. When looking at their procurement and supply chain organizations, evaluating risk is embedded in every decision, especially around product safety, shipping volatile chemicals, and reducing product recalls. Their procurement processes may include strict supplier auditing, certifications, and tighter coupling with the internal controls department.

8. **Brand reputation:** When a company values its brand, procurement strategies can be leveraged to improve its reputation in many areas, including fair trade and corporate social responsibility. While this value also originates from outside the organization, it does require the company to make decisions that hold themselves responsible and accountable for environmental, ethical, philanthropic, and economic impacts. This may lead the procurement department to work with suppliers whose products are neutral on greenhouse gases (environmental) or to not purchase from suppliers who use child or slave labor (ethical). Starbucks is an excellent example of this. It actively develops a supply chain that provides farmers equitable access to generating revenue by working directly with Starbucks. Instead of Starbucks working with a middleman, it builds facilities in that country to ensure local farmers are not cut out of profits. This investment from Starbucks aims to improve the lives of the farmers and local community members where they source coffee beans. This not only aligns with their brand's ethos, but also strengthens the customer relationship and improves customer trust and loyalty.

KNOW YOUR VALUE(S)

Many companies do not have a clear view of *what they want to be when they grow up*, or as the company's strategic direction changes, how does value change along with it. Consider a retail company founded in the 1990s that produced hemp-made T-shirts. The company-defined value in the 1990s may have been linked to growing revenue. In 2000, the value changed to expanding market share. In the following decade, the value shifted again to supply chain integration. In the next decade, the value was defined as product diversification and, again, 10 years later, environmental impact. Each time, the company chose to put more weight on one thing over another, and each time value was redefined, the company had to shift to support those values.

What if this same company did not redefine value when it needed to? Instead, its executives considered the company's value to be growing revenue and market share because that is what the company has been focused on for the past 30 years. The procurement organization would prioritize supplier relationships differently, retain key performance indicators that didn't change over time, and let opportunities slip by. This sets up the company for failure. Executives will either continue to support the values they were introduced to or decide the values are outdated and follow values they believe are more aligned with the current market. The employees receive inconsistent messaging from leadership and stretch themselves too thin trying to support everything, which leads to accomplishing nothing.

Companies that enjoy long-term sustainable success do so because they know who they are. They understand what they do as a company and can articulate their identity. They know who they want to be and why, which translates to what is valuable.

The executive board should reevaluate its strategic direction every two years. During this time, it reassesses its short-term objectives, which can also revise the organization's definition of what it holds as having the most significant value. If the procurement organization is not aligned with or aware of these changes, no matter how slight, it may focus its funds and resources in conflict with the rest of the organization.

> Realigning with the company's value should occur every two years.

The value defined by the procurement organization must align with the value defined at the executive level. If we consider the earlier example where the internal users hold more value to the company than the external supplier, then providing value to the internal user will ultimately prove the value of the procurement organization. This will lead to increased collaboration and raise the influence of the procurement organization. Measuring value is essential not just the first time you work with an internal user but every time. It is recommended to start small and expand rather than go big and lose credibility. To begin, consider the user's point of view and understand what is valuable from their perspective when working with procurement. Select the ones that align best with the company's values from those responses.

From that final list, start by focusing on one key area, such as how long it takes for the procurement organization to respond to a request. Specifically, what is the total cycle time from when a request is received to when it is completed? Select two to three of the most common types of requests. After defining the metrics, the next step is documenting how they should be calculated and identifying the required data fields. Finally, discover where that data resides and whether you can access it. If there is no data to support that metric, consider an alternative metric or recognize that this may not be something you can currently track.

Once value and relevant assumptions are defined, review them with the users you work directly with (also known as your stakeholders). By including your stakeholders in the conversation, you create an accountability partnership. Procurement is a central organization supporting all business groups. It should not be solely accountable; this is a shared responsibility because procurement and the business group own the successes and failures. There has been a long-standing gap in how procurement creates sustainable relationships with its stakeholders.

Next, use cases should be prioritized to determine where funds and resources should be focused. This step will validate the purpose and allow traceability of how decisions were made. Consider a matrix by looking at the following:

- Value
- Level of effort/time (some activities may be dependent on other activities)
- Cost
- Ease of execution (this may include technology and impact on users)

- Dependencies across other use cases
- Resource availability

These six variables can provide enough information to score the use cases and determine the sequencing and order in which they can be started. They can be layered on the roadmap to visually see what can be completed in the short term versus what can be started in parallel but have a longer lead time to complete. This methodology works because as new use cases are added, they can be evaluated and prioritized against others already in the process and queue.

When communicating with a stakeholder, certain activities may suddenly fall off the priority list; it is a lot easier when you have a consistent approach applied equally to everyone. This also works as the type of use case or activity changes over time. Remember, the organization refines its definition of value about every two years. When that occurs, the categories included in what is considered value will fluctuate as needed. There should be no need to overhaul the entire approach every two years. If that happens, the foundational methodology was built incorrectly.

The following list shares some examples of how value can be connected to specific metrics:

1. **Supplier performance:** This can be evaluated by monitoring delivery times, quality levels, and responsiveness to customer needs. Additional metrics may include the value of how proactive the supplier is in bringing potential risks to the procurement organization. More recently, as environmental, social, and governance criteria have become more popular, this could also involve evaluating how and where the supplier uses nonrecyclable materials in products sold to your organization. Monitoring performance has expanded into a significant enough activity that most procurement organizations have a dedicated group for this activity. It helps ensure internal stakeholders receive high-quality goods and services on time, thus improving productivity and reducing downtime.
2. **Risk management:** This involves the ability to identify and mitigate supply chain risks, such as supplier financial instability,

natural disasters, and compliance issues. A procurement organization that effectively manages risk can help protect the company from potential losses and disruptions and ensure business continuity.

3. **Innovation:** Procurement has been more involved in driving innovation in the supply chain by collaborating with suppliers to develop new products, processes, and technologies. This can improve product performance, reduce costs, and enhance customer satisfaction. A procurement organization encouraging innovation can help the company stay ahead of the competition.
4. **Process efficiency:** Procurement can redesign and simplify purchasing processes, reduce cycle times, and eliminate inefficiencies. This results in improved productivity, reduced costs, and increased agility in responding to changing business needs.
5. **Stakeholder satisfaction:** Procurement can improve stakeholder satisfaction levels by gathering feedback on their performance and identifying areas for improvement. This can improve internal and external customer satisfaction, collaboration, and organizational performance.
6. **Increased transparency:** This gives internal stakeholders greater visibility into the purchasing process, including supplier selection, pricing, and contract terms. This can improve reporting and data access. The goal is to enable self-service information that internal stakeholders can use to make better-informed, data-driven decisions.
7. **Cost savings:** Generally, this is defined as comparing the prices paid for goods and services to market rates and documenting the percentage reduced in the cost of goods sold. Procurement negotiates with suppliers, identifies cost-saving opportunities, and reduces waste and inefficiencies in purchasing. This can result in lower costs for the organization, which benefits all internal stakeholders. Cost savings is sometimes confused with cost avoidance or the action procurement takes to prevent a business user or group from spending unnecessary money in the future.

> The confusion exists because there may not be a clear definition with real-world examples of cost savings and avoidance. Many procurement organizations list cost avoidance as an alternative to tracking cost savings. Still, they may be unable to explain it to a business user in a way that makes sense to them.

Finally, it is essential to understand why value can be so difficult to show in procurement. The following subsections will summarize a few areas to be mindful of. Knowing where difficulties may be encountered can help you become better prepared.

Balancing Cost Versus Quality

Procurement will always experience pressure to reduce costs, sometimes conflicting with the need to maintain high quality. Finding the right balance between purchasing at a lower price and ensuring products or services meet quality and performance standards is sometimes tricky. Focusing too much on cost can lead to poor quality or higher maintenance and replacement costs in the long term, affecting overall value.

What has worked well is to draft a threshold that can help avoid going too far in one direction or the other. Start by drawing a line where cost is on one side and quality is on the other, then document the center point. Each procurement initiative will have elements to consider regarding costs and quality. How far you move toward cost will reduce what you can achieve in quality. This is a good starting point that can be refined over time.

Complexity of the TCO

The initial purchase price may be easy to measure. However, understanding and calculating the full TCO—such as maintenance, downtime, disposal, and operational expenses—can be complex and require detailed data and analysis. Failure to consider all aspects of the TCO throughout the entire life cycle can lead to underestimating long-term costs, diminishing overall value.

Managing Suppliers

Building and maintaining long-term supplier relationships that consistently deliver value requires significant effort, negotiation, and constant collaboration. It involves managing supplier performance, fostering innovation, and ensuring alignment with organizational goals. Procurement can struggle to unlock the full potential of suppliers without effective management and communication. This leads to missed cost savings, innovation, or risk mitigation opportunities. If procurement is unwilling to take the steps needed to manage this correctly, then a lot of time and effort is wasted that can be used to drive efficiencies elsewhere. Developing a supplier management team is not just another box to check off.

Supply Chain Risks and Disruptions

External risks like geopolitical events, natural disasters, pandemics, and changes in global economies can disrupt supply chains. This is another challenging area for procurement to secure reliable and consistent value. These risks can lead to increased costs, delays, or compromised quality. Unforeseen supply chain disruptions can derail procurement strategies, causing unexpected expenses and reducing value due to increased exposure to risk.

Siloed Organization

In many organizations, procurement operates in a silo that is disconnected from other functions like finance, operations, the data office, or research and development. Lack of alignment between departments makes integrating procurement's role into broader strategic goals challenging, limiting the organization's ability to drive value. This misalignment leads to inefficiencies and missed opportunities to leverage procurement's contributions to overall business value, such as innovation or sustainability goals.

Rapid Fluctuations in Global Markets

Procurement must continuously adapt to changes in consumer demands, geopolitical instability, price volatility, new regulatory requirements, and technological advancements. Even companies operating only within their home country will be impacted by what is happening around them globally. Keeping up with these changes while maintaining value can be overwhelming and exhausting. Yet slowing down can lead to missed opportunities for better pricing, innovation, or risk mitigation strategies that can reduce the overall value delivered.

Limited Data or Visibility to Data

Achieving value also requires access to accurate and available data on suppliers, market trends, costs, and performance. Many organizations struggle the most in this area with limited visibility, fragmented systems, or insufficient analytics capabilities. Without reliable data, procurement professionals have difficulties making informed decisions, forecasting costs, or identifying areas for improvement, which creates an obstacle in pursuing value.

Sustainability and Ethical Sourcing

Incorporating sustainability and ethical sourcing into procurement decisions adds another layer of complexity. Focusing on environmental and social responsibilities, cost efficiency, and quality expectations can be difficult to achieve simultaneously. Failing to meet sustainability targets or ethical standards can lead to reputational damage, regulatory penalties, or customer dissatisfaction, reducing the overall value delivered.

Stakeholder and User Alignment

Procurement must navigate competing priorities from internal stakeholders—finance, operations, and marketing—each with different cost, speed, quality, and innovation goals. At the same time, procurement must also navigate with individual users who interact with procurement at different levels of engagement at varying intervals throughout the year. Disconnection among stakeholders and users can lead to conflicting objectives and slow decision making, preventing procurement from fully capturing value across the organization. Clear and constant communication is the answer here. If not properly executed, procurement will spend most of its time and resources managing perceptions rather than realities.

CHAPTER 13

RETHINK

> We must rethink how we find the solutions to our business challenges.

WHAT IS DESIGN THINKING?

The underlying concepts of *design thinking* originated from 1940s physiological studies on creative thinking. Over the following decades, L. Bruce Archer and Christopher Alexander applied creative thinking to industrial engineering and architecture.

Don Koberg's and Jim Bagnall's revised 1981 edition of *The All New Universal Traveler: A Soft-Systems Guide to Creativity, Problem-Solving, and the Process of Reaching Goals* shifted design thinking away from the structured engineering methodologies and considered it for everyday problem-solving. Terms like *user-centered, human-centered, and design thinking* were cited across many disciplines in the 1980s and 1990s. They were often perceived as synonymous with each other in early development cycles.

- **User-centered thinking:** This approach involves users interacting with individual system components. In modern terms, this is more than just how the user interface (UI) is designed; it considers the environment, the tasks, the workflow, and the individual steps within an end-to-end process.
- **Human-centered thinking:** This method applies a human perspective when developing an interactive approach, focusing on the user's needs, equitable accessibility, and sustainable outcomes. The goal is to improve effectiveness and efficiency while maximizing human health, safety, and performance.

- **Design thinking:** This approach refers to people's reasoning when engaging with problems. It focuses on creating human-centered solutions that prioritize clarity over complexity. Design thinking favors purposeful solutions instead of overloading options and leans toward solutions that are intuitive or easy to follow at first glance. This is reflected as a body of knowledge, often as a series of steps or procedures.

RETHINK HOW YOU THINK

Practicing different ways of thinking is valuable, whether you are redesigning a process . . . or a bedroom. The underlying concept of design thinking is that each time you look at a specific challenge or problem, you recognize the outcome may be different.

For example, let's say that I reorganize my closet every two years. While it seems like a very similar problem each time, new variables need to be considered, and those variables change how I view the problem *and* the solution. Where am I on my professional journey? Am I going into the office and need formal attire, or am I primarily working from home? Other considerations may include the number of new closet additions over the past two years or the increase in winter clothing because I decided to learn to ski. These variables also change how I use or interact with my closet (i.e., the user experience). I may decide that I now prefer to hang my T-shirts instead of folding them and folding my sweaters because I recently learned I was stretching the fabric using hangers.

Taking all of these variables into account means that by the end of this process, my closet will be *designed* to work effectively for my needs at that point in my life. The closet is more intuitive because I know where everything is, and I am not overloaded with so many options that I lose sight of what is available in my closet.

The concept of design thinking guides problem-solving; when practiced correctly, it becomes easily accessible and natural. One key aspect of this methodology is learning how to break down a challenge into smaller, manageable components, which is discussed in the following sections.

Understand the Problem

This iterative and interactive approach starts with a deep dive into the root cause of a specific business challenge or question. At this stage, information is gathered through stakeholder interviews, focus groups, and data collection. This could also include documentation of the process steps across each user group that physically touches or interacts with the process. Interviewing individuals has some flaws, as they will only be able to communicate their experiences. It is also recommended that a detailed process map be created, which can uncover other challenges that are not yet visible to the individual user.

Do not make assumptions and try to minimize bias. For instance, suppose after two weeks of interviews and process maps, 15 problems, issues, or challenges were documented. However, it is important not to stop there. Take time to think through why those challenges exist and consider what the users were doing at the time the challenges were discovered. It is entirely possible those 15 problems can be drilled down into four common issues that can be mapped to one or more of the 15 problems initially outlined.

This part of design thinking is critical. If we had moved forward trying to solve those 15 problems, the rest of the process would have wasted time and energy trying to solve the symptoms rather than focusing on the real problem (the root cause). You may have already experienced this, where a team redesigned and implemented a new process but did not understand why the solution was not working and instead raised more issues. In those scenarios, the solution was not applied to the root cause of the problem.

Outline Options or Ideas

All potential solution options for the four business challenges identified in the prior stage should be listed in this stage. The goal is to list all the possible options, not just the ones believed to be best suited for the user or the organization, even the ideas that appear to be 100 percent wrong. Not documenting all the solution options opens the door for bias. This stage should also remove additional bias and any lingering assumptions from the prior stage that the team may have missed. It may also reveal overlapping options across more than one business challenge that could potentially lead the team down a new path.

> Failing forward will always be the right approach.

I once considered not documenting a revised process flow because I assumed the organization would never implement it. The solution option was not aligned with their current culture, and they were not ready for it as an organization. I eventually decided to include all options and outline the pros, cons, and impacts, both short and long term. After that discussion, the organization's leaders asked me to provide an interim solution they could implement as a stepping stone to get them closer to the option I had initially dismissed—the possibilities I assumed would not work.

This stage is for creative ideas and brainstorming; it is for considering all perspectives and scenarios. I strongly recommend avoiding terms like "think outside the box." *Do not think about any box—because there is no box.* The phrase implies there is still a box or a defined space that ideas must fit inside or outside. We want to go beyond that.

Drill into One Option or Idea

The next stage is to select one of the solution options and drill deeper to outline how to execute the idea. For example, the solution may be great, but it may also take longer to implement if it requires the creation of new custom integrations or requires data that is not available. The goal is not to consider that there is only one path to implementing an idea. The more you study, talk out loud, and collaborate with others, the more ideas you consider, which leads to new ideas.

There is no such thing as a bad idea at this stage. In my experience, being more imaginative and open-minded can lead to remarkable outlines the team could never have imagined in the prior stage. It is entirely possible this option doesn't have a good solution right now. If that occurs, step back to the preceding stage and select an option in which to drill deeper.

> Our most significant failures can lead to the most successful outcomes.

Test It

Now is the time to decide to move forward with the option from the prior stage. This may be just one component of the overall solution or one part of a process. For example, if a more extensive process is proposed, one business group must be selected to test the solution or test one component. This could be a focus group discussion or a presentation with key stakeholders. The phrase *test it* does not necessarily require that something is always built. It represents a point in this methodology to validate further that the option selected in the prior stage can be implemented *before* significant resources and funding are allocated to a long-term project that may not work.

The most important takeaway from this phase is *whether this works*; is there enough value to the outcomes compared to the execution time and cost? If this option is not viable, that is also okay; it is beneficial to document *why* it did not work. It is sometimes more important to document why it did not work compared to why it did. There have often been examples where options failed to achieve the desired outcomes, then later revisited when technology changes or the company's culture shifts.

Build It

By this stage, the business challenge, solution, and methods to execute the selected option are clear, with a path to manage it. This stage involves more internal identification of resources, funding approval, and receiving the green light to build it in the real world or in a commercial environment. It is also possible that the final solution may not require building something brand new but modifying an existing process. The methodology remains the same.

Key Takeaways

1. The more diverse the team members, the more valuable the outcome
2. Problem identification cannot occur in a vacuum
3. Document all options, not just the ones you believe will work or not work
4. Movement through each stage will fluctuate; there is no chronological order to each stage
5. Our most significant failures can lead to the most successful outcomes
6. Be comfortable with being uncomfortable

SOME EXAMPLES

Tesla

Tesla used design thinking concepts to rethink what the interior dashboard would look like in a truly electric vehicle (see Figure 13.1) versus trying to fit an electric vehicle dashboard around those found in traditional gas-powered automobiles. The result was to remove all the gauges typically found just behind the steering wheel. I recall the first time I drove a Tesla at night. I was surprised by how dark the dashboard was compared to the illumination I was used to seeing when driving any other vehicle. That is where design thinking helps. It moves us away from what we thought we knew as *normal.*

For example, do we need to know the revolutions per minute (RPMs) of a car we are driving? For 99 percent of drivers, that answer is no, not anymore. The typical driver does not require this information, and the latest generation of drivers may not even know what an RPM is or why it was necessary knowledge almost 65 years ago. Another example observed is the removal of the lever on the steering column that controls the wiper blades. New technology automates wiper blades to start once it begins to rain. The wipers automatically speed up and slow down depending on how much rain is detected on the windshield. Removing the manual lever reduces potential accidents because the driver does not

Figure 13.1 Tesla dashboard

need to adjust the wiper speed and can focus more on the road, where the driver's attention should be.

As you will notice in this picture of a 2020 electric vehicle (see Figure 13.2), a computer screen was added, but it still looks mostly like a traditional car. Gauges still exist behind the steering column, and all the buttons still exist on the steering wheel.

The design thinking methodology leads to innovation by removing assumptions and biases that prevent us from discovering what is possible. It helped the Tesla automotive company create a new way to conceptualize a vehicle's interior.

The design thinking methodology leads to innovation by removing assumptions and biases that prevent us from discovering what is possible.

Figure 13.2 Dashboard of an electric vehicle in 2020 (not a Tesla)

Zoox

Zoox is a brilliant example of a company that redesigned something from the ground up, completely discarding standard traditional concepts that dated back over a century. In this case, Zoox tore the vehicle down to the chassis and built it back from the bottom up, asking *why* all along the way. With a goal in mind to be completely autonomous, they had to question at each step in the process, "*Why does it have to be this way*?" This led to what we now know as the bi-directional self-driving electric vehicle (see Figure 13.3).

Kura Sushi

This is an excellent example of redesigning the current serving process of the traditional restaurant model. Imagine, for instance, that we just get seated at a table and are awaiting the server. Most often, the first pass at service is for drinks. When the server returns with our drinks, we usually order our food if everyone knows what they want (not always easy for a family). A refill of our water, another drink, or more ketchup is always contingent on the server. We need to wait on the server to consume anything at the restaurant. This means a lot of waste (waiting) in the process and creates a bottleneck.

Figure 13.3 Zoox bi-directional electric transportation vehicle

If we apply some of the design thinking concepts we have discussed, we first narrow our list down to what we want to solve. These become our business objectives:

1. Remove the server bottleneck
2. Ensure a positive customer experience

Kura Sushi's solution was to install a touch screen at each table to order hot food items and drinks. Kura also developed a conveyor belt system to deliver food. A lower conveyor belt is in constant motion and features only cold food items on small plates, while hot food items are delivered via the upper belt, stopping directly at the table where they were ordered (see Figure 13.4). The conveyor belt runs through the kitchen, where chefs prepare the items and add them to the conveyor belt (i.e., fruit, sushi, appetizers, desserts, salads, etc.). A robot serves drinks, also delivered directly to your table (see Figure 13.5).

When you finish your plate, you push it through a small garbage chute at your table. You are charged for each plate passing through the chute, the hot food items ordered from the digital menu, and beverages. The restaurant has full-time servers or associates. Their job focuses solely on satisfying the customer. The associate may remove bowls that could

Figure 13.4 Kura Sushi two-tiered conveyor belt

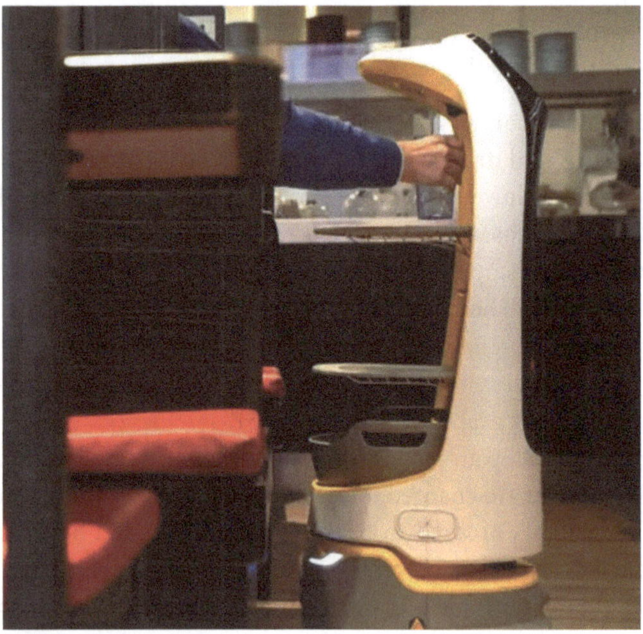

Figure 13.5 Beverage robot

not fit down the chute, but they are primarily there to make sure the customer has a positive experience and will want to return.

The final step was redesigning the physical layout to accommodate the new processes by placing tables next to the conveyor and leaving enough room for the robot and staff to walk through the aisles. The results are that staff members no longer deliver food—especially the wrong food—and those dining at the restaurant can order whenever they want instead of having to wait for the server.

READINESS CHECKLIST

The following checklist will assist in understanding whether you, your department, or your organization is ready to apply design thinking concepts:

- Is there a general understanding of design thinking concepts? If not, this could be implemented through formal training, lunch-n-learns, reading articles, and watching videos.
- It is estimated that six out of every 10 people are at least willing to try a design thinking approach. When creating teams of 10, most team members must be open-minded.
- Do you or your team members have experience gathering requirements through observation, research, establishing interview questions, and conducting stakeholder interviews that will lead to value-based outcomes supporting future stages?
- Do you or team members accept collaboration as a process tool and can communicate ideas effectively? This is often the most difficult to overcome since many company cultures do not incentivize or encourage collaboration.
- Do you or your team members understand and accept ambiguity? Design thinking is not black or white but rather a lot of shades of gray. Not everyone is comfortable with uncertainty or realizing a problem may not have a tangible solution.
- Do you or your team members know this approach may lead to failed results more often than successes? In other words, are you or they comfortable with experimentation through hypotheses and open to feedback on its ideas?

- Are you or your team members willing to be creative to generate innovative solutions to complex problems?
- Are you or your team members willing to imagine yourself in the users' shoes and separate what they need from what they want?
- Do you or your team members understand this process is not about a quick fix or lift-n-shift but rather about providing a sustainable, value-added solution? Many potential solutions will exist, yet most cannot be maintained in a post-production or steady-state business model.

This checklist can be used anytime, even if no project exists. Try applying it at home in smaller steps, such as changing the furniture layout to support your needs better or perhaps removing everything from your refrigerator and placing the items back in different locations, so it is easier to get to the items you use the most.

CHAPTER 14

LEADERSHIP

ROLES AND RESPONSIBILITIES

The role of the chief procurement officer (CPO) has evolved significantly over the past three decades, from focusing primarily on cost reduction and avoidance to revenue generation. This evolution has expanded the scope to encompass quality, value, and establishing long-term strategic partnerships with suppliers. When effectively managed, these partnerships enable companies to collaborate with suppliers, leading to process and packaging optimization that automatically improves efficiency and reduces costs.

Proctor & Gamble serves as a great example of this evolution. Their website and executives speaking at procurement and supply chain conferences reveal a history of successful collaboration with suppliers to redesign the packaging of their detergents. Working together as a team, this close partnership between procurement, suppliers, and other departments yielded a more compact container. The value was widespread across the entire supply chain, from reducing product development costs to increasing the delivery truck's load capacity and requiring less space on grocery and consumer shelves. Consequently, the need for frequent shipments decreased, significantly reducing carbon emissions and providing cost savings across key areas in the supply chain. This success offers a hopeful glimpse into the potential for growth through sustainable supply chain management.

Procurement officers have also been entrusted with revenue generation, showcasing the broadening scope of their responsibilities and their direct impact on business growth. The indirect procurement department for Avon Products (the company changed its name in 2021 to The

Avon Company) was involved in special projects from 2006 to 2008. During this period, they played a crucial role in developing a gift card program for Avon representatives. With over 60,000 representatives (at the time) and realizing the potential for online sales, the program aimed to boost revenue through gift card sales, introduce the online portal, and foster repeat business from the next generation of women. This example illustrates how procurement leaders can directly contribute to business growth, market share, and, indirectly, the stock price, underscoring the significance of their role.

Another revenue-generating program included extending corporate procurement contracts to Avon representatives. I led this strategic move after recognizing the mutual financial benefit to the Avon representatives and corporate procurement. Avon representatives could purchase office suppliers from the corporate contract and receive significant discounts they could not have achieved independently. Extending this contract to over 60,000 Avon representatives resulted in an additional three million dollars of annual spending. This additional spend allowed us to renegotiate the contract to include a higher annual spend threshold, which increased the discount on office supplies and also increased the annual rebate Avon could expect at the end of the year. Each year, that money would be invested back into Avon through one-off projects.

Also around the same time, Avon was trying to separate itself from its old brand identity, most notably shown by the classic television commercial "Avon calling." This TV commercial depicted how someone could buy Avon cosmetics: a mature-looking woman knocking on a neighbor's door and announcing the popular phrase, "Avon calling." This traditional approach to sales clearly did not appeal to the next generation of women (Generation X), who were not accustomed to having salespersons show up at their front door. Also, Avon needed to transition to online retail sales, which meant introducing a different buying channel to potential customers.

Changing Avon's brand was a strategic move and a significant step toward securing the company's future. However, rebranding the company can only go so far without public awareness of the rebrand. This would require a dedicated campaign for TV commercials and funding to buy those ads. However, the budget from the prior year was not enough to cover the new ad blitz to introduce the new branding.

To bridge the commercial funding gap, Avon used the yearly savings generated by the indirect procurement department. At the beginning of the year, the procurement department was given a savings goal to cover the cost of media buying and advertising agency fees for creative content. Through various strategic sourcing initiatives such as contract recognitions, request for proposals (RFPs), and consolidation of spend to fewer suppliers, the money saved at the end of the year was reallocated to the advertising department. The success of the company's rebranding was now linked to the savings generated by the procurement organization, thereby adding direct value to Avon. After that rebranding, the procurement department was not seen the same way. This led to an expanded role in integrating the procurement organization into more significant corporate initiatives.

Oddly, around 2010, despite some widespread success, the industry saw the role and stature of the CPO diminish. Some larger companies did not want to provide the perks or salary associated with an "officer" role and instead downgraded the title to SVP, VP, or head of procurement. The responsibilities did not change, and the role was the highest-ranking procurement role in the company. Still, it did not carry the same weight as other C-level officer roles (CEO, CFO, etc.), eventually leading to the procurement executive no longer having a *seat at the table.* At one large company, the new SVP of procurement was not provided with the perk of a daily car service to and from work as the other company officers received. This is a minor but real example of redefining the meaning of the role of the procurement leader to reduce overhead costs and the perks often associated with an officer role. While some companies still use the title *procurement officer*, it has diminished in status significantly over the past 15 years. For those that still do, there is evidence that the CPO's power has also slowly declined, combined with a diminished role. Others have observed that the role may have never really gained momentum in the first place. Looking back through history, the procurement executive role was not dedicated until the late 1900s, compared with the chief executive and financial officers, who have been around for over 200 years.

In addition, a large influx of start-ups began in 2020. Start-ups typically do not have dedicated roles for procurement executives; therefore, the procurement officer is not valued or positioned like those of the CEO, CFO, COO, etc. Ultimately, however, the title of the role does not matter as long as procurement has a seat at the table to help guide corporate strategic decision making. If they do not, you need to look at company culture and how much that company truly values what procurement can do to help shape success.

Value Creator

In the last few years, there have been some industry discussions to determine whether the procurement department can contribute beyond being a revenue generator and value creator. The debate remains ongoing because the definition of value differs across companies and between executive leadership and the procurement organization.

The procurement organization must deliver visible, tangible value at all levels across all business units in the company. Examples may include but are not limited to increasing revenue; proactively reducing risks; collaborating with suppliers to drive innovation and improve competition; ensuring compliance with policies and external regulations; supporting consumer demands for environmental, social, and governance initiatives; improving a sustainable circular economy; and strategically supporting corporate acquisitions. Here are a few items to keep in mind when framing a discussion around value:

1. **Define value with executive leadership:** Understand whether the definition of value is foundational or connected to their strategic goals. As those goals change, so does the definition of value, leading to constantly moving targets.
2. **Support the value:** Once identified, address what the procurement organization can do to support it. What existing projects can be leveraged, or what new projects should be created?
3. **Assess what is plausible—you cannot define success if you can't measure it:**
    a. Is data available to outline the baseline or the current state? But more important, will data continue to be available to measure over time?

   b. Are you identifying the right resources?
   c. Do these resources have the capacity and skills to support this project?

4. **Available data:** Having some data available is no longer enough to be successful. More specific data may need to be available to measure various value initiatives. This data may already be stored on a system somewhere but not available to the procurement organization. Even with the right resources, results may not matter if the data are irrelevant.
5. **Personal risk as a leader:** This is the most overlooked area of leadership, your personal risk threshold. Decisions made as a leader affect the company, the procurement organization, the procurement team, and the leader making the decision. Understanding tolerance, or how much risk you will absorb, is just as significant. For example, if the procurement organization cannot generate value or measure value, then personally, are you willing to move forward and commit as a leader? Remember, as a leader, your word and commitment carry more weight than others.

Some experts believe the procurement organization has remained largely stagnant over the past three decades, with *stagnation* defined as a lack of growth and minimal progress. This occurs when traditional concepts are unchallenged and stay the same: cost-centric decisions, failure to leverage technologies, or an overemphasis on short-term gains that limit future opportunities. The perceived lack of progress can have negative consequences if not addressed or resolved. There is some truth to the viewpoint that the procurement organization has not progressed far enough to become what a modern procurement organization needs.

Stagnation has caused the procurement organization to become more reactive than proactive. The lack of a proactive approach has even left other areas of the company feeling like they are consistently dragging the procurement organization forward. While there are pockets of forward-thinking or progressive procurement leaders, the challenge is that these pockets do not reflect the procurement organization across the Fortune 250 as a whole. The success of these progressive procurement organizations is attributed to a supportive corporate culture and proper executive leadership.

WORKING WITH THE NEW C-SUITE

Whether the title of chief procurement officer or head of procurement is used, the scope and responsibilities are generally the same; they act as the company's highest-ranking procurement leader. One of those responsibilities is collaborating with the executive leadership across the company. Some of the following common executive titles are still relatively new, but this list offers a look at a present-day C-suite:

1. Chief executive officer (CEO)
2. Chief technology officer (CTO)
3. Chief operations officer (COO)
4. Chief strategy officer (CSO)
5. Chief information security officer (CISO)
6. Chief information officer (CIO)
7. Chief data officer (CDO)
8. Chief analytics officer (CAO)
9. Chief data and analytics officer (CDAO)
10. Chief AI officer (CAIO)
11. Chief data and AI officer (CDAIO)
12. Chief transformation officer (CTO)
13. Chief digital officer (CDO)

Organizations may combine these roles. For example, the information officer may have the responsibilities of a data officer, whereas in other organizations, the data officer is a separate individual. Additionally, some of these roles may be in the early stages of maturity and do not yet encompass all areas of the organization. The most significant challenge is collaboration. Ten years ago, procurement leadership may have felt tension in collaborating with four or five of these roles. Now, that list has more than doubled. Steps to strengthen that collaboration include:

- **Define:** Confirm that the roles and responsibilities are clear across executive leadership. As the list of executive roles expands, there is more room for overlap and misunderstanding of who has the primary responsibilities for critical areas. If the roles are not defined clearly, take time to understand. This will minimize rework, duplicate efforts, miscommunications, and general confusion.

- **Prioritize:** Outline which leaders are more critical for you to engage with. Create a four-quadrant table listing the types of engagement required—inform, align, engage, and collaborate. Each one of these types has a varied degree of interaction. However, each executive role does not require equal two-way collaboration. As a procurement leader, there will be some executive roles where the desire for interaction is greater in one direction.
- **Influence:** The initial engagement may not always be easy for new procurement leadership, especially if they are new to a mature leadership group that has worked together for many years. It might be more challenging to interface with some. Observing and asking questions will enable visibility into how those relationships are established and how you can best leverage them. Identifying who has close relationships will provide alternative approaches, such as interacting with one role that strongly influences the role you desire to interact with.
- **Celebrate wins:** Ultimately, how you solve problems and your capabilities to *get things done* are measurements of success as a leader. One of the most difficult components of leadership is self-promotion or, in this scenario, promoting the procurement organization's wins. One great way to identify these wins is to request direct reports to identify all the *successes* their departments have achieved each month. This will provide a list of available options for communicating within the organization.

> Success in the organization is not a success if no one is aware of it.

THE FRONT-SEAT LEADER

Modern procurement is like a fine wine with notes of complexity and robustness in its aroma. It must balance the inconsistent changes in consumer demand with the limitations in producing goods and services to support those demands. Modern procurement is built on a flexible foundation that can adjust to frequent positive and negative disruptions while staying aware of how technology can be leveraged effectively. It has to recognize the importance of staying present but understand how critical it is to always look ahead.

This means a modern-day procurement leader must embody the skills to:

- Collaborate with executive leadership
- Become fluid in both strategic and analytical thinking
- Stay educated on the latest technology
- Manage resources effectively
- Delegate
- Stay present, yet always be looking ahead
- Respond to planned disruptions
- Manage the wide gap between today, tomorrow, and beyond

None of this can be accomplished if you do not enjoy waking up daily to build something. A modern procurement organization requires a front-seat leader.

A front-seat leader is a person who does not sit in the back seat of a car periodically telling the driver how to drive (see Figure 14.1). The backseat driver does not have the best view and often cannot see the larger picture. The person in the back seat lacks visibility to the dashboard with metrics and data. Just like in a car, this person would have difficulty hearing everything from the back seat during conversations. The backseat driver takes a more passive view, believing that other folks in the organization will *figure it out*. They are the exact opposite of a front-seat leader who has his or her pulse on the organization with access to the data and relationships needed to run it properly.

> Often, when a leader says nothing, they are really saying a lot.

One example of when effective front-seat leadership comes into play is when an organization faces technology disruption, such as AI. There

Figure 14.1 Back seat executive

is an expectation that the organization's workforce will not fully know what and how to leverage these technologies, so they will look to leadership for guidance. Like a child who falls and isn't sure whether to start crying or brush it off, they check for the parent's reaction. If the parent cries out and runs to her child, the child also believes they are in danger and cries. If the parent smiles and looks away, the child thinks everything is good and keeps playing. Similarly, employees look to corporate leadership to define what is important for the organization. They then use that information to determine where to prioritize their efforts. When an executive does not do or say anything, it often says a lot. They are passively communicating to employees that AI technologies, for example, are not important. Therefore, employees do not prioritize learning about AI because leadership has remained silent on the topic. Instead, they focus on other areas and miss out on future opportunities that could benefit the organization, such as leveraging AI technologies during RFP cycles.

To emphasize this analogy further, around 2021, IBM began developing TV commercials to communicate publicly how important AI technologies were for IBM's growth. Internally, their decision to shed departments that didn't align with this future resulted in mass layoffs. These decisions communicated how IBM would evolve to stay relevant in the market. The messaging was consistent, and consumers and employees knew precisely what IBM wanted to do and how they would achieve its goals. They hired data scientists, expanded employee AI training programs, and developed innovation centers to facilitate client workshops on how to best leverage AI technologies. In 2024, IBM was recognized across multiple AI and other industry magazines as a leader in AI consulting. This example illustrates successful front-seat executive leadership at IBM. The executive team decided what was necessary for the company's growth and direction. They were vocal internally and externally about that decision and what they would prioritize.

> The front-seat leader moves forward from the back seat to take an active role in leadership.

INDEX

Note: Page numbers followed by *f* and *t* refer to figures and tables, respectively.